ROBERT SELLERS is the author of eight books including the highly acclaimed *Very Naughty Boys*, the history of George Harrison's film company HandMade, described as 'essential reading' by *Empire* magazine. Most recently he published *The Battle for Bond* which *Film Review* called 'easily the best movie book of the year'. Robert contributes regularly to *Empire*, *Total Film* and the *Independent*. A former stand-up comedian, Robert lives in Harpenden with his wife and daughter.

Happy Birthday, David

With our love

John - Ken

xxx

ALSO BY ROBERT SELLERS

Sting: A Biography

The Films of Sean Connery

Sigourney Weaver

Tom Cruise: A Biography

Harrison Ford: A Biography

Sean Connery: A Celebration

Always Look on the Bright Side of Life:
The Inside Story of HandMade Films

Cult TV: The Golden Age of ITC

The Battle for Bond: The Genesis of Cinema's Greatest Hero

HELLRAISERS

The Life and Inebriated Times of Richard Burton, Richard Harris, Peter O'Toole and Oliver Reed

ROBERT SELLERS

PENGUIN BOOKS

This paperback edition published by Preface 2009

First published in Great Britain in 2008 by
Preface Publishing
1 Queen Anne's Gate
London, SW1H 9BT

An imprint of the Random House Group Limited

www.rbooks.co.uk
www.prefacepublishing.co.uk

Addresses for companies within The Random House Group Limited can be found at:
www.randomhouse.co.uk/offices.htm

The Random House Group Limited Reg. No. 954009

A CIP catalogue record for this book is available from the British Library

ISBN 978 1 84809 018 7

Penguin Random House is committed to a sustainable future for our business, our readers and our planet. This book is made from Forest Stewardship Council® certified paper.

Typeset in Dante MT by Palimpsest Book Production Limited,
Grangemouth, Stirlingshire

Printed and bound in Great Britain by Clays Ltd, Elcograf S.p.A.

To the hellraisers of the world, who have swapped vodka shots for cocoa, whores for a nice cuddly pair of slippers and a night in the cells for a book at bedtime

Contents

I'd like to thank the following who contributed to and agreed to be interviewed for this book:

Michael Anderson,
Vic Armstrong,
Ian Carmichael,
Ray Galton,
John Glen,
Piers Haggard,
Anthony Harvey,
James Hogg,
John Hough,
Waris Hussein,
Charles Jarrott,
Christopher Lee,
Mark Lester,
Richard Lester,
Euan Lloyd,
Peter Medak,
Brian Murphy,
Barry Norman,
Tony Palmer,
Richard Rush,
Ken Russell,
Ilya Salkind,
Alan Simpson,
David Storey,
Jack Wild,
Michael Winner,
Herbert Wise,
Michael York,
Roger Young

Credits

Spitting Image Sketch: © Spitting Image

Section 1. Richard Burton

Burton holding a skull © Getty Images; Smoking a cigarette © Popperfoto;Arms folded © Corbis; Wearing tweed © Movie Store; Burton and O'Toole © Rex Features (From *Becket*, DIR: Peter Glenville, PROD: Hal B. Wallis); Burton and Taylor © Popperfoto; *The Night of the Iguana* (DIR: John Huston, PROD: Ray Stark) © Time & Life Pictures/Getty Images; *Who's Afraid of Virginia Woolf?* (DIR: Mike Nichols, PROD: Ernest Lehman) © Pictorial Press; *Where Eagles Dare* (DIR: Brian G. Hutton, PROD: Elliott Kastner) © Pictorial Press; Burton, Taylor and O'Toole (From *Under Milk Wood*, DIR: Andrew Sinclair, PROD: Hugo French & Jules Buck) © Rex Features; In later life © Corbis; With a glass of wine © Rex Features

Section 2. Oliver Reed

Reed wearing a striped shirt © Popperfoto; Playing a werewolf (From *Curse of the Werewolf*, DIR: Terence Fisher, PROD: Anthony Hinds) © Rex Features; Wearing denim © Mirrorpix; Sporting a moustache © Mirrorpix; At Broome Hall © Getty Images; *The Three Musketeers* (DIR: Richard Lester, PROD: Alex Salkind) © Movie Store; 1970s sex symbol © Rex Features; With a pint of beer © Rex Features; Balancing on the bar © Mirrorpix; Night clubbing © Rex Features; Wearing a Scottish rugby shirt © Mirrorpix; *Gladiator* (DIR: Ridley Scott, PROD: David Franzoni, Branko Lustig & Douglas Wick) © Movie Store

Section 3. Richard Harris

Harris and a bottle mountain © Getty Images; *This Sporting Life* (DIR: Lindsay Anderson, PROD: Karel Reisz) © Movie Store; With beer bottle in scene from *This Sporting Life* © Time & Life Pictures/Getty Images; Hands framing face (From *The Bible*, DIR: John Huston, PROD: Luigi Luraschi) © Movie Store; Drinking at the bar © Mirrorpix; On the floor © Rex Features; King Arthur (From *Camelot*, DIR: Joshua Logan, PROD: Jack L. Warner) © Movie Store; Smoking a cigarette © Wire Image/Getty Images; *The Wild Geese* (DIR: Andrew V. McLaglen, PROD: Euan Lloyd) © Pictorial Press; Wearing a rugby shirt © Corbis; Harris and Ann Turkel © Rex Features; Wearing a beanie © Rex Features; *Gladiator* (DIR: Ridley Scott, PROD: David Franzoni, Branko Lustig & Douglas Wick) © Rex Features

Section 4. Peter O'Toole

Lawrence of Arabia (DIR: David Lean, PROD: Sam Spiegel) © Popperfoto; O'Toole and Siân Phillips © Time & Life Pictures/Getty Images; *Lord Jim* (DIR: Richard Brooks, PROD: René Dupont) © Rex Features; *What's New Pussycat?* (DIR: Clive Donner, PROD: Charles K. Feldman) © Getty Images; *How to Steal a Million* (DIR: William Wyler, PROD: Fred Kohlmar) © Pictorial Press; Wearing a bowler hat © Corbis; *The Night of the Generals* (DIR: Anatole Litvak, PROD: Sam Spiegel) © Rex Features; *The Ruling Class* (DIR: Peter Medak, PROD: Jules Buck) © Corbis; *My Favorite Year* (DIR: Richard Benjamin, PROD: Michael Gruskoff) © Rex Features; as Macbeth © Mirrorpix; *Caligula* (DIR: Tinto Brass, PROD: Bob Guccione) © Rex Features; O'Toole and Jeffrey Bernard © Mirrorpix; 2002 Oscars © Corbis

Select Bibliography

The following previous books on our hellraisers proved most useful:

Richard Burton by Fergus Cashin (W. H. Allen, 1982)

Burton: The Man Behind the Myth by Penny Junor (Sidgwick & Jackson, 1985)

Rich: The Life of Richard Burton by Melvyn Bragg (Hodder & Stoughton, 1988)

Richard Harris: Sex, Death and the Movies by Michael Feeney Callan (Robson Books, 2003)

Behaving Badly: The Life of Richard Harris by Cliff Goodwin (Virgin Books, 2005)

Peter O'Toole by Nicholas Wapshott (Hodder & Stoughton, 1983)

Loitering with Intent by Peter O'Toole (Macmillan, 1992)

Reed All About Me by Oliver Reed (W. H. Allen, 1979)

Evil Spirits: The Life of Oliver Reed by Cliff Goodwin (Virgin Books, 2000)

Other books proved helpful with miscellaneous stories:

The Street Where I Live by Alan Jay Lerner (Hodder & Stoughton, 1978)

A Divided Life by Bryan Forbes (Heinemann, 1992)

What's it All About? by Michael Caine (Century, 1992)

Parcel Arrived Safely, Tied with String by Michael Crawford (Century, 1999)

The Diaries of Kenneth Tynan by John Lahr and Kenneth Tynan (Bloomsbury, 2001)

Trevor Howard: A Personal Biography by Terence Pettigrew (Peter Owen, 2001)

Public Places: The Autobiography by Siân Phillips (Hodder and Stoughton, 2001)

Bruce: The Autobiography by Bruce Forsyth (Sidgwick & Jackson, 2001)

Robert Mitchum: Baby, I Don't Care by Lee Server (Faber and Faber, 2002)

And Why Not?: Memoirs of a Film Lover by Barry Norman (Simon & Schuster, 2002)

Adventures of a Suburban Boy by John Boorman (Faber and Faber, 2003)

Close Up: An Actor Telling Tales by John Fraser (Oberon Books, 2004)
Blow-Up and Other Exaggerations by David Hemmings (Robson Books, 2004)
From the Eye of the Hurricane: My Story by Alex Higgins (Headline, 2007)

I'd also like to thank the staff of the British Film Institute library for allowing me access to their vast collection of magazine and newspaper cuttings regarding our hellraisers.

HELLRAISERS

'God put me on this earth to raise sheer hell.'

– Richard Burton

'I was a sinner. I slugged some people. I hurt many people. And it's true, I never looked back to see the casualties.'

– Richard Harris

'Booze is the most outrageous of all drugs, which is why I chose it.'

– Peter O'Toole

'I don't have a drink problem. But if that was the case and doctors told me I had to stop I'd like to think I would be brave enough to drink myself into the grave.'

– Oliver Reed

Spitting Image television sketch

(A telephone rings. A hideously unrealistic Oliver Reed puppet, looking like a hybrid of Father Christmas and Hannibal Lecter, and sitting in a luxurious chair near a roaring open fire, picks it up.)

REED: Hello.
(Cut to a skeletal Peter O'Toole alone in bed.)
O'TOOLE: 023 0923, that is your number.
REED: Oh, O'Toole.
O'TOOLE: Oliver Reed, by my beard. Tell me, was I with you last night.
REED: (laughs) Indubitably. We quaffed a few as it were, and quaffed and quaffed again.
O'TOOLE: Well the damndest thing, I appear to have lost me leg.
REED: Yes, you bet it.
O'TOOLE: What!
REED: You lost your leg in a wager.
O'TOOLE: What bloody wager.
REED: You bet you could piddle on Nelson from one of the lions.
O'TOOLE: What about the sex change operation?
REED: Ah, you've noticed.
O'TOOLE: Noticed! I woke up this morning with a hangover and a pair of titties. I'm a bloody woman, Oliver. My didgeridoo's been turned inside out.
REED: It was double or quits.
O'TOOLE: Why didn't you stop me?
REED: I fancied a quickie.
O'TOOLE: My God, you didn't have me.
Reed: 'Course I had you wench, you were a woman.

O'TOOLE: I think I'm going to be sick again.
REED: Again.
O'TOOLE: Yes, I think I'm having a baby.
REED: Oh what a night, it shall be etched bold in legend wherever men revel and quaff.
O'TOOLE: God, God. What am I going to do? Once I was Peter O'Toole, now I'm Peter No Toole. A one-legged, pregnant single woman.
REED: Pity the GLC's been disbanded, you could have had a grant.
O'TOOLE: What am I going to tell people?
REED: Tell them; just tell them you went for a drink with Ollie Reed! Ha Ha.

Introduction

They are the four most extraordinary and controversial film stars Britain ever produced, men who at their peak had the whole world at their feet and lived through some of the wildest exploits Hollywood has ever seen. But all that fame had a price. Richard Burton's liver was shot by the time he reached 50; just one more drink would've killed him. Insurance companies wouldn't touch Richard Harris with a barge poll and his film career stalled for over a decade. Peter O'Toole's drinking almost put him in the grave before his 43rd birthday and his generally eccentric behaviour led to public humiliation and one of the biggest disasters the London stage has ever known. Oliver Reed ended up dying prematurely after an arm wrestling contest with a bunch of 18-year-old sailors on the eve of scoring his biggest ever movie triumph with *Gladiator*.

What follows is the story of four of the greatest boozers that ever walked – or staggered – into a pub. It's a story of drunken binges of near biblical proportions, parties and orgies, broken marriages, drugs, riots and wanton sexual conquests. Indeed if you or I had perpetrated some of the most outrageous acts it would've resulted in a jail sentence; yet these piss artists were seemingly immune from the law. They got away with the kind of behaviour that today's sterile bunch of film stars can scarcely dream of, because of who they were and because the public loved them. They were truly the last of a dying breed, the last of the movie hellraisers.

This book traces the intertwining lives and careers of Richard Burton, Richard Harris, Peter O'Toole and Oliver Reed, plus an assortment of other movie boozers who crawled across their path, people like Lee Marvin, Trevor Howard and Robert Mitchum. It's a celebratory catalogue of their miscreant deeds, a greatest hits package, as it were, of their most breathtakingly outrageous behaviour, told with humour, affection, lashings of political incorrectness and not an ounce of moralising. Enjoy it; they bloody well did.

An Aperitif

Throughout the history of movies there have always been hellraisers; actors and booze go together like Rogers and Hammerstein or eggs and bacon. Film producer Euan Lloyd, who worked over the years with Frank Sinatra, Robert Mitchum and Dean Martin, says that drinking simply went with the job. 'Whether it was lack of confidence or just habit, it was hard to tell, but a destroyer could comfortably swim in the ocean of liquid consumed by actors.'

Lloyd's association with Burton and Harris was the boy's own adventure, perhaps the archetypal hellraiser movie, *The Wild Geese*, which also starred veteran boozer Stewart Granger and Roger Moore, himself not averse to a bit of elbow-bending, but able to hold it more than most. By 1978, after decades on the piss, Burton and Harris were mere shadows of their former selves. One day during a break in filming they sat together under the African sun reminiscing and trying to make sense of their lives. 'We were like two old men,' Harris said. 'Once the greatest hellraisers in the world, we were now too tired to stand up and pee. After two hours of philosophical discussion, we came to the conclusion that the tragedy of our lives was the amount of it we don't remember, because we were too drunk to remember.'

So why did they do it, Burton, Harris, O'Toole and Reed, why did they drink themselves to death, or – in the case of O'Toole – come within a hairsbreadth of it? Burton said it was 'to burn up the flatness, the stale, empty, dull deadness that one feels when one goes offstage.' More likely it was to get over the realization that he was appearing in a piece of shit. Nor was he averse to getting pissed on the job. Maybe it went hand in hand with his reputation as a legendary womanizer: not long after starting his infamous affair with Elizabeth Taylor on the set of *Cleopatra*, Richard

Burton answered the phone at her home. It was Taylor's husband, Eddie Fisher, demanding to know what he was doing there. 'What do you think I'm doing?' Burton replied. 'I'm fucking your wife.' Probably emptying his drinks cabinet, as well.

Burton's intake was prodigious. At the height of his boozing in the mid-70s he was knocking back three to four bottles of hard liquor a day. On *The Klansman* he was drunk for the entire production. 'I barely recall making that film,' he confessed. Burton loved the sheer sociability of booze, drinking in pubs, talking with mates and sharing stories; he was a man who enjoyed life better with a glass in his hand. After sex it was the thing he loved most in life. Coupled with his nicotine addiction – it's rumoured he smoked 50 a day – Burton embraced that seemingly inbred Celtic desire to walk dangerously close to the precipice perhaps more than anyone.

Harris too loved the communal nature of boozing. He loved nothing better than going into a pub on his own and by the end of the evening being surrounded by a new gang of boisterous pals. 'Men, not women,' he'd state. 'Boozing is a man's world.' For years Harris habitually drank two bottles of vodka a day. 'That would take me up to seven in the evening, then I'd break open a bottle of brandy and a bottle of port and mix the two.' Asked by a reporter once to describe how much booze he'd consumed over his lifetime Harris was only exaggerating mildly when he replied. 'I could sail the QE2 to the Falklands on all the liquor I drank.'

There was also an element of being the naughty schoolboy about Harris's drinking, of showing off. 'I adored getting drunk and I adored reading in the papers what I had done the night before.' He knew full well what he was doing by getting pissed all the time and ending up in police cells or brawling in public, but didn't think it that awful. Neither did he hate himself for it in the morning or feel guilty. No, Harris just believed that the world and too many people in it were boring old farts and his mission was to live life to the fullest and spread a little joy around. 'So I did, and damn the consequences.'

O'Toole was another who loved the social life of a drinker, propping up bars in Dublin or London, nattering with saloon-bar poets and philosophers, putting the world to rights. 'But I don't really know what I get out of it,' he once said. 'What does anyone get out of being drunk? It's an anaesthetic. It diminishes the pain.' O'Toole would drink to excess for no good reason, as he became intoxicated quite quickly due to the delicate state of his insides; he suffered from ill health most of his life, particularly from intestinal pain.

Naturally eccentric, the drink merely compounded the affliction, and fame when it came threw a spotlight on it so all the world could gawp and gasp at his escapades. This was a man who travelled the world yet never wore a watch or carried a wallet. Nor upon leaving home did he ever take his keys with him. 'I just hope some bastard's in.' More than once, on the occasions when someone was not, O'Toole had to explain to the police why he should be breaking into his own property.

There was an undercurrent of violence to his drinking, too. At his hell-raising peak the gossip columns were filled with accounts of booze-fuelled antics: a brawl with paparazzi on the Via Veneto in Rome, a fistfight with a French count in a restaurant, his fleeing Italy on the eve of being arrested, even the beating up of a policeman. O'Toole's social life often was in danger of eclipsing his talent. 'I was silly and young and drunken and making a complete clown of myself. But I did quite enjoy the days when one went for a beer at one's local in Paris and woke up in Corsica.'

For Reed, like Burton and Harris, it wasn't so much drinking he loved but the fact that it took place in pubs. He loved the companionship, the camaraderie with other men, the chance to challenge people to drink contests or bouts of arm wrestling. All his life he preferred the friendships he made in pubs to those on a film set. 'You meet a better class of person in pubs.'

He also loved the loss of inhibitions in a person when they drank and so found great sport in getting anyone in his vicinity totally smashed. 'People make so much more sense when they're drunk and you can get along famously with people you couldn't bear at other times.' Journalists who visited him were invariably plied with unhealthy amounts of drink and staggered home after the encounter with the battle scars of a war correspondent.

Reed was proud of the fact that he could drink any man under the table. His favourite tipple was 'gunk', his own invention, an ice bucket with every drink in the bar poured into it. The *Daily Mirror* reported a doctor's findings that the safe limit for any man's consumption of alcohol was four pints a day, and then printed a story that Reed had managed to knock back 126 pints of beer in 24 hours and photographed him performing a victory horizontal hand-stand across the bar.

Reed's antics were perhaps unmatched by any other hellraiser – and they are legion. He once arrived at Galway airport lying drunk on a baggage conveyor. On an international flight he incurred the wrath of the pilot by dropping his trousers and asking the air hostesses to judge a prettiest boy contest. All this led one journalist to say that calling Oliver Reed unpredictable was like calling Ivan the Terrible 'colourful'.

All these men played up to their boozy, brawling, madcap image; some resented the press label of hellraiser, others wallowed in it, turning it almost into a badge of honour and a second career. 'What that group of actors had was a fine madness, a lyrical madness,' said Harris. 'We lived our life with that madness and it was transmitted into our work. We had smiles on our faces and a sense that the world was mad. We weren't afraid to be different. So we were always dangerous. Dangerous to meet in the street, in a restaurant, and dangerous to see on stage or in a film.'

Director Peter Medak recognizes that this element of danger was a significant part of the hellraiser's make-up. 'It was the same with Burton and O'Toole, and Harris and Reed, there was this terrible sense of danger around them, you didn't know if they were going to kiss you, hug you or punch you right in the face. They were just wonderful.'

Legends are Born

Like father, like son. Richard Walter Jenkins, the father of Richard Burton, was a fearsome boozer, a 12 pints a day man, incapable of passing a pub without stepping inside for a quick one. 'My father considered that anyone who went to chapel and didn't drink alcohol was not to be tolerated,' said his son. A coal miner and inveterate gambler, Jenkins thought nothing of buggering off for days on end, his family unsure if he was alive or dead; once, for three whole weeks only to turn up as if nothing had happened. Yet his charm beguiled all those who met him. Burton claimed his father looked very much like him, 'That is, he was pockmarked, devious and smiled when he was in trouble.' Others thought the future film star got his handsome looks from his mother, a real Welsh matriarch who was responsible for keeping the household going, with scant help from her husband who was often penniless a few hours after getting his wage packet.

Stories are many about Burton's father. How he never arrived at a rugby match because the route to the stadium was cruelly lined with pubs. How he was burnt in a pit explosion and covered in bandages, looking like Boris Karloff as the mummy, but still insisted on going out boozing where his mates charitably poured beer down his throat. At closing time he stumbled home but bumped into a work colleague who had a score to settle. Trussed up as he was Jenkins stood no chance and had his teeth knocked out and was bundled over a wall. The family didn't find him until the morning.

Burton's grandfather, Tom, was just as much of a character. He too had been crippled in the mines, and celebrating a big win on a horse called Black Sambo one night got dreadfully pissed. In his wheelchair he raced downhill all the way home yelling, 'Come on Black Sambo,' but lost control and crashed into a wall. The old fool was killed instantly.

Richard Jenkins (later Burton) was probably spoon-fed such tales about his bonkers relatives from the day he was born on November 10th 1925. His chances of escaping them, however, or the environment in which God had chosen to dump him, the bleak coal-mining village of Pontrhydyfen, South Wales, were thin at best. To have achieved the fame and fortune that he did was nothing short of a miracle, especially coming from a household of 13 siblings. Having escaped his Welsh heritage Burton's patriotism for his country never dimmed, although its glow was barely visible from the tax haven of Geneva.

With a father who was absent most of the time, or wandered through life in a beer-induced haze, Burton was made to feel even more isolated when his mother died not long after his second birthday. For the rest of his life he'd regret not having even one recollection of her. Burton went to live in Port Talbot with his elder sister Cecilia. With household finances there on an altogether better keel, life suddenly became easier, although the threat of poverty was never far away.

In reaction perhaps to the crummy hand fate had dealt him Burton, from an early age, got into trouble, dirtying or tearing his best clothes, kicking the soles off his school shoes and worse, starting a smoking habit aged just eight. He'd scrape the money together to buy a packet of five Woodbines and illicitly smoke them while watching his favourite Western serial at the local cinema, popularly known as the 'shithouse'. Fighting was another occupation and Burton punched his way to the top of several local gangs. His dad declared proudly, 'You've got a face like a boot. Everybody wants to put his foot in it.'

But Burton's real passion was sport, principally rugby. 'I would rather have played for Wales at Cardiff Arms Park than Hamlet at the Old Vic,' he once said, meaning every word. Wherever he was in the world or whatever he was doing Burton always managed to get hold of important rugby results. During one matinee stage performance he installed a portable radio in the wings and kept straying across to it all afternoon to keep tabs on a crucial Welsh international, whether stage directions merited it or not. Often he'd travel to Cardiff from London to attend the big matches. After one such outing he and his brother Ifor were involved in a brutal and bruising encounter with English supporters. Burton would later trace the beginning of his lifelong painful and ultimately crushing spinal problems to the beating he received that day.

On the field the young Burton was a fearless player, never pulling out of heavy tackles, despite the opponents sometimes being miners and therefore big bastards. He was also loyal. When a teammate was picked on by an opponent Burton laid the bully out cold when the ref wasn't looking.

By 15 Burton was an independent, tough and troublesome man-boy who'd already developed a taste for beer, and who brazenly answered back to his teachers when he thought he was in the right. He bragged too of having girlfriends from the age of 12. One early date didn't go exactly to plan. From adolescence Burton suffered terribly from boils on his neck and face. He even had nicknames for them. One Olympic contender was smack bang on his arse and when this poor girl inadvertently grabbed hold of it Burton let out such a scream that she ran off terrified.

Being academically gifted Burton was saved from a life of drudgery down the mines but when his family hit a rocky financial patch he was forced to quit school and take a job as a shop assistant, his way out of the valleys through education seemingly strangled at birth. It was then that acting presented itself as a new means of escape when Burton joined a local club and began performing in shows, so impressing the youth leader who managed to persuade the council to readmit the boy to school after almost two years' absence. It was an unprecedented move.

On his first day back Burton lobbed his gym shoe across the classroom smashing a window. The tearaway hadn't gone away. He got into numerous fights, would return to school reeking of beer after lunch and at half time in rugby matches gathered the team around while he coolly smoked a fag. There's a story of him pissing out of a carriage window as the train roared by a station platform filled with people, and also of belting a teacher who had hit a friend for something he hadn't done. So his fearlessness was still there, too.

This was wartime and Port Talbot with its large steelworks was a target for the German Luftwaffe. But the air raids didn't trouble Burton who'd stay in bed while the rest of the family rushed to nearby shelters. On the evening of his first trip to London there was a heavy bombing raid. While other hotel guests scattered for safety underground Burton casually walked up onto the roof to watch the whole glorious spectacle. As during the rest of his life, he was unafraid of the obvious dangers around him.

* * *

Unlike Burton, Richard Harris was born into relative luxury, on October 1st 1930. His father, Ivan, was the owner of a local mill and bakery and his house in Limerick, Southern Ireland, was a large affair with maids and gardeners and big cars in the drive. Then suddenly, almost overnight, it was all gone when the bakery closed down. 'One day was luxury, the next morning my mother was on her knees scrubbing floors,' Harris recalled. 'I was too young to understand anything, but I knew we'd lost a lot.' In order to survive Ireland's worsening economic situation the family moved into more modest accommodation.

The Harris brood was a large one, as families were back then, and Harris all but got lost amidst the scrum of seven brothers and sisters. 'What's his name again?' his father frequently asked over the top of his newspaper. 'Dick,' said mother. 'Oh yeah, Dick, I remember.' Harris learned early on to be a rabble-rouser, an attention seeker, it was all he could do to make his presence felt in the household, but he was usually ignored until such boisterousness inevitably led to friction. Sometimes he'd flee home, sleeping rough outdoors. No one ever came looking for him, knowing full well that he'd eventually return meekly to his bed. But all this fostered in him a feeling of neglect and isolation. 'I never got to know my parents and they never got to know me.'

Instead Harris channelled his pent-up energy into sports, becoming a natural athlete, and also into a good deal of larking about. He was banned from virtually all his local cinemas for causing a nuisance. As keen film fans but always short of money, his mates would pool their resources to buy a single ticket and then Harris would go in and as the lights dimmed let his friends in through the fire exit or a window in the toilets.

School and Harris didn't mix either and he was often expelled, once for setting fire to the toilets, another time for attacking a nun. She took exception to Harris's boisterousness and thwacked him with a ruler, as nuns in Irish schools tended to do. Harris wrestled the ruler back from her and hit out violently. In his own words Harris was 'wild and uncontrollable'.

Had Harris been able to avoid school he would have, the underlying reason being his inability to read fluently. 'I just couldn't hack it.' It wasn't until he was well into his 30s that Harris learnt he was dyslexic. At secondary school he survived by focusing on rugby, and like Burton became obsessed with the sport, dreaming of one day playing for his country. Aged 12 Harris was already a big bugger and a real bruiser on the pitch, able to dish out punishment as well as receive it. One such occasion was when he was a player for a local junior team and took on the legendary professional front row forward Ducky Hayes. 'If the stand was full of surgeons they couldn't have done anything for my nose I got such a wallop,' Harris ruefully stated afterwards. Carried off, his face smeared in blood, Harris was treated in the casualty department of the nearby hospital, and with his face heavily bandaged and only the slits of his eyes visible, sportingly returned to the field of play to be greeted with shouts of derision such as: "Tis the return of the Phantom; no, 'tis the Mummy.'

Harris ended up breaking his nose a further eight times in subsequent collisions with various walls, doors and fists. The last time he broke it was when he plunged headfirst through the windscreen of a car. It was reconstructed using bone from his hip as there was no bone left in his nose. 'Each time a girl kisses my nose,' he joked, 'she doesn't know how close she is.'

Away from the sports field and in the classroom Harris tended to doze off or fart to get attention, the lesson going completely over his head. The teachers simply gave up on him. Even caning or the occasional whack didn't work. At one exam he made houses out of the test papers and when he'd exhausted that outlet simply put his head on the desk and fell asleep. This don't-give-a-fuck attitude was like a magnet for the other kids who gravitated towards him as their natural leader. It was a role Harris happily cultivated. Nor did he much mind his dunce status. One story had a student complaining that Harris was sound asleep during a lesson, to which the teacher replied, 'For God's sake don't wake him.'

Such attitude surely would've seen Harris booted out had it not been for the rugby coach who kept the lad on because he was the best second row forward amongst the pupils and the school prided itself on its junior rugby team. Harris's parents, both very much the outdoor type, forgave their son's academic lapses on account of his prowess on the rugby pitch. Just as well. Harris left academic life with nothing much to show for it. Even when his teacher secretly passed him the answers for the intermediate exam, in a bid to help him on his way, Harris, with days to prepare, still flunked it.

To the north west of Limerick, in County Galway, is the picturesque Connemara, birthplace of another legend who could booze for Ireland. Peter O'Toole arrived just two years after Harris on August 2nd 1932 and like him, and akin to Burton's rabid Welsh patriotism, being Irish was the most important thing in his life. O'Toole said it accounted for his passion, his unruly behaviour, his disregard for authority, his natural capacity for acting, and of course his love of drinking. It was to an isolated cottage in Connemara that O'Toole would always retreat whenever illness or personal tragedy befell him. It was his sanctuary. 'I go to Ireland for a refit, just like a car.' He liked to brag to journalists the preposterous notion that he was descended from the ancient kings of Ireland. Throughout his life O'Toole would also never venture out of his front door without wearing something green, usually socks. It was his own private homage to the fact that in the late 19th century the British authorities made it a capital offence for any Irishman to wear his national colour.

Perhaps O'Toole's attachment to Ireland is so strong because he was forced to leave it at an early age. When his father, Patrick Joseph O'Toole, couldn't find suitable work any more he moved the whole family to England and a small terraced house with an outside loo in a working class area of Leeds. O'Toole was a year old. The area was well known for its large population of Irish expatriates. 'A Mick community,' O'Toole described it. His father never again set foot on Irish soil.

The Leeds neighbourhood where O'Toole grew up was rough. Three of his playmates went on to be hanged for murder: one strangled a girl in a lover's quarrel; one killed a man during a robbery; another cut up a warden in South Africa with a pair of shears. It was, he recalled, a heavy bunch.

Although it was his mother, Connie, who instilled into O'Toole a strong sense of literature, by reciting poems and stories to him, by far the biggest influence on his life was his father. Patrick was an off-course bookie, illegal before the war. He was feckless, a drunk and occasionally violent. 'I'm not from the working class,' O'Toole liked to say. 'I'm from the criminal class.' One day Patrick stood his son up on the mantelpiece and said,

'Jump, boy. I'll catch you. Trust me.' When O'Toole jumped his father withdrew his arms leaving his son splattered on the hard stone floor. The lesson, said his father, was 'never trust any bastard'. One Christmas Eve Patrick came home rather the worse for wear. The excited young O'Toole asked him if Father Christmas was coming. Patrick went outside, burst a paper bag, came back and told his son that Father Christmas had just shot himself.

When his occupation turned legal Patrick became a familiar face around the racecourses of Yorkshire. The young O'Toole idolized his father and never forgot the times when he was allowed to accompany him to the racetrack. Sometimes Patrick would miscalculate the odds, or would lose so heavily on one of his bets that he would not have enough cash to pay off his winning customers, so, immediately after the race was over, Patrick would grab little Peter's hand and say, 'C'mon, son, let's be off!' and the two of them would slip through the shrubbery and disappear quickly from the track, not to return for a few weeks.

To grow up with a father who lived so recklessly inevitably led to O'Toole approaching life in a similarly happy-go-lucky way. The whole family income rested on success or failure at the racetrack. 'When he'd come home after a good day, the whole room would light up. It was fairy-land. When he lost, it was black. In our house, it was either a wake or a wedding.'

Patrick also liked to drink and wasn't averse to picking a scrap with a policeman when drunk. Father and son often got plastered together, like the occasion in London when Patrick came down to celebrate the birth of a grandchild in 1959. The O'Tooles got customarily slaughtered and as everyone retired upstairs to bed Peter lay spread-eagled on the floor: 'Not asleep, but crucified.' Patrick tried lifting his flagging son to his feet, but to no avail. Instead he opened another bottle and joined him on the floor. That's where the pair were found the following afternoon.

O'Toole can thank his father not just for his love of booze, but for his sheer durability. 'He was physically quick – whatever else I got from the old sod I got that. A little while before he died he was hit by a car as he came out of the bookies and knocked into a saloon bar without being much damaged.' Alas, O'Toole also inherited a lifetime of ill health. As a child he suffered from TB, a stammer and poor eyesight that resulted in several major operations. The constant illness played havoc with his education. Although he could read by the age of three, O'Toole did not attend school on a regular basis until he was 11 and then only stayed for two years. He disliked school intensely and was a rebellious and poor pupil. Being devout Roman Catholics the O'Tooles entrusted their son to the goodly care of nuns and Jesuit priests, but it was an experience that led O'Toole to later describe himself as 'a retired Christian'. In art one day he drew a vibrant picture of a horse. When asked by a nun whether there was something else that might be added to the picture, the young O'Toole agreed and drew a huge dangling dick with piss coming out of it. Wildly, and with both hands, the nun began to flail the boy. Other nuns rushed over to join in.

In a 60s interview with *Playboy* O'Toole heavily criticized his religious upbringing and the Catholic Church in general. For weeks after he got angry letters from priests and nuns. 'They were shocked. I wrote back saying I was shocked – what were they doing reading *Playboy*.'

Whereas O'Toole and Burton hailed from the working classes and knew poverty as children, Oliver Reed knew only privilege, with a nanny, a maid and a butler serving the household. Born on February 13th 1938 in Wimbledon, South London, Reed said his earliest memory was of seeing patterns sprawled across blue skies during dog fights in the Battle of Britain. Evacuated from London to the Berkshire countryside Reed happily played in fields, drank lemonade in the village pub and waved to pilots from the bottom of his garden as they taxied their planes along a nearby runway for take off. One day a blazing aircraft narrowly missed obliterating the house and ditched in the next field. Villagers ran to the crash site where children were already clambering over the smoking husk for souvenirs. Reed could see the pilot slumped over the controls of the downed Messerschmitt. It was the first time he'd seen a dead man and he began to cry.

Reed's introduction to the opposite sex was equally vivid and a result of that age-old game of doctors and nurses. Barely five Reed had just pulled the knickers down of an obligingly cooperative local lass when her mother walked into the room. That little girl grew up into the actress Samantha Eggar and fate made sure she and Ollie would make a movie together, where they laughingly recalled the incident. 'I didn't attempt to consummate the memory,' said Reed.

Perhaps in the hope of ending such liaisons, at age seven Reed was bundled off to boarding school by his divorced parents and left to feel even more abandoned and betrayed. Nor did he take much to education. Often his impatience resulted in a smack across the head from a ruler, or he'd be lifted from his desk by his ear and deposited in the corridor. His antics, Reed realized, drew the attention and enjoyment of his mates and he began wearing the persona of class clown with pride.

When his family could no longer afford the school fees Reed went to live in Tunbridge Wells to be looked after by a series of nannies and au pairs. One particularly nubile au pair, Swedish of course, called Ingmar, took Reed and his brother David into bed with her one evening telling them that if they all stripped off and squeezed together their joint temperature would shoot up from 98.4 to 160. Every few minutes Ingmar would diligently slide a thermometer under their little cocks and say, 'Not yet varm enough.' To get things really moving Ingmar helpfully guided Ollie's hand onto hers as she repeatedly slotted the thermometer in and out of her rapidly dampening vagina, while at the same time pressing his free hand onto her breast until his fingers felt the stiffening of her nipple. Every time she presented the thermometer to be read all the boys could say was, 'Wow!' and think what a great science experiment they were having. Today if Ingmar had been a man and Reed and his brother little girls it would quite rightly be a case of child molestation. 'Later in school,' said Reed, 'when boys would say that girls get excited and get babies if you push your donger into them, I mourned for Ingmar.'

A succession of schools were unlucky enough to have Reed fostered upon them and in every one he sank to the bottom of the class as he daydreamed his time away, the bane of many a teacher's life. He had particular trouble with reading and writing due to poor eyesight. Like O'Toole he underwent a series of operations but still the problem persisted. It wasn't until his late thirties, the same age as Harris, that Reed uncovered his dyslexia.

By the time Reed was 11 he was already built like the proverbial brick shit house, a fearsome image slightly offset by the fact he still wore short trousers, at his father's insistence. 'I looked like Charles Bronson dressed up as a Boy Scout.' But no one dared tease him. It was Reed who did the bullying, able to pick on feeble youngsters at will. Hanging on the ropes in the gym one day Reed watched as one such weakling entered. 'Hello, Cammel,' Reed said. 'Oh, hello.' Reed was having none of that. 'When you speak to me, Cammel, you say sir.' 'Sorry, sir.' 'That's much better, Cammel.' Reed moved onto the wall bars. 'Do you know what tits are, Cammel?' 'Sort of birds, sir.' 'No they're not, Cammel. Tits are round and hang around ladies' chests.' Reed was swinging about like Tarzan as he elucidated on the subject. 'Tits don't fly, Cammel, tits wobble.' A matron entered, her face purple with rage. 'You filthy boy,' she hollered. 'Wash your mouth out with soap and water, you disgusting boy.'

In the headmaster's office Reed watched as he carefully selected a vicious looking cane and struck him hard on each hand. 'That didn't hurt,' announced Reed. Silence. 'Right lad, if that's the way you want it.' This time the headmaster raced up and delivered such stinging blows that Reed's fingers swelled up like sausages. 'That didn't hurt either,' said a defiant Reed. The headmaster yanked Reed over and walloped his backside. 'That hurt sir. That hurt like bloody hell.' 'Don't swear at me, boy.' Another wallop. 'Get out.' By this time the headmaster was physically shaking with temper, or 'probably excitement' Reed guessed. The incident made him a hero to the other boys but it resulted in his expulsion and yet another new school.

The last port of call in Reed's whirlwind tour of academic establishments was another boarding school. On his first night he was subjected to an initiation test. Stripped, blindfolded and with ointment rubbed on his cock for good measure Reed was made to crawl along the floor to kiss the Blarney Stone. 'Start kissing, Reed,' one of the elder boys announced. Reed imitated loud snogging noises until his head was thrust forward so his nose touched bare flesh followed by a jet blast of foul air into his mouth. The blindfold was removed and there was the Blarney Stone: 'It was the bare arse of the fattest boy in the school. He was amazing. He could fart at will.'

Finding time not just to bully the smaller boys, Reed also bullied the other bullies. Such behaviour was not by choice. He'd observed and learnt that, like life outside, it was survival of the fittest, the strongest succeeded while the weak got abused and ignored. As for sex, it was never mentioned.

Some of the older boys already had pubic hair and to the general amazement of onlookers could make their cocks stand up in the shower. There was also a lot of mutual masturbation going on, but most of his fellow pupils 'were no wiser about the facts of life than Irish virgins entering a Victorian nunnery'.

Sport was seen as the great antidote to sex and Reed excelled, particularly at boxing. In the holidays he earned extra cash by going three rounds against booth fighters in fairgrounds. He even turned semi-pro for a while, until some guy punched him so hard in the face his nose broke and had to be reset. So boxing was out. 'I won my first fight, lost the next, and decided I didn't like getting hit.'

After his expensive education Reed ended up an O-level dropout, possessing a mathematical mind, in his words, 'as astute as a calculator without a battery'. His father summed up his son's future chances. He'd be a burglar or an actor.

Where Reed fled the stuffy confines of academia Richard Burton embraced it. Readmitted to school, a man among children, he quickly came under the scrutiny of teacher Philip Burton, who saw in this rough diamond something extraordinary. Happy to play Eliza Dolittle to Philip Burton's Professor Higgins, the youngster moved in with his teacher and subsequently became his legal ward as well as adopting his name, thus Richard Jenkins became Richard Burton.

It was now that Burton started to drink heavily, maybe in a bid to win the respect of the area's tough drinking miners. Drink also became one of the few things that linked him to his father, who he hardly had any contact with any more and who as he got older meant increasingly little to him. It was Philip Burton who now took that role upon himself. When he heard in 1957 that his father was dead, Burton's immediate reaction was, 'Which one?'

When the young Burton confessed to Philip his ambition to be an actor, the teacher supported and coached him. When the eminent playwright Emlyn Williams was looking for supporting actors for his new play Philip Burton lost little time in putting forward his 18-year-old protégé. His impressive audition won him a place in a national tour. Burton loved it, chatting up chorus girls and boozing with the rest of the cast. His understudy was another son of a miner and future film star, 14-year-old Stanley Baker, and together they set themselves up to be hellraisers to the world. They'd have punch ups in their dressing room and break furniture and windows. Williams had to assume the role of headmaster and threaten them both with punishment if it happened again, but sure enough come the next evening the two were going hell for leather once more.

Although girls were easy to come by sex was still a great mystery to Burton, who would always be wary of his reputation as a pin-up idol. 'Stripped, I am monstrous.' Yet Philip Burton testified that from the age of 15 girls used to hang around Richard, 'like cats after cream'. On tour he and Baker would leer out of their dressing room window at the chorus girls sunbathing topless on the roof of the adjoining theatre and try to hit their tits with ammo from their peashooters. In the evening, boozed up, they'd attempt to coax them up some back alley for a quick fumble, or maybe something more. For Burton it wasn't really the art of theatre that hooked him into acting but the side benefits, the boozing and the girls. 'We ran totally wild,' Baker recalled.

In April 1944 Burton's academic prowess won him a place at Oxford University. He later confessed to feeling terrified on his first day. Here was a boy from the valleys, the son of a miner and a barmaid, in the hallowed halls of academia, the seeding ground for Prime Ministers. One student he met and befriended there was future actor Robert Hardy, who was instantly struck by Burton's greatness. 'I had never met anyone like him before nor have I since. Put half a dozen hellraisers in a room with him and he would be their chief in ten minutes.'

Hardy has spoken of Burton having almost an aura of danger around him that was intoxicating. All the students went after girls, but Burton invariably caught them. Everyone drank, but Burton out-drank them all to the extent that he won the nickname of 'Beer Burton'. He could down two pints of college beer in 10 seconds, a record that's never been beaten. His reputation as a drinker was so great that one night a student spiked his beer with wood alcohol causing Burton to crash down a flight of stairs. On a return visit to Wales one of his aunts asked what he'd learnt at Oxford. 'Who can drink the most beer,' Burton replied.

Amidst his drinking debaucheries time was found to do a little acting, notably as the lead in a university production of *Measure for Measure*, before an audience that included John Gielgud and Terence Rattigan. The performance took place outdoors and so consumed by the role was Burton that at one point he rammed his fist against the wall of a church dislodging a piece of centuries-worn masonry. A spray of dust hit his eye and he staggered off-stage half-blinded with the audience roaring with laughter. Despite the incident Burton was a smash and celebrated in style at the after show party. It took place in a very grand house in town and Burton was led to a display of exotic looking drinks he'd never seen before. Compelled to try them all Burton duly did and passed out. Waking up at dawn he raced back to college, now locked up, and was forced to climb the railings. But he slipped and was impaled on a spike. 'As I remember it,' said Hardy, 'the spike went slap up his arse.' Bleeding profusely Burton had to be lifted off the spike but refused to see a doctor as he knew it would surely lead to him being grounded. He didn't care; the night had been his.

Burton left Oxford in the autumn of 1944 to join the RAF. His eyesight was below par, which disqualified him from being a pilot, much to his annoyance, so he trained instead as a navigator. With the war practically over by the time training was complete Burton spent most of his time drinking and playing rugby. The only action he saw was in barrack room and pub brawls; his worst injury inflicted by a commando who broke his nose with a single punch. But Burton could dish it out too, once duffing up a Welsh sergeant for trying to conceal his heritage by putting on a phoney Yank accent; an unforgivable sin. Another evening, while celebrating his 20th birthday, Burton got pissed along with a gang of mad Irishmen. Running amok through the barracks they took it upon themselves to demonstrate that it was indeed possible to punch out a window without cutting one's fist. 'It was all quite innocent,' said Burton. But they smashed 179 windows and ended up with seven days' punishment.

Burton also showed no fear where women were concerned, having had the nerve to pick up the casting director at his first ever audition. But he could be a shit with them, too, thoroughly devoted but a week or two later moving on to the next one. It was a conveyor belt of crumpet. Burton was even caught *in flagrante delicto* with a high-ranking officer's wife. His knowledge of the opposite sex was once even used to defend an Italian POW accused of raping a local girl. Burton knew the lady in question, as did most of the camp, and his line of reasoning in court was that she more likely raped him. The case was dismissed.

It was always hoped that Richard Harris would go into the family business when education was finished with him. His father's bakery had gone but the flourmill was still in operation, though struggling. He coped with the job for a while, but his heart just wasn't in it. Harris wasn't the business type at all; he could hardly add two and two together. His idea of fun was brawling on the rugby pitch with his chums before going off to the pub to get royally hammered.

Harris's lifelong love of booze was instilled in him from an early age. Actor and friend Ronald Fraser recalled that Harris once told him that 'he was pissed from the day he was out of short trousers.' One of Harris's favourite teenage tales involved driving a massive haulage truck to Dublin when aged 17, on an errand for his dad. Ordered to be back home promptly by 7.30 that evening he headed for the nearest pub after making the delivery. 'Fuck it,' he said. 'I'll make it on the back roads in no time.' Pissed, Harris set off and soon up ahead was a bridge warning 'Clearance 12 feet'. Thinking he could just make it Harris sped on but hit the thing, lifting it off its pillars. At the other end was an unimpressed copper. Flagged down Harris opened his window and said, 'Sorry, officer. You see, I'm just delivering this bridge to Limerick.'

During another delivery trip Harris amazingly knocked over a double-decker bus and lost his driver's licence. 'I am a bit short-sighted,' he explained to the judge hearing the case, who responded by commending Harris for having performed on the highway, 'an audacious and historic feat'. Years later he was up on another driving charge and the judge reportedly told him to acquire a helicopter. 'That way jumping red lights wouldn't be such a problem.'

A loud and eccentric drunk, Harris got away with murder while under the influence – 'I was a rude, bombastic, opinionated, beautifully ignorant loudmouth when I got drunk' – because he could win you over with an abundance of Gaelic charm. Harris could call your wife a fucking whore and still elicit a smile. His boozy antics often sailed pretty close to the wind of illegality, but he didn't care about the consequences unless word got back to his dad. He once stole the West of Ireland Tennis Championship trophy on the eve of the final. When his father found it stuffed behind the sofa in the house he exploded with rage and ordered his son to return it. Harris planted it in a hotel toilet and anonymously tipped off the police. Another time he was arrested for being drunk and disorderly in town and taken to the police station. After a caution he was released, but the local press got to hear about it and ignoring Harris's objections ran the story. Ivan read it and went mad. Harris never forgave the paper and Ivan too never forgave his son for the public embarrassment he'd caused the family.

Perhaps these wild exploits were indicative of a restless character that knew life was taking him nowhere. One afternoon Harris stopped in the street to catch his reflection in a glass door. 'Who are you?' he asked. 'I'm the Dickie Harris you haven't found yet,' the reflection answered. 'Catch me if you can.' Whether it was fate or just coincidence, around this time Harris began showing an interest in acting. Walking past a theatre, bored one day, he saw a sign. 'You too can be an actor,' it said, and Harris thought, 'Why not?' He was 17.

When he joined a local dramatic society no one singled Harris out as being particularly talented, although he'd yet to fully commit to a life on the stage. One thing he was committed to was women. 'I was always a horny bastard. I just didn't let it rip till I was 15 or so.' Hardly the matinee idol type, but ruggedly attractive all the same, Harris was seen as a good catch among the local lasses. But life did seem to be passing him by. While he indulged in a rampant sex life his friends were starting to get married, have children and move away. There were no thoughts of a definite career, either. Secretly he knew he'd never make the professional grade as a rugby player and his father's mill was out of the question. During a labour dispute over shorter hours and higher pay Harris had sided with the workers, a stance that didn't surprise his father, but pissed him off all the same. 'Dickie,' he said one day, 'you're a pain in the arse. And something else, while we're at it, you're fired.'

Peter O'Toole left school at the earliest damn opportunity. He'd no qualifications, as he had not sat a single exam. His only ambition was to flog second hand Jaguars. After a stint working in a warehouse wrapping cartons, O'Toole landed a job on his local paper, the *Yorkshire Evening News*, thanks to one of his priests pulling a few strings. Starting as a tea boy, O'Toole steadily moved his way up in the four years he worked there, even doing a stint as a journalist, reporting on stories with the likes of Keith Waterhouse and Barbara Taylor Bradford. 'But I soon found out that, rather than chronicling events, I wanted to be the event.' Already O'Toole sensed that his life was not going to follow the more conventional path of many of his contemporaries. As a teenager he had scribbled an oath in his notebook: 'I will not be a common man because it is my right to be an uncommon man. I will stir the smooth sands of monotony.'

As a junior reporter O'Toole was a regular pub goer, despite being years shy of the legal drinking age of 18. He'd get away with it by his sheer size and a few helpful props, a heavy raincoat, a cigarette, newspaper and a cloth cap that he carried around with him for the specific purpose of upping his age a bit. 'It didn't always work but it was well worth a try and, anyway, what could they do, shoot me?'

Previously O'Toole's sexual experiences had been limited to joint masturbation sessions with another boy when he was 12. 'I joined the fraternity of MM, Mutual Masturbation, which was regarded as a healthy alternative to ordinary sex. But I got over it. You could say I pulled myself together.' Aged 15 O'Toole decided it really was about time he sowed some of his oats in a more rewarding direction. With a friend he trawled the streets of Leeds in search of suitably obliging women. They found two likely candidates on the steps of a church. O'Toole guessed they were probably semi-professional hookers. After a few minutes of idle chit-chat O'Toole took the initiative by thrusting one of the women's hands down his trousers. She laughed and said, 'Put that on the mantelpiece. I'll smoke it in the morning.' Back at their digs O'Toole's hoped-for initiation into the dark, secret world of adult sex was not a success. He achieved penetration and so it counted as a bona fide shag, but afterwards he was so wrapped up with guilt about what he'd done he decided to confess. The priest in the confessional booth asked just two questions. 'Was it a woman, my son?' And, 'Was she married?' O'Toole can't recall taking confession since.

Free of school and independent at last, Oliver Reed had taken to nocturnal jaunts to London's West End, particularly the sleazy nightspots of Soho. In a strip joint he broke up a fight and so impressed the management that he was hired as a bouncer. He couldn't believe his luck, here he was being paid to stand and watch women take their clothes off. But after a month the club was raided and Reed bolted out of the toilet window and ran all the way to Waterloo station and a train home, never to return.

His next job was as a hospital porter. He had to collect the recently departed from the wards and take them to the mortuary. As a gag one night his fellow porters wrapped him up in a sheet, put him on a trolley and wheeled it into the office. The duty nurse had to check the dead person for rings and other personal items and as she lifted the sheet and reached for his fingers Reed grabbed her hand and sat bolt upright. 'She nearly jumped out of her knickers.'

It was national service next for Reed and because of his stint as a hospital porter he was put into the Royal Army Medical Corps. He hated the idea after discovering that there were no nurses with black stockings. 'Only nurses with black hairy legs.' But Reed soon settled into army life, finding the institutionalized discipline not too far removed from his experiences at boarding school. Posted out to Hong Kong the still virginal Ollie got in with a gang of experienced Jocks who took him one night to a brothel. Walking in through the door Reed was met by row upon row of white arses merrily bonking away. The going rate was two dollars for a quick one, and one dollar for a wank. The prospect of landing a dose of VD, rife in Hong Kong, caused Reed to go for the safer option of a wank. 'But my seven and a half pence wank was a disaster.' The woman's age was something approaching 75 and she alternately terrified and repulsed Reed who failed to achieve an erection, no matter how hard the old bird pumped at it. Eventually she gave up and waddled off. 'Leaving me with my thing hanging out, still limp.'

Regimental orders meant that excessive drinking was kept to a minimum, though Reed and his comrades always had a massive booze up at least once a month. On one highly memorable occasion they got slaughtered absolutely free of charge when the platoon was given a guided tour round a local brewery. Bored with all the technical cobblers it was the free samples they were after and eventually the men were led into a large room where a solitary pipe gushed forth beer like a burst water main. The sergeant in charge pointed to a row of mugs hanging on hooks on the wall. 'Take a mug apiece,' he said. 'You've got exactly one hour.' There was a stampede, like kids let loose in a candy store. When time was up the soldiers could barely stagger to the waiting truck, which took the bumpiest road in all of China returning them to camp. 'The amount of vomit that was deposited in the back of the lorry had to be smelled to be believed,' Reed later recalled. He also realised why their choice of vehicle was a tipper lorry. Back at barracks the commandant ordered the back end to be tipped up and out slid the vomit and the soldiers in one big revolting pile.

The Plastered Fifties

After his stint in the RAF Richard Burton was unsure whether to go back to Oxford or try his luck at acting. The decision was made for him when Binkie Beaumont, London's top theatrical impresario who'd seen Burton act at Oxford, offered the Welshman a lucrative contract. That settled it. In London Burton teamed up again with fellow boyo Stanley Baker and embarked upon a sexual rampage, notching up nurses, usherettes, shopgirls and actresses with equal abandon. Their appetites knew no sane boundary.

In a theatrical environment the opportunity for excessive shagging was far greater than in any other sphere of life simply because the prevailing tone of theatre land was gay, and so if you were something of a stud then actresses fell over each other to get you into bed. The best example of all was Rachel Roberts, later Mrs Rex Harrison, who took it upon herself to seduce platoons of young actors whom she surmised were undecided which way to swing sexually, among them Laurence Harvey and Robert Shaw. In the morning she'd wave them on their way with the cheery words, 'You see, lovely. Stop worrying, you're not queer!' She certainly bedded Burton, although no sane person would've marked him down as 'confused about his sexuality'.

Burton quickly garnered a reputation as a fine actor and in 1948 Emlyn Williams wrote the part of a young boy especially for him in his film *The Last Days of Dolwyn*, about a Welsh village that must be evacuated so it can be flooded to make way for a reservoir. Williams ranked Burton as a natural, despite the fact he had trouble emoting innocence or vulnerability. In one scene Burton just had to look casually at a girl dancing, but all his face registered was a dark ferocity. 'Maybe he had never been innocent,' concluded Williams, who referred to Burton as being born 'with the devil in him'.

Burton's smoking habit also irked his director who worried it might bugger up his voice, which even then had the timbre of the soul of Wales about it. In the end Williams offered him £100 (a hell of a sum in those days) to give up fags for three months. Burton's face lit up and he took the bet, but after six weeks caved in. 'Self-indulgence overcame greed,' he confessed.

Williams also deeply disapproved of Burton's sexual appetite. 'Having discovered sex,' Burton said, 'I began looting and plundering it with great delight.' Exasperated Williams said Burton really ought to settle down, and why not date one of the nice girls in the cast, pointing as he spoke to a pretty actress called Sybil Williams. Burton took the advice and the couple were soon seriously dating. Right from the start of the relationship Sybil knew about Burton's reputation and his numerous affairs, but was content with the fact that most of them were only one night stands. Burton himself always took great care for his nocturnal romps to remain as secret as possible. 'Mustn't hurt Sybil,' he'd say. It didn't take him long though to realise that here was a diamond indeed and they decided to marry only a few months after meeting, in February 1949, setting up home in fashionable Hampstead.

Impressive roles began coming Burton's way. He played Henry V for BBC radio, arriving at the audition clearly pissed but still getting the job. This despite arguing with the producer that no one was going to tell him how to play Shakespeare and threatening at one point to throw him through a window.

He appeared in a West End play, *The Lady's Not For Burning*, directed by John Gielgud who wrote in his diary about Burton, 'He was a real pub boy, had a great stable of ladies. At the very first morning of rehearsals he began to yawn and look at his watch, already eager to get back to the pub for a drink.' 'He was already a star,' fellow cast member Claire Bloom noted, 'a fact he didn't question.'

Claire also noticed Burton's drinking. He'd line up glasses of beer interspersed with glasses of straight whisky and knock them back in turn. The other young members of the cast tried to compete but Burton could drink the lot of them under the table. Boilermakers were a particular favourite drink of Burton's at the time. He was once challenged by an entire 15-strong rugby team, all Welsh miners, to a drinking contest and downed 19 of them. Alas the next day he was in no fit state to remember who won.

Inevitably the cinema was soon interested in Burton; his first British pictures, largely forgettable, included *Waterfront* (1950), about a drunken sailor who returns years later to the Liverpool family he deserted. The director was also somewhat green, it being only his second feature, but Michael Anderson has nothing but fond memories of the young Burton. 'He was certainly not difficult in those days; indeed he was very helpful and generous as an artist, helping out other actors in the cast who were even less experienced than he was.'

Anderson later became a director of international renown with films like *The Dam Busters* and *Logan's Run*. He'd also work with Richard Harris no less than three times and learnt that the best way to deal with actors with a hellraising reputation was to make them feel secure with their director. 'They needed to feel comfortable, that they were listened to, that their point of view was at least appreciated, so that they weren't just being ordered around like cattle.'

There was one actor on *Waterfront*, however, that even Anderson could not control, the irrepressible Robert Newton, most famous for his film portrayals of Bill Sikes and Long John Silver. 'The problem with Newton, who had this huge drinking problem, was to keep the booze away from him. Somehow I think he always managed to get hold of a drop of something and often was never quite as fluent in his delivery of lines, but that was all part of his charm, that was his performance, that's what he did that made him so great. He was famous for occasionally pronouncing long "aghhhs" in a scene. I found a couple of times on *Waterfront* it was when he couldn't remember a line, he would look up at the ceiling and go, "Well, I, er, aghhh." He was thinking of the next line. It became a trademark.'

Filming *Waterfront* Newton often gave Burton a lift to the studio in his battered old Bentley. One morning Burton arrived to see Newton unusually the worse for wear, brandy flask in hand, and unshaven. It was winter and the car had a thin covering of frost and refused to start. Newton handed Burton his flask, went back into the house and returned with a horsewhip and began laying into the bonnet. When they tried the ignition again the Bentley revved up. Drinking all the way to Pinewood they arrived late on the set. Newton's dresser was hurrying him along with his costume when the bell rang for the commencement of filming. Newton dashed for the set, his dresser rushing behind him desperately trying to point out the fact that he wasn't wearing his trousers or indeed any underpants. The set was awash with technicians and actors as Newton arrived. 'Oh sir, you can't go on like that,' the dresser yelped. 'And why not?' queried Newton. 'Because there's something missing, sir.' 'Missing. Missing!' Newton bellowed before looking down at the awful evidence. 'Thank you for pointing it out. Very grateful,' Newton said as he lifted his shirt. 'Make-up!'

Newton's drinking was sometimes so excessive that he'd lose all memory and sense. He once got so inebriated that he showed up on the wrong movie set. The director was slightly bemused by his appearance but managed to put the star in four scenes until people from the movie he was really supposed to be in came to haul him off. When he was performing at the St James's Theatre in London the curtain failed to rise one evening and the audience grew restless and started to slow clap. At last the curtain moved to reveal the sozzled figure of Newton. Silence fell upon the auditorium. 'Ladies and gentlemen,' he bellowed. 'The reason this curtain has so far not risen is because the stage manager has the impertinence to suggest that I'm pissed!'

Michael Anderson directed Newton again on the mammoth *Around the World in Eighty Days* (1956), but almost didn't because the producer Mike Todd was nervous about casting him due to his reputation. Todd confronted Newton with, 'Your friend David Niven says you are a big drunk.' The actor replied, 'My friend Niven is a master of understatement.' In the end Newton agreed to have it in his contract that he wouldn't touch a drop for the entire shoot. He kept his word. 'But when the picture was over,' says Michael Anderson, 'he went on a binge about a month later and I think it killed him.' Newton was indeed dead before *Around the World* opened in cinemas.

Invited to watch the shooting of *Waterfront* was Euan Lloyd, then publicity manager of the Rank Organisation. Years later the press thought him mad for casting Burton and Harris together in *The Wild Geese*. 'But that could have applied equally to Paul Soskin, producer of *Waterfront*,' says Lloyd. 'Robert Newton was "King Lush" in the eyes of the world and the young Burton tried hard to keep up with him.'

In the bar at Pinewood Lloyd and Burton got acquainted, their friendship sealed when the actor learnt of his birthplace: Rugby. Lloyd found himself an 'honorary' member of Burton's club of Welsh rugger supporters, made up of fellow actors Stanley Baker and Donald and Glyn Houston, whose voices were heard annually on the terraces of Twickenham when Wales and England clashed before 50,000 fans. 'This handsome young star with a Churchillian voice sent from heaven could do no wrong in the fifties,' says Lloyd. 'And every beauty in town, young and old, craved his company. With booze spurring us on, some of us found ourselves in competition for favours. At a movie premiere I met a gorgeous young starlet and was invited to call on her the next day. All spruced up, cologne applied, I arrived on her doorstep at the appointed time and rang the bell. A long delay, some off-stage noises were heard, and eventually (but slowly) the door was opened. As I entered her hallway I caught a short glimpse of a male head lowering itself out of the kitchen window . . . it was Richard, the Welsh bull! Spotting me he yelled, "A try for Wales, I think!"'

Sacked by his father and now free from any obligations to work in the family business Richard Harris had reached a momentous moment in his life. He'd decided to emigrate to Canada, to escape the stifling middle-class conventions of his upbringing and the religious bigotry and hypocrisy of rural Ireland. The fact that Harris had just split up from his first ever serious girlfriend probably pissed him off, too. Then his whole world fell apart when he was diagnosed with TB. Canada was out, as were any hopes he may have fostered about a rugby career. He never did play again. Instead Harris was confined at home for nearly 22 months, six of which he lay inert in bed, 'playing a staring game with the damp Irish walls that caused my TB in the first place'.

It was here that he first dreamt of escape into an acting career and began sending off letters to drama schools in London. His TB finally beaten, Harris promised himself never to be shackled and imprisoned again, and set out to pursue a life of sensory overload, willingly embracing his demons. The death of his sister from cancer also deeply affected him as a teenager. Within a year he saw his mother turn into an old woman through grief. He knew then that life was short, that you could die tomorrow or next week. 'So I wanted to embrace it all. I had a terrible desire to let nothing pass me by.' It was a personal journey that nearly killed him.

When he heard the news that his son was leaving for England Harris's dad's only comment was, 'For God's sake, let him go.' Harris gave himself just one year to succeed in London, and the friends and family members who waved him off at the station couldn't help thinking he'd be back in Limerick soon, tail between his legs. Arriving in London Harris took the cheapest lodgings he could find and on his second day auditioned for the Central drama school. He was 25 years old amongst other applicants barely out of their teens. He looked physically out of place too. The mid-1950s was the age of the Rank matinee idol as personified by pretty-boy actors like Dirk Bogarde who spoke with clipped upper class accents and were sexually non-threatening on screen. Harris was Irish and though his accent was moderately decipherable his native brashness and swagger, combined with his loud personality, grated with some people. At the end of his audition piece the panel said, 'What right do you think you have to enter our profession?' Harris wasn't going to take that one on the chin. 'The same right you have to judge me.' He was shown the door.

His next port of call, LAMDA, was more successful, even though he arrived covered in muck and leaves after falling asleep in a park; he was accepted on a two-year course. He'd fallen in love with London, the neon-lit nightlife of Soho, the smells and new experiences and the kind of fascinating women he could only have dreamt of meeting along Limerick High Street. Inevitably Harris turned almost overnight into a gung-ho womanizer, often moving from flat to flat as love affairs dictated. It was as if he'd found a great new sport and was training like mad for the Olympics.

Such behaviour rankled with some of his drama school contemporaries, as did his exuberant personality and aura of 'look at me'. He had a problem with the teachers too; old fogies in grey suits telling him to treat Shakespeare with reverence and pronounce his verbs like Olivier. Fuck off, thought Harris. As usual he wanted to do things his way. To prove his point he hired a venue off Leicester Square (so grubby it eventually was turned into a strip joint) to put on his own stage production. But it proved a disaster and closed after just a few performances.

The consequences of Harris's bold theatrical enterprise were severe. He was left wiped out both physically and financially. Without the money for rent he slept for a while on top of the bar of a mate's pub and then under piles of coats on the Embankment. When it rained he scraped enough cash together for a bed in a local doss house. Later he camped in doorways along the Earls Court Road, close to LAMDA, which he still falteringly attended. When one day he collapsed from hunger during class a fellow student took pity and offered him accommodation at his small flat. Harris had entered what he was to call his starvation period.

By 18 Peter O'Toole had decided journalism was not for him, a view shared by his editor. Obsessed by theatre O'Toole had joined a local drama group with the intention of becoming an actor, only for this ambition to be curtailed in 1950 by National Service. Undecided about which of the armed forces to enter he finally opted for the Navy, gamely bullshitting that he came from a long line of Irish salty sea dogs. 'I preferred the sea and I vomited over every square inch of it.'

O'Toole arrived at Victory barracks Portsmouth with a ragtag assortment of other recruits and after a visit to the demon barber and collecting ill fitting uniforms, next on the agenda was an intelligence test. 'It was here we realized that we had amongst our group either a total nut case or a man of genius!' one of his naval comrades later recalled. O'Toole was given a series of wooden pegs, some round and some square. The idea was to fit the round pegs in the round holes. For O'Toole that was too easy. In front of the RN shrink and keeping a straight face, he spent about half an hour trying to force the square pegs into the round holes. Other officers were called to witness this feat and when they had given up in despair, and called off the test, a huge grin appeared on O'Toole's face. Next was a series of questions to ascertain whether or not the recruit was officer material. O'Toole answered only one of the 20 questions. How would he lift a heavy barrel over a 30-foot wall using only two ten-foot lengths of rope. O'Toole replied simply, 'I'd call the chief petty officer and say to him. "Get that barrel over the wall."'

After all that O'Toole became a signals operator in the submarine service – 'can you think of anything more unsuitable than that, I get claustrophobic in a lift' – and was ordered to the North Atlantic. It didn't take long for him to rebel, explaining to the ship's doctor that he had a hereditary in-growing toenail (fictitious, of course) and as such he could be injured for life if he had to wear regulation boots. O'Toole became the only member of the ship's company to be allowed to go ashore in anything other than boots. At a later stage, he acquired an imaginary curvature of the spine and was allowed to sleep in a camp bed rather than the conventional hammock. He was also arrested for taking extra rations of rum ('because it was a cold day') and again later for insubordination. It did look as if the Navy and O'Toole was an ill-matched pair. 'I would stand alone on deck at night talking to sea gulls for hours.'

It was all really part of O'Toole's grand scheme to get out of the services as quickly as he'd got in. 'What was I doing marching to the left and marching to the right? What was I doing darning socks? It was a bloody nightmare and I tried everything to get out.' One attempt consisted of drinking 18 bottles of wine, taking a lot of aspirins and a drug that was supposed to turn his features a deathly grey, but it didn't work.

Given the task of decoding weather forecasts sent in code by a Wren ashore O'Toole, plainly going against the spirit of the test, avoided the hour and a half it took to decipher the message by simply telephoning the woman and getting her to read it out in English. But somebody ratted on the girl and she was booted out while O'Toole got thrown in the brig. Even worse was the occasion his ship visited Sweden. A big ceremony was planned for the British admiralty to walk ashore by jetty to greet the Swedish king, but when a fog descended the fleet got lost and couldn't find the correct place to dock. O'Toole was hurriedly sent out in a boat with a walkie-talkie to tip off the admiral where the king could be found. Alas O'Toole accidentally dropped the radio into the sea. He was jailed once again.

While in Sweden O'Toole did manage to find an unorthodox cure for the stammer and lisp that had been plaguing him since childhood. Playing in a Navy rugby team against one made up of thugs from the Swedish police force, O'Toole caught the ball and fell on it only for a hulking great Swede to kick him full on the chin, slicing his tongue in half. He was rushed to hospital and the tongue was stitched back together, resulting in his speech impediment disappearing completely.

The hospital discharged him when it was time for his ship to set sail and put him on a train. He had been riding for half an hour when he found out he was going the wrong way. There was O'Toole, unable to speak English let alone Swedish, but luckily the nurse with him managed to find the way to the harbour – just in time to see the fleet sailing off into the distance. O'Toole later swore he hired a funfair boat and paddled out until it came alongside the supply ship and they threw a rope ladder down to him.

By hook or by crook O'Toole continued to try and get out of the Navy. 'I started pointing out the ridiculousness of the whole situation to them. I can't really say how much of what I was doing was pretending, or when my pretence became real. But I was released as mentally unsuitable after 18 months.' He'd later describe his time there as, 'a total waste for everybody, particularly His Majesty.' As a grand gesture, and to purge the Navy out of his system before resuming civilian life, O'Toole took his uniform and threw it in the Thames. Now it was back to Leeds and, he hoped, a career on the stage.

Free from his National Service and back in civvie street, Oliver Reed too was bursting to become an actor, but in the movies, not theatre. He'd briefly contemplated becoming a salesman but ditched that after his father said he wouldn't be able to sell a packet of crisps. Luckily Reed's uncle happened to be Carol Reed, director of the classic *The Third Man*, but his advice – to hobnob with the movers and shakers of the film community at fancy hotels and restaurants – proved useless; Reed hadn't even got a shilling to put in the gas meter and was living off spaghetti and tomato soup. One piece of advice from his uncle that he never forgot was to go to the cinema as often as he could. Why bother enrolling in drama school when he could watch and learn from the Hollywood greats right up there on the movie screen?

But Reed still had to get his foot in the door somehow and eventually found work as a film extra. 'I went round and I lied to everybody. I said I was in a repertory company in South Africa and in Australia – in Wagamoomoo, hoping that they wouldn't be able to check up – and they didn't.' A couple of walk-on parts followed in films like the Norman Wisdom comedy *The Square Peg*.

Socially Reed fell on his feet too when he was invited to share a flat in Belgravia with two girls who worked at a swanky West End nightspot as 'hostesses'. Reed loved playing practical jokes on his Irish drinking pals by inviting them over and getting one of the girls to walk through the lounge into the kitchen wearing nothing but bra and panties. While he carried on talking as if this was the most natural thing in the world his pals would sit there goggle-eyed. After a bit the other girl would glide through topless. Unable to contain themselves any longer his mates bellowed. 'Jesus, Oliver! What the fuck was that?' Reed said later, 'I was swamped with visits from drunken Irishmen.'

Attending numerous auditions and touting his photo round all the agents, Reed found nobody was interested in hiring him. As a star he used to love going back to visit those same agents bragging, 'Hey, remember me? I'm Oliver Reed. You used to tell me to piss off.' It was at one of these auditions that he met his first wife, Kate. As they began dating Reed was already seeing someone else, a ruse that was discovered when he was in hospital suffering from German measles and both girls turned up at the same time to visit. Kate had brought with her a box of 100 fags that she proceeded to shower over his head. Forced to choose between both women Reed picked Kate, though he was less than enthused with her idea of getting hitched immediately. But it was either that or goodbye.

Reed gave a slightly different reason as to why he got married in a 1970s *Penthouse* magazine interview. 'I was twenty-one, and I liked screwing the girl I was with; typical middle-class attitude. She was Irish, typical working-class girl, and she said, "Right, you've got to marry me if you want to go on doing that, baby!" And I said, "Yeah, yeah." She was a little spitfire, who wanted me to sign a contract saying I wasn't going to fuck anybody else.'

The couple married on New Year's Day at Kensington Register office and as the nephew of Carol Reed Ollie made his debut in the newspapers. They went to live in a house in Ladbroke Grove that belonged to Reed's aunt and which shuddered every time a train went by. They shared it with an old colonel, installed there by the aunt to see that Reed didn't demolish the property, as he had a habit of inviting friends round for destructive punch-ups. The two men ignored each other for weeks until one night they went to a pub together to celebrate St Patrick's Day. No sooner had Reed opened the saloon door than a man accosted him. 'Are you Irish?' Reed thought about it for a few seconds. 'What if I am?' A fist suddenly flew into his face along with the words, 'Sod off you paddy bastard.' The man had gone into the pub with the sole intention of picking a fight with an Irishman, any Irishman, and chose Reed instead, the only bloody

Englishman there. The Irish clientele leapt to Ollie's defence, kicking the shit out of his attacker, throwing him outside in the gutter and then pissing over him. Determined not to allow so minor an incident to dull their evening Reed and the colonel proceeded to have a ball. Staggering home shit-faced afterwards they continued to drink until dawn. 'Thank God St Patrick's Day only happens once a year,' the colonel announced in the morning. 'We've polished off my entire month's supply of liquor.'

Richard Burton continued to appear in some very indifferent British movies, compensating himself by seducing female members of the cast. On *Green Grow the Rushes* (1951) Burton tried to get future Bond and *Avengers* girl Honor Blackman into the sack. But the actress failed to fall for the hell-raiser's charms, and made her feelings clear when he attempted to woo her: 'You didn't really want somebody in your bed spouting Shakespeare.' She later recalled, 'Most of the time, he was drunk. We were staying in these little chalets and he came home one night and got into bed with me. I kicked him out eventually. He wasn't my idea of heaven.'

That summer Burton was asked to undertake a season of major Shakespearean roles at Stratford. During rehearsals for *Henry V* Burton, dressed in full armour, whiled away the hours by drinking 18 bottles of pale ale. As the battle of Shrewsbury approached our Dick was overwhelmed by a desire to urinate. 'Can we stop,' he asked, peering into the darkness of the stalls where Anthony Quayle sat directing. 'No, Richard.' There was clear exasperation in his voice. 'It's very late, not now, Richard please. We'll have a break in half an hour or so.' 'Right,' said Burton. 'Watch this.' An incredulous cast stood gawking as the Welshman relieved himself and 18 bottles worth of pale ale seeped through his costume and collected in a large puddle on the wooden floor.

Pissing and Shakespeare were curious bedfellows for Burton during his Stratford run. Playing in *Henry IV Part 2* with Michael Redgrave, having been on the booze all day, Burton was in the middle of a scene when he felt his bladder near to exploding. 'Luckily the old fellow was pointing upwards,' Burton later related. 'And the costume was pretty heavy, so none of it leaked out. It was all swilling about inside.' Burton told this story on the set of his last movie, *1984*. A few years later its director, Michael Radford, went to see a house that was for sale. The owner happened to be an actor and Radford mentioned that he'd once worked with Burton. 'The nearest I ever got to Burton,' said the actor, 'was at drama school. We did *Henry IV Part 2*, and I wore the very costume that Burton had worn.' 'Was there anything funny about it?' Radford asked, convinced Burton had been telling porky pies. 'As a matter of fact – yes,' replied the actor. 'It was stained yellow.'

Burton's Shakespearean performances at Stratford were the stuff of legend with critics citing him as the heir to Gielgud and Olivier. But he was now under contract to Alexander Korda, the British film tycoon, who had decided that it was time to win over Hollywood and lent Burton to 20th Century Fox for a three-film package worth $150,000, more than all the actor's family could earn in a lifetime. Burton had always coveted a film career. At a party with other young hopefuls, each was asked to declare their ambitions. 'I want to be the greatest Juliet since Ellen Terry,' said one. 'I want to play Hamlet as it has never been played,' said another. 'How about you Richard,' they finally said. 'What do you want to be?' Burton's reply: 'Rich.'

At his farewell party Burton stayed up till dawn and drank himself senseless and had to be hauled onto the plane to Hollywood. He was flown over the Atlantic comatose, stopping over briefly in New York for more drinks. It was a further 11 hours to LA, a journey made tolerable by yet more booze. Unshaven and shattered Burton was taken by limo to his hotel room, where he devoured a bottle of scotch thoughtfully left there by the management. Hours later he was centre stage at a Hollywood party regaling everyone with recitals of Shakespeare and Dylan Thomas. Some thought him too overbearing, but none were left in any doubt that here was someone very special. The party had been organised by Lauren Bacall and Humphrey Bogart, fans of Burton from his stage work. Bogart adored Burton and the feeling was mutual. They became lifelong friends and shared many marathon drinking sessions together. 'He was my kind of man,' said Burton. 'If you challenged him to put his hand through a plate-glass window, he'd do it. And keep on drinking with the other hand.'

Once Burton challenged Bogie over a point of acting and the Hollywood legend stormed out of the room returning with his Oscar, which he thumped down on a table. 'You were saying?'

Bogart's penchant for alcohol was awesome. He once said, 'I don't trust anyone who doesn't drink.' Returning from a holiday in Italy he told reporters. 'I didn't like the pasta, so I lived on scotch and soup.' On location for *The African Queen* Bogart was the only one who didn't succumb to disease and diarrhoea because he never drank the water, surviving instead on pure scotch. When asked if he'd ever been on the wagon Bogie replied. 'Just once. It was the most miserable afternoon of my life.'

One glorious story has Bogart losing his way home after an all-night drinking session. Finding himself in an unfamiliar Hollywood suburb as dawn rose Bogart spied a woman cooking breakfast in a nearby house. Peering through the window his face startled the woman until she recognized it. 'My God,' she cried out to her husband. 'It's Humphrey Bogart!' 'What about him,' her husband shouted back. 'He's in our front yard.' 'Well invite him in.' Bogart sat down for breakfast with the couple and their kids, wolfing down bacon and eggs while mesmerizing them with tales of Hollywood. When he'd finished he stood up, said thank you politely and then walked out the way he'd come in.

Near the end of his days, Humphrey Bogart reflected upon his life and declared that things had gone downhill after a single bad decision. 'I should never have switched,' he explained, 'from scotch to martinis.'

It didn't take long for the Hollywood gossip mongers to seize upon the potential of Burton, spreading rumours that his philandering had already broken up nine marriages in the movie capital. Back home Sybil papered the toilet with articles that had him climbing drainpipes for a romantic rendezvous, or being visited in his dressing room by naked women. She had no choice but to grin and bear it, for Burton was indeed a wild stallion around Hollywood. Married or single, he didn't discriminate. At one party he locked eyes on a rather famous Hollywood actress and instructed his friends to keep a watch on the husband while he took her outside for a quick one. Quick it was; both were back through separate doors and mingling with party guests before the husband had even noticed his wife's absence. Co-star Raymond Massey was asked in an interview if he thought there was any woman Burton had failed to win. 'Yes. Marie Dressler,' said Massey. 'But she's dead,' came the reporter. 'Yes, I know,' was his reply.

Sometimes Sybil's tough exterior did crack; she was after all only human. Burton was having an affair with Jean Simmons, then married to Stewart Granger. One New Year's Eve party the lovers remained interlocked just that little bit too long after the stroke of midnight and Burton got a severe slap in the face from Sybil, who then left in a rage. Many considered Burton a total shit during those years. He picked up women in cinemas, pubs, shops; you name it. He even made love to a maid within hours of speaking his marriage vows. Friends were often roped in to cover for his affairs persuaded by Burton's pleading: 'I'll never hurt Sybil. I'll never leave Sybil.' But as time went on he seemed not to care who knew about his infidelities. This was the way he lived his life.

Ironically it had been Stewart Granger who told Burton to look him up when he got to Hollywood. He'd been so dazzled by Burton in a West End play that he went to his dressing room afterwards to congratulate him. Burton was standing there naked save for a jockstrap and a glass of beer. 'When you come to Hollywood we must meet up,' said Granger. 'Hollywood!' said Burton. 'I'm not going to Hollywood.' 'Oh yes you are. That's for sure.' One wonders if Granger ever forgave Burton for dallying with Jean Simmons. They only ever made one film together, *The Wild Geese*, appearing in just two scenes, and in both the antipathy between them is tangible.

Apart from copious amounts of shagging ('knocking off everyone there was in sight') Burton also managed to find the time to do a bit of acting in Hollywood, though sadly in some pretty lamentable films. The first, *My Cousin Rachel* (1952), was a vehicle for Olivia de Havilland, though it was Burton who came away with an Oscar nomination, his first. It was on this film that Burton physically destroyed a whole set: 'And as far as I remember Olivia de Havilland was on top of it.' Burton couldn't remember his lines in a scene where he was supposed to climb up a wall to greet Miss de Havilland above. 'I just couldn't remember what I had to say,' he recalled with some amusement on a Parkinson TV show. 'So I climbed up once and slithered down in a temper because I'd forgotten the lines. Went up again, slithered down. Went up again, slithered down. I must have gone up about ten times. Finally I went raving mad and started to kick the set and the whole thing started to fall in. I was very clever to get out of the way. Miss de Havilland didn't forgive me for a long time.'

Burton was rather prone to fly into rages when he didn't meet the high demands he set himself. Once, after fluffing the same line repeatedly, he deliberately charged headfirst into a plaster wall. Hollywood had rarely seen such eccentric behaviour.

What Richard Harris called his 'starvation period' ended when he joined Joan Littlewood's Theatre Workshop, an influential company housed in London's East End. It came about purely by luck when he overheard someone in a pub saying they hadn't finished casting a production. Borrowing fourpence for the phone Harris called them only to hear that the vacant part was for a 50-year-old. That didn't stop him. 'I look fucking 50,' he bellowed down the line. 'I haven't had a good meal for four months and I haven't slept for days. Just take a look at me!' His blarney won him an audition and the part. It was a production of *The Quare Fellow* by Brendan Behan, who attended rehearsals, sitting chain smoking and coughing in the stalls, occasionally interrupting the actors saying, 'Did I write that? I'm a fucking genius.' Fellow Irishmen Harris and Behan became lasting friends through their shared love of alcohol. Behan had once dragged a cello halfway across Dublin to a pawnshop that he knew would give him the price of a round of drinks.

Brendan Behan was born in Dublin and lived his childhood in the slums of the city. His family was strongly republican; loyalty to the IRA was expected, and from the age of nine he'd served in a youth organization connected with the IRA. When he wasn't in the pub, Behan was invariably in jail. He was sentenced to three years in Borstal for attempting to blow up a battleship in Liverpool harbour. Later he was sentenced to 14 years for the attempted murder of two detectives. In 1946 he was released under a general amnesty, but was in prison again in 1947, serving a short term for allegedly helping an IRA prisoner to escape.

During his years in prison, Behan started to write plays and stories that colourfully depicted the life of the ordinary working men and would lead to him becoming one of the most famous Irish writers of his time. He had long been a heavy drinker, describing himself, on one occasion, as 'a drinker with a writing problem' and claiming, 'I only drink on two occasions – when I'm thirsty and when I'm not.'

Behan was once hired to write an advertising slogan for Guinness. As part of his payment for this, the company offered him half a dozen kegs of their stout. After a month the company asked Behan what he had come up with; Behan had already managed to drink all of the beer they had given him and hurriedly produced the slogan: 'Guinness Makes You Drunk'. Not surprisingly he didn't win the contract.

A lifelong battle with alcoholism ended Behan's career in a Dublin hospital on 20th March 1964, at the age of 41. His last words were to several nuns standing over his bed, 'God bless you, and may your sons all be bishops.'

Littlewood's company saved Harris from a fate worse than death – having to go back to Limerick – and he befriended fellow actor Brian Murphy, later to achieve TV fame in the classic 70s sitcom *George and Mildred*. 'We got on rather well and I liked Richard very much. He was incredibly determined. He said to me that he was going to be a film star and I say to this day, he's the only person that I have worked with who set his sights high on becoming a film star and achieved it in a very short time. He seemed to me to be very calculated.'

Once he started making movies Harris would sometimes pop back and catch one of Joan's productions. 'He sat in the box,' Murphy recalls, 'and laughed uproariously. I told him, "Christ Richard you behave more like a bloody star in the audience than you ever did on stage." Certainly he would make sure everybody knew he was there.'

With his first regular income from acting (however meagre) Harris decided to get married. For some months now he'd been dating drama student Elizabeth Rees-Williams. They'd met at a café in Earls Court and she was smitten with him immediately. 'There was this energy, this powerhouse, this charisma.' They moved in together but lived in virtual poverty. Later, when Elizabeth discovered she was pregnant, she had to make her maternity clothes out of an old pair of curtains.

It was a passionate affair, both of them rebellious spirits. Harris saw Elizabeth almost as 'forbidden fruit' with her father being Liberal Peer David Rees-Williams, the 1st Baron Ogmore, who sat in the House of Lords. When it came time to meet Elizabeth's posh parents Harris had to borrow a suit, tie and shoes but couldn't find anyone to lend him some socks so, not wanting to reveal the true state of his poverty, for the whole evening tried desperately to keep his trouser legs tugged down. Obviously he failed because when the couple announced their wedding plans Lady Ogmore gave out 'a sort of wail of despair' as Harris remembered it. Other reports say that she threw her arms in the air and ran screaming from the room. Lord Ogmore insisted Harris couldn't marry his daughter until he could afford to keep her. Harris hit back, 'I'm a thespian, I can command high fees at Stratford. I've wonderful contacts, you know, old Ralphie Richardson and Johnny Gielgud and all those splendid theatre queers.'

In spite of parental grumbles the marriage went ahead on 7th February 1957. It was a grand affair taking place at the Church of Notre Dame in Leicester Square with a reception at the House of Lords, attended by 300 guests, most of them Ogmore friends and family. Hardly any of the Harris clan showed up. Living at the time in a tiny bedsit and on the breadline, here was Harris rubbing shoulders with Lord So and So and Lady Whatsit. The irony of it all must have brought a huge smile to his face.

With the little money he'd received upon demobilization Peter O'Toole hitchhiked around the theatrical cities of Britain, spending his money on theatre seats rather than hotel rooms, with the result that he often slept rough. In a field in Stratford he took refuge atop a haystack that turned out to be a dung heap with just a thin covering of straw on top. The next morning, still potless and now smelling like a fox's fart, he ate at a café and made a break for it when the waiter wasn't looking. Years later he returned to Stratford in triumph and visited the very same café, this time to leave a massive tip.

After breakfast he caught a train to London and immediately made his way to RADA, only to be told at reception that he couldn't get in without a proper academic background. O'Toole went ballistic. By sheer luck the school's principal, Sir Kenneth Barnes, overheard his protest and set up a private audition. Impressed by the young rascal he decided to take a chance and a scholarship was granted. O'Toole's life was about to change as he found himself in a vintage year of aspiring actors that included Alan Bates and Albert Finney. 'That was the most remarkable class the academy ever had, though we weren't reckoned for much at the time. We were all considered dotty.' All of them lived in virtual poverty, O'Toole subsisting on a diet of spaghetti and tomato sauce. Broke, he lived in a succession of dingy bedsits; even for a time on a barge that sank one night during a party after too many revellers came aboard.

Predictably O'Toole's three-year stay at RADA was not without incident. On his way to a school production he was a passenger in a car that hit a ten-ton lorry on the A1. So severe was the accident that the driver, O'Toole's friend, was crippled for life. Taken to hospital for X-rays, his leg bursting with pain, O'Toole discharged himself after being kept waiting for hours, took a train to London and found a sympathetic doctor to bind up his injured leg and pump him full of painkillers in order to give his performance. Returning to hospital the next day the X-ray proved that O'Toole had a broken leg.

Over the years cars and O'Toole have never been the best of friends. He once fell asleep while driving on the M1 and woke up to find himself careering down the grass of the central reservation. 'There was nothing for it but to put my feet up on the dashboard and wait for the crash.' He survived undamaged and walked to the nearest town to phone the AA to ask them to tow the wreckage away. 'I never did see that heap again.' He also wrote off an MG sports car. One woman who accepted a lift from O'Toole swore afterwards that she would never do so again. During the journey he ignored a keep left sign on the grounds that it was 'silly' and narrowly avoided driving down a flight of steps. On another journey, this time with actor Kenneth Griffith, O'Toole was speeding along a high road when Griffith said, 'I say, old son, you're doing very well but should you be trying to change gear with the hand brake?'

O'Toole thought nothing of getting behind the wheel intoxicated and didn't bother with such trifles as owning a driving licence, claiming he'd learnt to drive perfectly adequately whilst on holiday in the Swiss Alps. Finally in 1959 he decided maybe he did need a licence after all. On the morning of the test he was a little hungover but brimming with confidence. In the time it took to execute a three-point turn and head back out into the street, connecting with a pillar on the way, the shaken examiner requested to be driven back and O'Toole to withdraw from the vehicle. Not to be outdone O'Toole bought an Irish driving licence for 30 shillings. When stardom and riches came along driving was wisely dispensed with and O'Toole hired a chauffeur instead.

During this time a friendship was struck with Wilfred Lawson, whom O'Toole would describe as an 'eccentric, perverse old bastard'. Lawson, famous for his part on stage as Eliza Doolittle's father in *My Fair Lady*, became O'Toole's acting mentor and was a notorious drunkard. In the days when plays went out live on television Lawson was muddling through his lines one night when he suddenly dried. Luckily his fellow actors were able to cover for him and when the scene ended Lawson breathed a huge sigh of relief and said, 'Well, I fair buggered that up, didn't I,' not realizing he was still on-air.

Lawson had also made the acquaintance of Burton, perhaps sensing that both men were at the vanguard of a new form of realism in acting and therefore represented the future. More likely it was because they made for good drinking companions. During lunch in a pub Lawson ran into Burton and invited him to the matinee of a play he was appearing in at a nearby theatre. Since he wasn't in the early scenes Lawson offered to sit with Burton in the stalls. About 20 minutes after curtain up Burton started to get rather anxious that Lawson had not yet left to don his costume or make-up, instead just sitting there enthralled by the spectacle. Suddenly he tapped Burton's arm and said. 'You'll like this bit. This is where I come on.'

Lawson would meet quite a bizarre final curtain, suffering a fatal collapse while having a death mask made for a film.

Still determined to be an actor Oliver Reed went to casting director after casting director looking for work. He knew full well what went on in the industry, that powerful people, both male and female, took advantage of young actors. Reed himself had been told that to get on in the business he might have to take his trousers down. One particular director who had invited him over to his house for a private audition was a notorious homosexual. Kate knew of his reputation and wrote 'This is mine' in blue paint on her husband's cock. On Reed's back she scrawled the legend: 'Get off!' At the director's home Reed was plied with endless glasses of whisky. 'I thought, he's trying to get me pissed and the next thing he will do is unzip my flies and it will spoil everything when my diseased-looking little thing falls out with writing all over it.' To prevent such a catastrophe Ollie decided to casually toss into the conversation the fact that his uncle was Carol Reed, which made quite an impact. There were no more whiskies after that; instead the director merely handed Reed a sausage roll. 'Not the one he had originally intended.'

* * *

Hollywood seemed to suit Richard Burton, but the films he was being asked to appear in did nothing for his stature as an actor. There was a war film, *The Desert Rats* (1953), where he played an English captain out to nobble Rommel, played by James Mason. Set in North Africa, but acted out near Palm Springs, it also reunited him with Robert Newton. One weekend they decided to cross the border into Mexico. Because American citizens were allowed in without visas, unlike Brits, both men assumed American accents. 'We became absolutely paralysed with tequila,' said Burton. 'And on the way back we were so stoned that we completely forgot about our accents, and we landed in the pokey for the night.'

Burton next made *The Robe* (1953), which sealed his position in Hollywood as a major new talent. Burton played Marcellus, the Roman centurion charged with overseeing the crucifixion, but when he wins Christ's robe in a bet his life is changed forever. It was a huge production but clunky beyond belief, the kind of Hollywood religious film for which the makers themselves should have been crucified.

Burton was making crap in Hollywood and he knew it. 'If you're going to make rubbish – be the best rubbish in it.' One night over drinks he poured out his woes to Laurence Olivier, in Hollywood at the same time making not dissimilar pieces of garbage. 'What on earth are we doing?' said Olivier. 'You know, there's only one thing that can save us. We have to go and find some babies to reassure ourselves that there's some kind of future.' So, pissed of course, Burton and Olivier drove round Beverly Hills in the middle of the night looking for a baby. They knocked at doors of houses with lights still on and in one of them a rather startled couple produced a baby for them. 'To this day, I don't know who it was,' recalled Burton years later. 'I think we both wept a little. Our fans of the future, we must have said. Then we went back home.'

Despite churning out crud Burton impressed the head of 20th Century Fox, Darryl F. Zanuck, and was offered a seven-picture deal worth one million dollars. But Burton showed incredible balls by refusing, having already promised to play Hamlet at London's Old Vic for £45 a week. Zanuck hit back, determined to keep Burton, saying the actor had already signed the contract and by leaving was in breach of the agreement. Burton answered by claiming that his agent had been the one who signed the contract, and had done so without his permission. The result of all this was that Zanuck and Fox took Burton to court for breach of contract.

The showdown arrived and there was Burton on one side of the courtroom while on the other side stood Zanuck, one of the most powerful men in Hollywood, and half the lawyers it seemed in America. 'I didn't have a lawyer,' revealed Burton. 'I played it very English, very Ronald Colman.' At one point one of the lawyers jumped up and shook his fists at Burton and said, 'You shook hands with Mr Zanuck on this agreement. You shook hands with Mr Zanuck in his own office.' Burton was incredulous. 'I don't believe Mr Zanuck said that because he's an honourable man. But if he did say it, then he's a fucking liar.' The courtroom erupted and the session was cancelled. The next day the phone rang at Burton's hotel and there was a woman at the end of it. 'Did you call Darryl F. Zanuck a fucking liar?' she asked. 'Yes, I think I did,' said Burton. 'Then you need help. I'll be right round.' The woman was a tough American lawyer who did indeed help disentangle Burton from this legal mess, impressing him so much that he made her his business manager.

Just before leaving Hollywood Burton was invited to a party in Bel Air. As he was introduced to a group of people by the obligatory swimming pool a girl sitting opposite took off her sunglasses and looked at him. Burton met her eyes and was momentarily stunned by her beauty. She took a sip of beer and then went back to her book. For the rest of the party Burton couldn't take his eyes off her. She, in return, totally ignored him. Her name was Elizabeth Taylor.

Back from Hollywood Richard Burton returned home to a hero's welcome from the locals, except his dad who merely said, 'Well Rich, how are you getting on?' as if he'd only been away for the weekend. He never quite got a handle on the fact his son was a massive star and only ever saw a couple of his films because there were simply too many pubs between his home and the local cinema. It took great persuasion to get him to attend a showing of *My Cousin Rachel*, only for him to walk out when Richard poured himself a drink on screen. 'That's it,' he said and was off to the pub.

Soon it was back to London for Burton and the Old Vic to play *Hamlet*, where he found comfort and much more in the arms of co-star Claire Bloom, despite the actress once referring to him as, 'that uncouth man'.

The affair started as mischief really. Bloom had a guardian at the theatre, actor William Squire, whose job was to keep undesirables at bay, especially Burton, who now took this as a challenge. In a nearby pub Burton sidled up to Squire to make inquiries. 'Look, it's no good Rich,' Squire said. 'She won't do it with anybody, especially not you.' Burton's dander was up. 'I bet I'll get there.' Squire was adamant he wouldn't. 'Want to bet?' said Burton. Squire thought about it. 'A pint,' he said finally. 'You're on,' said Burton, rubbing his hands. Later that week Squire was sitting in the stalls watching Burton perform on stage when Claire, who was sitting next to him, sighed. 'You have to admit,' she gushed, 'he is rather marvellous.' Squire saw his pint bet disappearing fast.

Burton reigned supreme at the Old Vic, achieving the kind of fame usually reserved for pop stars. At the last night fans nearly tore the place apart looking for him and he had to be smuggled away in a taxi. His stamina and energy equally amazed colleagues. Here was a man who could go out on the piss all night and be in punctually next morning for rehearsal, while the rest of the company suffered horrendous hangovers. Burton once revealed that up until the age of 45 he never had a single hangover. After that, though, his hangovers were sometimes so severe that he couldn't even get out of bed.

Practical jokes took up much of his time, too, such as the occasion when he tried to take a horse upstairs into a restaurant. But he responded even better when they were played on him. While appearing as Henry V at Stratford Burton showed off his physical prowess by hitting a springboard and leaping upon his horse to begin the famous 'Once more unto the breach dear friends' speech. At one performance fellow Welsh actor Hugh Griffith shuffled onto the stage in disguise and moved the horse. When Burton bounced up in the air he almost missed the thing completely, managing just to hang on with one leg, but upside down, his bollocks shattered and in utter agony; 'Once more unto the – arghhh.'

Richard Harris, now married with responsibilities, had begun winning regular roles at Joan Littlewood's theatre, including his Shakespearean stage debut in a modern dress version of *Macbeth*. It was only a small part but so proud was Harris that he invited his family to attend the first night. As he marched onto the stage, dressed as a soldier brandishing a sword, his mind went blank. As he opened his mouth, hoping the line, any line would come out, it wasn't his voice that filled the auditorium but his mother's booming out from the front row, 'That's my son. Isn't he marvellous.' Stranded on the stage, utterly alone with everyone looking at him Harris needed to get off fast. Raising the sword high he yelled the first thing that came into his head – 'Grrrr' – before exiting ignominiously, stage right.

Harris also went with the company on tour in Europe and managed to get stranded. The company were in France and on their way to a festival in Switzerland when the train stopped in Lille. Harris and a couple of others, including Brian Murphy, got off to have a bite to eat in the buffet. 'We leisurely strolled back,' recalls Murphy, 'but then we saw that our train was leaving so we ran like hell and got to the end only for this huge guard to push us off back onto the platform. So there we were, alone, and we had nothing on us because our jackets were in the train along with our passports. We tried explaining what happened but our French was minimal, so Richard tried demonstrating, he ran up and down the platform pretending to be the train and the guard pushing us off. Of course the looks on the faces of the station officials were totally blank. They must have thought, who the bloody hell have we got here.'

Adding to their woes was the fact it was Sunday so the local British dignitary was off somewhere playing golf. With hardly any money and nowhere to go the group ended up sleeping in a field. 'For much of the time Richard was regaling us with stories or impersonations to keep us amused,' says Murphy. 'He was a brilliant mimic and on trips and things would have us all quite helpless with laughter. Then when he ran out of steam his head would drop forward and he'd go to sleep. The next morning we woke up surrounded by cows looking very inquisitive. Back at the station the British consulate had organised for us to take any train bound for Zurich. Joan and the company had landed the day before, of course, greeted with a red carpet and a small band. Although apparently much of the company was scattered rather like us in distant places.'

The pay was meagre and Harris and his wife remained pretty much on the breadline. Things got so bad that Elizabeth pawned her jewellery in order to survive. Just as Harris was contemplating quitting acting the breakthrough arrived when he caught the attention of a TV director looking for someone to play an IRA rebel. Flat-broke Harris smashed the gas meter in his flat for the bus fare to the audition. Kept waiting in the office for an hour Harris burst in and screamed in the director's face that he was a fucking pain in the arse, a display of raw emotion that got him cast on the spot. It was a fat fee too. 'I fell on my knees and kissed the ground at his feet for that loot.' The play aired in March 1957 and Harris proved a screen natural: the TV critic of the *Daily Mirror* singled him out as someone to watch. After years of demanding attention, suddenly it was all there in his lap. But Harris wanted more.

Offers started to come in, such as supporting roles at the Bristol Old Vic opposite Peter O'Toole. It was the beginning of a lifelong friendship between the two men and countless marathon booze binges. Harris described this period as, 'Golden days. We kept each other up half the time, we never slept. It was days of chat and yarn-spinning and great, legendary boozing.'

During every intermission Harris and O'Toole propped up the bar of the local, managing to get back just in time for curtain up in the second half. One matinee they overstayed their welcome and a stagehand burst into the saloon bar screaming, 'You're on!' Both men leapt to their feet and made it back into the theatre in 15 seconds flat, but O'Toole was first. Crashing into the wings, he hurtled past the backstage crew and tumbled onto the stage, almost falling headfirst into the audience. A woman in the front row sniffed his breath. 'My God, he's pissed drunk.' O'Toole lifted his head. 'You think this is bad. Wait till you see the other fella.'

Harris delighted in his friendship with O'Toole. They shared a passion for rugby and went to Twickenham whenever they could. 'O'Toole was a poet and a warrior. I loved every moment with him.' One prestigious bash they attended was presided over by Lord Ogmore, Harris's father-in-law and president of the London Welsh Society. The place was of course full of Welshmen but Harris and O'Toole's Irish revelries went so far over the top that Ogmore was besieged by threats to resign from the society unless the pair were ejected. Harris and O'Toole were indeed booted out.

They got up to other laddish japes in London. At one time they were both competing for the affections of the same woman and after a night of drinking went their separate ways, only to bump into each other 20 minutes later outside the girl's block of flats. The game was up and so a deal was struck. O'Toole would try to smooth talk his way into her bedroom using the intercom, while Harris would climb the drain pipe up to the sixth floor and try to attract her attention that way. First come, first served, as it were. 'I nearly killed myself with my mountaineering efforts,' Harris later recalled, 'but eventually reached her balcony and peered in. Peter had literally that moment walked into the room to claim his prize. As they headed to the bedroom, he looked back and saw my dishevelled figure and winked. I nearly fell down just from laughing.'

There is another version of this story, told from O'Toole's point of view. The pair were searching for this woman and drunkenly knocked on her door in the middle of the night. When there was no answer O'Toole scrambled up the drain pipe, knocked on the window and gained entry. 'But when I look back,' recalled O'Toole, 'there's Harris still on the ground. He must not have had my experience growing up with drain pipes in Limerick.' When Harris did try to climb, he got about four storeys up before the drain pipe broke away from the wall, leaving him in midair. So O'Toole and the girl summoned the authorities. 'When they'd got him down, I shouted from the window, "Officers, arrest that drunken Irishman. He was trying to break into our home!"'

O'Toole was fond of scaling walls. Delighted to hear one day that his old RADA chum Frank Finlay was in town and a guest at the local YMCA, O'Toole decided at past midnight to pay him a visit, only to discover the entrance locked. Undeterred O'Toole climbed his way four storeys up and, bottle in hand, manoeuvred his way along the narrow ledges to Finlay's room and hammered on the glass like a mad thing. 'Open up, open up.' A bemused but delighted Finlay was only too happy to oblige.

Peter O'Toole's time at Bristol was spent playing a variety of roles, big and small. He'd had no formal education to speak of, so RADA and the Bristol Old Vic constituted his only real schooling, and he revelled in it, whether playing Shylock in *The Merchant of Venice* or Mrs Ali Baba in the Christmas panto *Aladdin*. He didn't even mind having to sell ice creams in the interval. One evening, still dressed as Mrs Ali Baba he sold an ice cream to Cary Grant.

One early stage performance required him to speak only one line as a peasant in a Chekhov play: 'Mr Astrov, the horses have arrived.' Trying to make the most of this meagre role O'Toole decided that the peasant was the young Stalin. Going on stage consumed with hatred for the whole aristocracy, having worked on his make-up for hours using early photographs of the dictator, O'Toole could feel an electric spark of anticipation coming off the audience. He glared at Dr Astrov, paused and snarled quietly, 'Mr Horsey, the Astrovs have arrived.'

Occasionally the Bristol Old Vic brought its shows down to London. One in particular, a musical, *Oh My Papa*, in which O'Toole played opposite Rachel Roberts, was a complete stinker and people quite rightly booed at them from the stalls. Afterwards O'Toole got drunk on home-made mead and was arrested at three in the morning for harassing a building in Holborn. He spent the night in the cells and in the morning told the court, 'I felt like singing and began to woo an insurance building.'

When he wasn't at the pub O'Toole was busy making home-made whisky. 'We made gallons of it. We had a distillery. The only trouble was we couldn't find anything to store it in. So we got some of those big carboys they keep acid in and filled them with the stuff. Judging by the taste of the whisky, we left some of the acid in.'

By far the pinnacle of O'Toole's time at Bristol was his performance as Hamlet. Critics dubbed it an 'angry young Hamlet', alluding to the New Wave of British acting that was brushing away the cobwebs of staid middle class theatre. There was a revolution going on and post-war British dramatists typified by Noel Coward and Terence Rattigan were being dumped in favour of more gritty and controversial kitchen sink playwrights like John Osborne, thanks to his play *Look Back in Anger*. Cinema too was changing. The stiff upper lip and anyone-for-tennis brigade personified by Richard Todd and Kenneth More were being usurped by a new breed of tough working class actors: O'Toole, Harris, Albert Finney, Michael Caine and others. A revolution incidentally spearheaded by Burton.

These working class rising stars all knew each other, drank together, threw up together and caused trouble together. 'We were all mates,' recalled Caine. 'Raving it up around the pubs and clubs.' Their drinking and revelling was a two-finger salute to the middle class acting establishment, putting a landmine under the Olivier and Gielgud generation. This was a new breed and nothing like them had been seen before or since. For them acting wasn't a vocation. 'We didn't want to be the best actors in the world,' said Harris.

'We didn't want to be the best King Lear or be the new Olivier. What a boring ambition.' Instead they wanted to experience everything that life had to offer and have as good a time as they could. Yes they were talented, supremely so in some cases, but they were also totally fearless and the noise they made was their way of saying – we've arrived, ignore us at your peril.

It was an interesting period in British cultural history that gave birth to the hellraisers. Burton, Harris, O'Toole, Reed and the rest all shared the common experience of being war babies, of being bombed, of being evacuated, of facing compulsory military service. 'It's one of the most incredible experiences in the world, being bombed,' O'Toole has commented. 'You play this mad, demented, passive role. I tell you, if you haven't been bombed, you haven't lived. Perhaps if more people had been bombed, they might be less generous in their supply of bombs.'

Then there was rationing: no meat, no food, and no booze. But actually the post-war restrictions were worse. Years after the war Britain was still a country in the grip of austerity and belt tightening by the government. They had economic miracles in Germany and Japan. 'And all we were getting was Stafford Cripps [Labour's Chancellor of the Exchequer after the war] saying, "eat nuts." Bollocks,' railed O'Toole. 'We didn't want any of that. We wanted the roaring twenties, please. There were some of us who saw it as our duty to be truants from the system. The drinking was liberation from the fear and the restrictions of the war years. The frivolity and the fun had gone. Booze was a way of recapturing it. We certainly had a bloody good time.'

O'Toole liked to quote the often repeated line that if you could remember the sixties, you weren't really there. 'Well, we were doing that in the fifties. I can remember how the decade started, and how it ended but, sadly, nothing in between.' As students and young actors they had no money but had youth and stupidity in abundance, so often would save on heating by having parties on the Circle line on the London underground. It was warm, there were chairs and they'd take a battery-operated gramophone and play each other's 45s. Did they drink? 'Of course we did, baby,' says O'Toole. 'We'd get off at Sloane Square, pop out to the pub, get some more booze and get back on again. Great fun! And the sixties were only a continuation of that.'

* * *

While O'Toole, Harris and Reed were busy trying to make a name for themselves, Richard Burton was already a huge star, jetting back out to Hollywood to appear in more brain-dead but successful epics. There was *The Rains of Ranchipur* (1955) in which he played a Hindu doctor opposite Lana Turner, a film so dire that Burton later quipped, 'It never rains but it ranchipurs.' Then came *Alexander the Great* (1956) with Burton playing the titular hero in a blond wig that resembled a cowpat. His leading lady was, interestingly, Claire Bloom. After he had won the earlier bet by seducing her into his bed the couple had begun a torrid affair and although Burton's wife Sybil was on location with her husband in Spain this didn't stop our Dick. Claire was desperately in love with Burton and he knew it, treating her dreadfully sometimes, even prepared to totally humiliate her seemingly on a whim. One day on the set he announced to some of the crew that he was going to shag Claire in a nearby secluded stream. 'Why don't you watch from over that hill?' he kindly suggested. That afternoon Burton did indeed perform to an audience of randy grips and stunt men.

His next venture was another season at the Old Vic, which included *Othello*, alternating the lead role with that of Iago (generally considered to be the longest role in Shakespeare) with another actor. One Saturday lunchtime Burton was invited to attend a charity cricket match organized by the Lord's Taverners. Amongst the group was a young actor, Ian Carmichael, soon to become a star himself in a string of classic British comedy films like *I'm Alright Jack* and *Lucky Jim*. 'We had all downed a considerable number of pints,' recalls Carmichael. 'And my turn had come round once more. "Same again?" I enquired of all concerned. I then said to Burton, "Shall I skip you this time?" Burton stared back at me. "Why the hell not!" "You've got a matinee, haven't you?" I asked. "Yes," said Burton, "but it's only Iago this afternoon." The Welsh have great constitutions.'

Burton was now famous and rich enough to become a tax exile – he had calculated that if he made £100,000 in a year in England the bloody tax man would grab £93,000 of it, while as a Swiss resident he'd pay no more than £700 on the same amount – so in 1957 he moved to Celigny, a small village on the outskirts of Geneva. A regular visitor there was Brook Williams, the ten-year-old son of Emlyn, who remained a close friend of Burton's for the rest of his life. Burton enjoyed attending Brook's school plays where he often took with him a flask, not filled with tea, but strong martini. He'd pour it out into a plastic cup during the performance and blow on it to keep up the charade.

Not surprisingly Brook hero-worshipped Burton and became an actor himself, also a heavy drinker. In adult life Williams ran into personal problems and couldn't find work, so Burton took him under his wing, plonking him on the payroll. Williams became the star's minder, drinking companion and general lackey. Watch a Burton film and Brook Williams' bemused mug is in it somewhere.

Financially Burton's self-imposed Swiss exile made perfect sense, but it did mean that he cut himself off from the renaissance in English theatre and film happening back home. He was in danger of losing ground to that new breed of British actor he himself had helped pave the way for.

After his TV success Harris sparked interest from Associated British Pictures and the casting director there wasted little time in recommending the Irishman to director Michael Anderson, who was casting one of the main parts in his film *Shake Hands with the Devil* (1959). 'Harris arrived at the interview,' Anderson remembers, 'and as he walked into the room he said, "Well it's nice to see all you film folks, but I want to tell you up front, I don't do film, I only do stage work." I said, "Well why did you come?" And he said, "I wanted to see what you was all about, you know, you hear a lot about films these days. I've read the script, it's a good script but no, I don't think so." And he got up and started to walk towards the door where he turned round and said, "Who's in it?" And I said. "James Cagney." He said. "I'll do it."'

The part was an IRA gun runner and the film was shot in Ireland, where its subject matter caused a modicum of controversy. Though Harris was raw and unfamiliar with film acting technique Anderson recognised in him a spark of talent. 'He had such a screen personality and put in gestures and little method things that weren't in the script but stood out a mile. He was unpredictable in a scene; you never knew quite what he was going to do which made him so exciting. He was so different to Burton who had been disciplined on the set when I'd worked with him; Harris was not.'

Already Harris was carving out something of a reputation for questioning his directors, not blindly following instructions but his own instincts, a habit that would lead to violent clashes in the future. 'After just a few days on *Shake Hands* Richard would come on the set and say, "I don't know if I want to do it this way," and we'd talk about the scene and once I'd persuaded him that's the way it should be done and the way I wanted it there was no problem. But near the end of the picture we were rehearsing a scene and Harris wasn't there. I put all the chalk marks on the floor where the actors would stand and the crew were making bets that Harris would never stand on those marks, he'd do something totally different. So Richard came in and said, "What are we doing then?" I made up some bit of business and said, "I think if you go over to the window . . ." He said, "I don't think I'm going to go over to the window, I think I'll come up here." And he went right on the marks that I'd put on the floor.'

Though he shared few scenes with Cagney, Harris was in awe of the Hollywood legend, remembering the days when he'd seen him in action, blasting gangsters to kingdom come at his local fleapit. It was also a great opportunity to see a master at work and Harris exploited it to the full. 'He was fascinated with Cagney and would watch him work,' Anderson recalls. 'He was taking it all in.'

Money was now rolling into the Harris coffers so fast that he and Elizabeth didn't have to live on stew made of Oxo cubes and carrots any more. There was also a new propensity to brawl as frequently as he was able; and there was the drinking. More so than before, going on booze benders had become Harris's main pastime. After one evening he awoke in a prison cell. The sergeant asked him if he knew why he'd been arrested. 'No,' said Harris. 'I haven't a fucking clue.' Harris had a good capacity for hard liquor and, just like Oliver Reed, liked the way other people's inhibitions were loosened by it. There was also the Irish tradition of late night get-togethers where drink played just as much an important part as the reveries, the songs and the nostalgic stories about back home. 'I never touch a drop when I'm happy,' Harris reasoned. 'But it's a well-known fact that Irishmen are never happy.'

Harris was a boon to the publicity department of his new employers, whose stable of bland film stars didn't excite the press much. It was usually a case of coming into the office on Monday morning to find all the telephones ringing and wondering, 'God, what's Harris done now.' During a celebrity bash at the Royal Festival Hall one of Harris's friends accidentally broke a glass but the management mistakenly charged the group for ten replacements. When they refused to correct the error Elizabeth Harris got up and said, 'All right, if you're going to charge us for 10 glasses we still have nine to go.' One by one she threw the rest of the glasses to the floor. When the couple left Harris saw a group of cops huddled outside that he assumed had been called to deal with his wife's behaviour. Deciding to take pre-emptive action he rugby charged them, shunting the constables through a plate-glass shop window. No one was hurt, save Harris who had several stitches to a gash in his hand. Amazingly he escaped with just a caution.

To consolidate his success as Hamlet at the Bristol Old Vic Peter O'Toole took on the important role of a cockney sergeant in the play *The Long and the Short and the Tall* about a bunch of misfit British soldiers lost in Burma during the Japanese campaign of WWII. It was to be presented at the prominent showplace for young acting talent, the Royal Court in Sloane Square. As was his routine O'Toole, along with other cast members Robert Shaw and Ronald Fraser, drank in the local pub prior to curtain up. Sometimes with only minutes to spare they'd stampede back into the theatre, rub dirt over their faces and change into a khaki uniform looking as if they'd spent an hour in make-up to achieve the desired bedraggled jungle look. They made such a habit of sitting in the pub all possible hours that a line eventually had to be rigged up from the theatre so the stage manager's 10-minute call could be heard at the bar. The director Lindsay Anderson was almost driven bonkers, while the expert hired to make the actors look like real soldiers suffered a nervous collapse and left.

Someone else who had a torrid time was the young Michael Caine, hired as O'Toole's understudy. Caine would stew in suspense backstage as to whether O'Toole would return from the pub in time. This lasted three months and every night was torture. There he'd be, dressed up and ready to go on when O'Toole would breeze in offering a hearty hello to the panic-stricken youngster. One evening the curtain was actually rising when O'Toole ran in screaming, 'Don't go on Michael' as he bounded into his dressing room, shirt and trousers being cast asunder. Caine's other functions were to bring in booze, find out where the best parties were and acquire girls. 'I'd have made a wonderful pimp,' he later joked.

One Saturday night after the show O'Toole invited Caine to a restaurant he knew. Eating a plate of egg and chips was the last thing Caine remembered until he woke up in broad daylight in a strange flat. 'What time is it?' he enquired. 'Never mind what time it is, what fucking *day* is it?' said O'Toole. They located their hostesses, two dodgy looking girls who told them it was five o'clock on Monday afternoon. Curtain went up at eight. Luckily they were still in London and made their way to the theatre just in time. The stage manager was waiting for them with the news that the owner of the restaurant had been in and henceforth they were banned from his establishment for life. Caine was just about to ask what they'd done when O'Toole whispered, 'Never ask what you did. It's better not to know.' Ah, the voice of experience. After that Caine made a point of never going out on the booze with O'Toole again.

At the time Robert Shaw was the big cheese actor, so his dressing room had the only toilet and O'Toole had to make do with a big sink. One night after the performance, he was standing in his dressing room, peeing in the sink, when he heard an unmistakable voice behind him. 'Hello, my name is Katharine Hepburn.' O'Toole pretended to be washing his hands and quickly shoved himself back in his trousers.

Hepburn was in London filming *Suddenly Last Summer* with Montgomery Clift, and she commended the performance of this young actor O'Toole to the movie's producer, Sam Spiegel. Spiegel called O'Toole and asked him to take a screen test. A silver Jaguar arrived, driven, O'Toole recalled, by a particularly surly chauffeur, to ferry him to Shepperton Studios. Spiegel had wanted O'Toole to stand by for a weekly fee, ready to take over Montgomery Clift's role as a doctor in the film; he apparently doubted that the oft-ailing Clift would be able to finish it. The unfriendly driver who had fetched O'Toole worked for Clift and realized a coup was in the making. Once there O'Toole was hustled onto the set of a doctor's office, where, holding an X-ray as a prop, his screen test consisted of his own impromptu wisecrack: 'Mrs Spiegel, your son will never play the violin again.' The producer was not amused and O'Toole was quickly dispensed with; indeed Spiegel never forgot the insolence of the young actor and just a few years later almost thwarted O'Toole's bid to land the role of his lifetime – Lawrence of Arabia.

Most evenings after the show O'Toole enjoyed a long walk around Covent

Garden. Sometimes if he was in the mood he'd scale the wall of Lloyd's bank. The first time he took his future wife Siân Phillips on one of these nocturnal jaunts she was startled when he began his ascent of the north face of the bank thinking it to be, 'mad, dangerous behaviour'. But after a few nights of it the actress came to accept this as unremarkable, as far as O'Toole was concerned.

At the time O'Toole and Siân were staying rent free with actor Kenneth Griffith who admired O'Toole greatly but had grave doubts about the couple's wedding plans. 'You cannot marry this wonderful man,' he said one day to Siân. 'Understand, he is a genius, but he is not normal.' Siân started to get similar words of warning from quite a few of O'Toole's friends, and some of her own. She ignored them all. 'I was so deliriously in love I couldn't understand why everyone around me was worried.'

Griffith would remain one of O'Toole's most loyal and longest lasting friends. The two first met while working on a TV play in 1957. O'Toole woke up pissed one morning, no clue as to where the hell he was, remembering only that he'd written down on a piece of paper that he had to turn up for rehearsals for this play. Arriving late, with the rest of the cast already assembled and waiting, he burst through the doors. 'Sorry I'm late, darlings.' In an instant he fixed eyes on Griffith, thundered across the room, picked him up and kissed the startled actor on the cheek. 'I think you're bloody marvellous,' said O'Toole. It was an odd introduction.

Despite Griffith's misgivings O'Toole and Siân were very much in love, but certainly an unusual alliance. Looking at her decorative if drab wardrobe of black and violet clothes one day O'Toole said, 'You look as though you're in mourning for your sex life. Give it here.' Gathering up armfuls of shoes, gloves, frocks, hats and suits he flung them all out of the window. Siân looked at a thousand pounds worth of clothes on the wet cobbles below. 'What will I wear now?' she howled. O'Toole's reply was instant. 'My clothes.' They became the only couple in town with a shared wardrobe of cotton trousers, lumberjack shirts and fisherman's sweaters. Their marriage in Dublin, which consisted of a pub-crawl picking up well-wishers along the way, wasn't so much a ceremony as 'just an excuse for a piss up' in Siân's words.

It was the sheer unpredictability of the man that had so attracted Siân to him in the first place. Quite often she didn't know what the hell he was going to do next. Once he showed up in a sports car yelling, 'Get your passport, we're off.' Heading for Rome they took a wrong turning and ended up in Yugoslavia: the beginning of a grand mystery tour around Europe. For Siân each day was a challenge and an hilarious adventure. O'Toole was the perfect travelling companion. 'He had an aura, always. When we first went on holiday, we were mobbed. People wanted to travel with us, talk to us, but he hadn't done anything then. He wasn't famous. But even when he was nothing, as it were, you knew he was something.'

Still, his manic driving did tend to shred the nerves, either bombing down the autobahn or hurtling round the bends of alpine roads. After he'd taken a friend back to Amsterdam, the unfortunate woman later confided to Siân, 'He should never drive *anything*. He's lovely, but I thought we were going to die on that journey.'

They finished the holiday off with a trip to Wales to stay with relatives of Siân, but even a country cottage O'Toole managed to turn into a disaster area. One night he suddenly decided to do the cooking himself, although Siân had never seen him actually cook anything before. 'I can make the best French toast,' he stated. Minutes later the stove exploded into flames. They tried to extinguish the fire but it was impossible and both were driven out into the garden where they watched in the rain as the kitchen burnt down.

Instead of cashing in on the New Wave of British theatre exploding back home, Richard Burton was stuck making crap international films like *Sea Wife* (1957) in Jamaica, with Joan Collins cast, if you can believe it, as a nun. Naturally Burton made a pass at Joan, which was rebuffed. Unperturbed Burton slunk off, according to Joan, to shag half the island's female population. 'Richard, I do believe you would screw a snake,' she told him. To which Burton glibly responded, 'It would have to be wearing a skirt, darling.'

Bitter Victory (1957), a psychological war film, was another project that Burton felt was beneath him and so he frittered away the time haranguing his fellow actors and drinking himself every day into a stupor. Burton was rather prone to either sinking into a film role with utter conviction if he saw it as a challenge, or playing it with open contempt and boredom. If the film was a piece of shit Burton knew it in an instant and went on auto-pilot.

With a worrying number of film flops stockpiling behind him Burton agreed to do a play on Broadway, filling his spare time boozing royally in the bars of New York. He'd stroll into a club already pissed at midnight and be found there the next morning still telling tales, still knocking back double vodkas and beer chasers. Burton at this time never drank before 5pm when working, but his fortune was such that he could afford to hire a manservant, one of whose duties was to make sure that at 5pm on the dot a large vodka and tonic was ready to hit his outstretched hand.

While on Broadway Burton enjoyed an affair with his co-star Susan Strasberg, daughter of acting guru Lee. The romance lasted for several months and Burton didn't hide it at all. He even went home with her to meet her parents and introduced Susan to members of his family he'd flown over from Wales to see the show. Even when Sybil flew in he carried on regardless. When the play ended its run, so Burton terminated his association with Susan and returned to England to make the film version of the hit play *Look Back in Anger* (1959) with Claire Bloom. Susan was left devastated and followed him, turning up unannounced at the studio. All of which made things cumbersome for Burton who now had a mini harem of mistresses. No sooner was Susan through the door of Burton's dressing room than she was unceremoniously bundled into a toilet so Claire Bloom didn't catch sight of her. Humiliated, Susan considered jumping into the Thames off Waterloo Bridge. Instead she flew home.

Harris had made such a strong impression with Michael Anderson on *Shake Hands with the Devil* that the director cast him in his next production, the seafaring epic *The Wreck of the Mary Deare* (1959) opposite two more film greats, Charlton Heston and Gary Cooper. 'It was interesting,' recalls Anderson. 'When Harris first came on the set and I introduced him to Gary Cooper and Heston he said, "How are you then, nice to see ya." He wasn't at all impressed. That was Richard, he was his own man. As far as he was concerned he had his job to do, they had their job to do and he was certainly not intimidated by these big stars or anything else.'

Nor did Harris allow himself to be overawed by the fact that he was making his first movie in Hollywood, even though the flight over was almost his last when one of the plane's engines burst into flames and they were forced to make an emergency landing. 'He took the whole thing in his stride,' says Anderson.

Sparks flew, however, during shooting when Harris and Heston failed to get on. Harris found epic cinema's leading man to be prudish and stuck up. 'He'd played in Shakespeare and to listen to him you'd think he helped the Bard with the rewrites. He was a prick, really, and I liked tackling pricks.'

Again Anderson came away impressed with Harris the actor. 'He would improvise such wonderful things. We had a section of ship on the stage which was on rockers and he had to spit in this scene. So he spat overboard and with his head he turned as though he were watching the spit go down stream. Well, nobody in a million years would've thought of that bit of business, so you really believed that ship was moving. It was those little things that he would do out of the blue that were stunning, I'll never forget that.'

When the film proved a sizeable hit it was enough to convince Harris what his future course should be: all out pursuit of Hollywood fame and fortune. But he'd pay a hefty price for it. He was drinking more and more, not caring about the consequences. 'It wouldn't touch the taste buds, just hit the stomach, bounce back into my head and keep me going for a little bit.' Friends noticed that his temperament was starting to change, he was being vicious to people in a way he hadn't been before, mostly towards his wife. When unleashed the Harris fury was deeply frightening and something to behold. When he returned home late one day tanked up, Elizabeth made a perfectly justifiable remark about his condition only to see him turn into a raging inferno. Grabbing a nearby wardrobe he lifted it above his head and threw it at her. Friends, not unsurprisingly, wondered how long such a marriage could last.

Harris's habit of bringing home his drinking pals was causing Elizabeth severe distress too. She felt like an outsider in her own home. The poverty that existed in the early part of their marriage she could cope with. 'But this lack of privacy was beginning to destroy me.'

After his success in *The Long and the Short and the Tall* Peter O'Toole started to get movie offers. But even in those early days his behaviour and drinking had become legendary within the business and who knows how many film offers went down the plughole because of it. On one occasion he went to see future 007 producer Albert R. Broccoli, then looking to replace an actor who had a drink problem on one of his films. Alas O'Toole stumbled into Broccoli's office and a bottle of whisky fell out of his overcoat pocket.

While still at RADA O'Toole had appeared on film and television carrying out stunt work under various pseudonyms such as Walter Plings, Charlie Staircase and Arnold Hearthrug but his first proper credit was a small role in Disney's *Kidnapped* (1959), based on the classic Robert Louis Stevenson book. Amazingly on his very first day on the film O'Toole overslept. An angry film company rang to ask, 'Where is Mr O'Toole?' Kenneth Griffith answered and bullshitted as best he could. 'This is a very large house, I'll see if I can find him.' Griffith raced upstairs and popped his head round O'Toole's bedroom door. He was fast asleep. 'O'Toole. You are 45 minutes late.' Lifting his bedraggled head off the pillow O'Toole asked if his car had arrived. 'No,' said Griffith, struck by the question. O'Toole's head crashed back onto the pillow. 'No car, no me.' And he went back to sleep. 'From that day to this, there has been a Rolls-Royce waiting for him,' Griffith once revealed. Maybe in this one anecdote, we have the true definition of what makes a star. As Griffith wryly commented, he himself was never late for work, always turned up on time under his own steam, yet stardom and fame eluded him. From the very beginning O'Toole had star quality and behaved as a star should; in other words, a monumental egoist and royal pain in the ass.

The star of *Kidnapped* was Peter Finch. The Australian was a mighty drinker, so not surprisingly the pair became great pals. As a young actor Finch lived in Sydney and worked a lot on radio. One morning he woke up still pissed from the previous night and with just an hour before he was due on air. In order to sober up, and arrive on time, Finch jumped into the bay and swam a mile across Sydney harbour. He surfaced at the botanical gardens and arrived barefoot and soaking at the studio, ready for work.

Even after he'd made it as a matinee idol and international film star Finch remained a fearsome drinker. One night while driving him along Sunset Strip in Hollywood his exasperated wife looked across at Finch drinking from a bottle of tequila and just saw red. Opening the door she threw him out and sped off. Guilt kicked in about half a mile up the road so she reversed back to look for him, but he was gone. Anxious for the rest of the night she was about to call the police when Finch stumbled into their flat at five in the morning and fell into bed. Not a word about the incident was ever spoken.

O'Toole and Finch piss-ups were mighty affairs and although they never made another film together little excuse was needed to indulge themselves. When Finch was working in Ireland in the early 60s O'Toole joined him one night for a drink but the pub refused to serve them because it was after closing time. Both stars decided that the only course of action was to buy the pub, so they wrote out a cheque for it on the spot. The following morning after realising what they'd done the pair rushed back to the scene of the crime. Luckily the landlord hadn't cashed the cheque yet and disaster was averted. O'Toole and Finch remained on friendly terms with the pub owner and when he died his wife invited them to his funeral. Both knelt at the graveside as the coffin was slowly lowered in, sobbing noisily. When Finch turned away, unable to stand it any more, O'Toole saw his friend's face change from a look of sorrow to one of total astonishment. They were at the wrong funeral. Their friend was being buried 100 yards away.

O'Toole's bit part in *Kidnapped* led to a sizeable role in *The Day They Robbed the Bank of England* (1960), about a group of Irish patriots who plan to steal the British government's gold reserves. But seeing himself for the first time on screen was a calamitous experience and from that day on he never watched his own films, not even *Lawrence of Arabia*, instead giving his premiere ticket to a friend and asking afterwards, 'How is it?' He finally caught up with his most famous film when it premiered on British TV over Christmas 1975, giving up after 40 minutes as the memories came flooding back. 'I kept thinking things like, weren't we doing that bit when Omar Sharif got the clap? No, no, that bit was the day I got the clap. It makes serious viewing extremely difficult.'

His next film, *The Savage Innocents* (1960), where he played a Canadian explorer who befriends an Eskimo was even more of a calamitous experience. In one scene the two men have to make a sledge in order to escape the Arctic wastes but the scriptwriter hadn't been able to figure out exactly how they were supposed to achieve this. O'Toole helpfully suggested the Eskimo eat his character and make a sledge out of his bones and skin. 'We want a happy ending,' said the director. Filmed at Pinewood the snow was in fact tons of salt mix and two polar bears brought in from Dublin Zoo weren't deemed white enough against the salt so were covered in peroxide which drove them nuts. O'Toole left this sorry mess scratching his head as to whether he would ever make it in the movies, especially when he saw the final cut and discovered that his voice had been dubbed by another actor. Throwing a fit he demanded that his name be removed from the film's opening and closing credits.

The Soused Sixties

More crap films followed for Richard Burton as he entered the 1960s. Making *Ice Palace* (1960) in Alaska, a lame action drama, to overcome the horrendous hurdle of getting up at 5am every morning he simply drank his way through the night, usually in the company of co-star Jim Backus (famous as the voice of Mr Magoo). 'Here we are,' Burton would say to Backus, 'drinking at three o'clock in the morning, sitting on top of the world and making this piece of shit.'

Burton was quite conscious of the fact that he was appearing with alacrity in a steady stream of drivel. Later in life he admitted to having made more than his fair share of lousy movies, and not always just for the money. 'I have done the most utter rubbish just to have somewhere to go in the mornings.' His pursuit of fame was mixed up in all this, too. Make enough films, one of them might score at the box office even if the others crash and burn. Burton wanted fame more than anything else. In the early sixties he went for the first time to Eastern Europe and, attending the theatre one evening, was forced to wait in a queue, something he'd not done for quite some time. As none of his films had been released behind the Iron Curtain no one recognised him. He related this incident to a journalist. 'Wasn't that nice for a change,' the man said. Burton stared back, 'No. I hated it.'

Drink still, to a large extent, controlled his life, though the loyal Sybil had learnt to tolerate it in silence. Sometimes Burton would slip into bed beside her at some ungodly hour, too drunk to take his clothes off. One night he got into bed with a lighted cigarette and fell asleep with it still in his hand. Luckily Sybil was awoken by the smoke from the smouldering bedclothes but couldn't stir Burton no matter how hard she shook him. Panic stricken she ran through the house alerting the staff who together carried Burton from the bedroom to the safety of the garden. Only then did Sybil realise that no one had brought out their daughter Jessica, asleep on the top floor. Sybil dashed back into the smoke-filled house and rescued the little girl in the nick of time.

Even during interviews Burton didn't hide the fact that he drank like a fish, not giving a stuff if it was reported or not. As the decade progressed journalists came to regard interviewing him as a perilous business because the actor usually expected the reporter to match him drink for drink. Burton would drain his glass, hand it to an acolyte to be refilled and then frowningly instruct his reluctant drinking companion to 'finish that up, it's time for another one'. During one interview Burton played a practical joke on his interrogator, challenging the reporter to a booze contest. Burton's butler served the drinks and the journalist ended up comatose under the table. Burton stood over him triumphant, a wide smile on his face. Only later did the journalist discover that every time he was served with double whiskies, Burton's glass was filled with iced tea.

After his run in with Heston, Richard Harris faced the even more fearsome Robert Mitchum in his next film *A Terrible Beauty* (1960), an IRA drama shot in Ireland. At first Harris disliked Mitchum but warmed to him when the Hollywood legend came to his aid during a pub brawl. Another time Mitchum sat drinking in a Dublin bar when a short Irishman came up and poked him in the ribs with a pencil. 'Hey movie star, give me your autograph. It's for my wife.' Mitchum eyed the midget up and down with undisguised disgust. 'Will you look at the little leprechaun,' and then told him to wait until he'd finished his drink. But the man persisted. Finally an exasperated Mitchum snatched the paper and pencil and wrote: 'UP YOUR ARSE – KIRK DOUGLAS.' The man was not best pleased and threw a punch, but Mitchum just sat there looking at him. 'If that's the best you can do, little lady, you better come back with your girlfriends.' The man did indeed return with some rather hefty mates. Mitchum head butted one of them, sending him reeling before two more came into the attack. Harris leapt into the fray and a massive punch-up ensued resulting in the police being summoned to break it up.

In between film roles Harris returned to the theatre in a play he pursued fervently, *The Ginger Man*. It was when he'd been cast that the trouble really started. Harris threw himself into the role like no other, rehearsing 40 hours non-stop, half-pissed, and then collapsing with exhaustion. 'I can't do the fucking thing,' he'd yell and storm off to the pub. Co-star and friend Ronnie Fraser was always the one sent to retrieve him. During these hours Harris introduced Fraser to what became his drink of choice, vodka, lime and soda, a love affair that almost wrecked Fraser's life.

For months *The Ginger Man* consumed Harris's entire being, to the detriment of his home life, which, combined with his constant drinking, led to regular arguments. Before the play opened Elizabeth left, taking their child with her. When told of this event years later Harris said, 'Did she? I wasn't fully aware.' *The Ginger Man* was hailed as another *Look Back in Anger* and Harris as theatreland's new angry young man. But the rave notices went over the Harris bonce. 'By the time we opened, I was living on Pluto.' When the production moved to Dublin, with Harris eager for a triumphant homecoming, the play ran into censorship trouble over its sex scenes and angry mobs barred the actors from getting into the theatre. The play was abandoned after just a few days.

Harris drowned his sorrow in booze. He drank every kind of alcohol but had a particular liking for brandy. His tolerance of spirits and beer was high, but brandy brought out the worst in him. His fits of temper were legendary. Sometimes they would arrive without warning, like on a trip to Spain when he suddenly leapt out of a taxi, dodged onrushing traffic on a main road, and ran to the nearest house where he began attacking a solid oak door with his bare hands. The elderly owner of the property emerged only to grab a chair and sit down on the porch to watch the spectacle of this mad stranger pounding away with bloody fists.

Harris truly hit rock bottom when his mother died of cancer. At the funeral he hid behind a tree weeping, unable to witness the coffin go in the ground. Mentally he was all over the place and convinced himself that the world was going to end in 1965. 'We'd been fucking around with nuclear science like lunatics for 20 years,' he rationalised. 'I had no faith in humanity. I thought we were fucked.' Harris had something of a fascination with death. For years he'd play a macabre game where he'd disguise his voice and pretend to be a policeman and phone his wife and close friends to report that Richard Harris, film star, had been killed in a nasty accident.

Things brightened up considerably when he and Elizabeth patched up their marriage, although friends admitted that Harris just wasn't cut out for domesticity and warned Elizabeth that her husband liked chaos and that more rows were inevitable. They were right.

His film career, however, was progressing very nicely thank you with roles in ever more prestigious productions, including the screen version of *The Long and the Short and the Tall* (1960) co-starring Laurence Harvey in the role O'Toole had played on stage. Harris and Harvey spent each lunchtime in the Red Lion pub, just across the road from Elstree studios. Director Leslie Norman got increasingly frustrated as, even though they returned on time, they were always pissed. It was a relationship between actor and director that never improved, as Norman's son Barry, the film critic and writer, recalls. 'Harris was a bit of a bully, and my father was not about to be bullied by an actor, so they were at loggerheads. In later years Harris avoided being interviewed by me because I remember him saying once, "I don't want to talk to him, his father hates me."'

As senior member of the cast Richard Todd took it upon himself to get things under control and one evening invited Harris for a chat in his dressing room. Todd ordered Harris, in no uncertain fashion, to stop behaving like an asshole. Expecting a torrent of abuse back Todd instead watched in amazement as tears welled up in Harris's eyes as he apologised and promised to cut down on his drinking for the rest of the film.

In later years Harris and Harvey became great drinking pals. One game they enjoyed playing was to visit as many bars as possible and down a different drink in each one. The last man standing was the winner. Sometimes these pub-crawls went on for hours as they went from regular pubs, to nightclubs and then the all-night drinking dens Harris knew and loved. One famous session started at lunchtime, went through the night and found the pair still drinking at dawn in Covent Garden.

Harris then made a brief cameo in the war classic *The Guns of Navarone* (1961), co-starring Gregory Peck and David Niven. Niven had been in the army and loved to recall the occasion when he was a guest at a posh military function. Sitting next to his commanding officer Niven was desperate for a piss after drinking far too many aperitifs, but couldn't leave the table before the royal toast at the end of the meal. The Colonel remained silent throughout the meal as numerous courses came and went, accompanied by countless glasses of wine, until by the time the cheese arrived Niven was in agony. He was saved by the intervention of a knowing waiter who placed an empty magnum of champagne underneath his chair. Gripping the huge bottle with his knees Niven proceeded to blissfully piss away for several minutes. Suddenly his CO remarked in a booming voice. 'I have fucked women of every nationality and most animals, but the one thing I cannot abide is a girl with a Glasgow accent. Pass the port.' It was the one and only time the Colonel ever spoke to Niven.

After a couple of negligible film appearances it was back to the theatre for Peter O'Toole, becoming at 26 the youngest leading man ever at Stratford. Director Peter Hall was scrambling for a replacement for Paul Scofield, who had suddenly left the Royal Shakespeare Company, when he remembered how mesmerised he'd been by O'Toole at Bristol, recalling particularly his 'enormous hooter of a nose'. It was indeed perfect for one of the lead roles in the forthcoming season, that of Shylock in *The Merchant of Venice*. O'Toole was summoned but when he arrived at the first rehearsal Hall was shocked to see he'd had a nose job, that big nose was no more. 'What have you done?' said Hall. 'I'm going to be a film star,' O'Toole answered back.

Playing Shylock one night, during the intense court scene, O'Toole spied a packet of fags close to the front of the stage. 'I was wondering what they were doing there, my cue came and I was off, "Now we have expressed our darker purpose..." It was the wrong play. I'd gone into *King Lear*.' Despite the occasional lapse O'Toole was a hit from the first night and critics hailed him as a major new force in acting. Even Elizabeth Taylor was interested in him playing opposite her as Mark Antony in *Cleopatra*, a role that eventually went to Burton. 'I'm marvellous. I must be,' O'Toole announced. The BBC even sent an interviewer down to profile him but the man clearly hadn't done his homework: 'Well, what have you done?' he asked. 'Eh,' said a startled O'Toole. 'Let's see,' the interviewer continued, scanning his rough notes. 'There was that army thing. Come on, come on, what else have you done?' O'Toole had had enough of this. 'Well, I played the dame in *Puss in Boots* once.' The BBC man's face turned sour. 'Look, we don't have to do this interview, you know.' 'In that case,' O'Toole replied, 'I suggest you fuck off.'

It was also at Stratford where O'Toole's reputation as a hellraiser was sealed. 'The best that you can do when you are drunk is to meet your mates, have a lot of giggles, break glass, kick people and get into trouble,' he once declared. At one after show party O'Toole held court on stage sitting on a throne, sustained by two pedal bins on either side of him, one full of beer, the other of hard liquor into which he would alternately scoop two-pint mugs. At another party ex-RADA chum Roy Kinnear watched O'Toole down a bottle of whisky without pausing for breath. O'Toole's favourite pub in Stratford was the Dirty Duck where he broke the house record by downing a yard of ale (that's two and a half pints) in 40 seconds. 'You only do that kind of lunacy because there's nothing else to do,' he excused. O'Toole went back to Stratford late in the 60s and on a visit to the Dirty Duck tried to repeat his earlier feat, without success. 'Either I wasn't that parched or my stomach had shrunk. Frankly I just don't have the stamina any more.'

This tearaway existence (not for nothing did he earn himself the nickname 'the wild man of Stratford') finally caught up with O'Toole when his doctors ordered him to cut out the booze. For the rest of the season O'Toole made a great show of downing large quantities of milk. He was acutely aware of his tearaway image though and played it up to the hilt. 'I get drunk and disorderly and all that, but I don't really think it's true that there is any danger of me destroying myself.' Maybe others, though. Fellow cast member Denholm Elliott, himself a boozer, found O'Toole so overpowering that he could hardly bear to be in the same room. 'I get awfully nervous with the kind of actor who looks as though he might be about to hit you, even though he never does.'

To escape the rigours of the theatre O'Toole went on a grand tour of Italy with Kenneth Griffith, both men finding themselves staying near Lake Como. One evening O'Toole received some news that distressed him greatly and dashed out into the night leaping onto a wall that overhung the lake. 'Griffith,' he shouted. 'It's got to end!' And into the water he went – feet first. 'At that moment, *Lawrence of Arabia*, *The Ruling Class*, *The Lion in Winter*, *My Favourite Year* were in mortal jeopardy,' is how Griffith later recalled it. 'However, fate is fate, and at that particular point, unknown to either of us, Lake Como is only two feet deep.'

This wasn't meant as a real suicide bid; O'Toole says he has never contemplated suicide, despite bouts of depression, the 'black dog', as he calls it, which plagued him all his adult life. He tried psychiatry, without much help. Asked once if anyone in the world really knew him, he laughed and after a moment's silence said, 'I think probably my mother and father had a better hint of the plot than anyone else. My sister once turned round to the very famous actress I was about to work with and said to her, "At the end of the picture, will you tell me who my brother is? What goes on in there, in the fucking thing he calls a mind?"'

Oliver Reed's film career started as near the bottom as it was possible to be, as an extra. Working at Elstree, he had a few lines in the Tony Hancock comedy *The Rebel* (1960). Reed went searching for his drinking pal Ronald Fraser, working at the same studio. He knocked on his dressing room door only for it to be opened by Richard Harris. 'What do you want?' the Irishman snarled. Reed asked if Fraser was there. 'Yes, he is,' said Harris and slammed the door in Reed's face. The two hellraisers never crossed paths again until the 70s when they began a mock-macho rivalry, threatening each time they met to knock seven sacks of shit out of each other.

The Rebel was written by Hancock's regular writing team, Ray Galton and Alan Simpson. The comedy giants, who later went on to create one of the all-time great TV sitcoms *Steptoe and Son*, were often on the set and in Reed sensed that here was someone out of the ordinary. 'He was mesmerising and it was obvious that the camera loved him,' remembers Simpson. 'But he kept fluffing his lines. Now on a film you have a tight schedule and for one little speech there's a limit to how many takes they're going to do. And he was so good, but he kept fluffing it and the director yelled, "Cut. Go again." I think they got up to seven takes and Reed fluffed every one.' The producer was standing next to the director and witnessing all this, shaking his head in dismay, according to Galton. 'He was saying to the director, "He's got to go, if he doesn't get it right now he's got to go, we can't waste any more film, it's costing money." I don't know whether anybody said anything to Oliver because on the next take he was absolutely perfect and it made the final cut.'

In between bouts of waiting for the phone to ring for possible jobs, Reed was invariably in the local boozer with an ever-widening circle of friends. At the time he lived in Wimbledon in a house that had several balconies and he wasn't averse, at some risk to himself, to leaping from one to the other. Reed had invented a pub-crawl that took in the eight public houses that circled the Common. The rules were simple; everyone had 15 minutes to down a pint of beer in each establishment before dashing on to the next one. It would take something like two hours to complete the route. Arriving back at the first bar Reed nearly always wanted to repeat the whole circuit again and would have to corral his mates into joining him, though they'd all pass out halfway through leaving Ollie on his own. Even he only ever managed to complete the course a second time on one rare occasion.

Staggering back home from the pub with a mate Reed sometimes enjoyed testing his friend's loyalty and bravery by lying spread-eagled on the road with him in front of oncoming traffic. The first to get up and leg it was chicken.

It was around about the start of the 60s that Reed became an unlikely horror star. An audition for the Hammer film company, who just a few years before had become notorious and hugely successful for a string of horror pictures like *The Curse of Frankenstein* and *Dracula* landed Reed a day's work as a nightclub bouncer in *The Two Faces of Dr Jekyll* (1960). Now he was off to Ireland for bigger and better things as a villainous nobleman who slays Peter Cushing's Sheriff of Nottingham in *The Sword of Sherwood Forest* (1960). It was a dream come true for Reed, running around a forest with a sword emulating his childhood hero Errol Flynn. The great swash-buckler of Hollywood's golden age had only recently died. Reed was in a pub when he heard the news and ordered a Guinness; standing to attention he downed the pint in a single gulp.

Reed's breakthrough arrived when Hammer cast him in the title role of *The Curse of the Werewolf* (1961). It was Hammer's make-up artist Roy Ashton, who had turned Christopher Lee so effectively into Frankenstein's monster, who suggested Reed would be perfect for the role because of his powerful bone structure. 'And the fact he resembled a wolf when he was angry.' It took five hours every day to complete Reed's make-up. 'Then I'd just be ready and they would shout "Lunch everybody," and I'd be left strutting around the studio covered in fur and teeth. I would slowly make my way to the restaurant and drink three pints of milk through a straw, and people would shout out, "There's that well-known homosexual actor!"'

At the close of the day Reed would have to spend an hour and a half peeling the make-up off hair by hair. 'Sometimes I wouldn't bother taking it off completely. It was great fun sitting in the car at traffic lights.'

After yet another string of dud movies salvation was at hand for Richard Burton when he was asked to play King Arthur in a new Broadway musical – *Camelot*. The show's lyricist, Alan Jay Lerner, was a big Burton fan and one night tried to keep up with him drink for drink and failed utterly. 'It was no classified secret that Richard's devotion to the bottle was almost religious, and his capacity was one of the wonders of the 20th century. If the Atlantic Ocean had been made of whisky, Richard would have been able to walk across.'

During the run Burton took on a bet that he couldn't down an entire bottle of 100% proof vodka during the matinee and then a fifth of cognac during the evening performance without any ill effect on his acting abilities. His co-star, Julie Andrews, unaware of the bet, would be the judge. 'What did you think I was like today then, love,' Burton asked as they both left the stage to rapturous applause. 'A little better than usual,' was Julie's reply. The two stars actually got on surprisingly well. When Burton later claimed that she was the only one of his leading ladies he'd never slept with, Julie responded, 'How dare he say such an awful thing about me.'

Burton was a rock as the production literally fell apart around him. On its pre-Broadway run the opening night lasted an epic four and a half hours and critics labelled the show 'a disaster area'. Then Lerner, who had only recently got over a nervous breakdown, collapsed and was rushed to hospital. Well again, he was carted out only for his vacant room to be occupied by his writing partner in *Camelot*, Moss Hart, who had just suffered a heart attack over the strain of hammering the show into a workable length. When it finally opened on Broadway reviews were mixed and members of the audience walked out, some nights as many as 300; it looked doomed. Everything changed when Burton and Julie Andrews guested on the hugely popular *Ed Sullivan Show* and the next day there were queues around the block; *Camelot* was a hit. It so nearly wasn't and Lerner owed Burton so much – he acknowledged that without him *Camelot* would never have been the huge success it was; Burton was endlessly patient and tolerant about being messed about, having lines and whole songs changed night after night, and by keeping his own spirits high he did much to prevent the whole company's morale from sinking.

Camelot was a massive hit, one of the biggest Broadway had ever seen and celebrities crowded into Burton's dressing room every night, including copious amounts of groupies. Some cast members felt that one of the show's songs 'I wonder what the king is doing tonight' might as well have been 'I wonder who the king is screwing tonight'. Like bees round a honey pot the company gathered to listen to his tales of growing up in Wales or his early days in Hollywood, always with a drink, or several. Lerner was constantly amazed by Burton's capacity for booze, 'when any normal man would have been placed on the critical list'. Amazingly, despite arriving at the theatre most nights considerably plastered, Burton never missed a single performance. There were some nights he'd arrive so smashed, his voice sounding like a car crash, that Lerner was sure he was incapable of going on, but something almost mystical happened when Burton walked on the stage: his voice would return resplendent and he'd deliver a brilliant performance. So intrigued by this feat was Lerner that he sought medical advice on it. 'Welsh livers and kidneys seem to be made of some metallic alloy, quite unlike the rest of the human race,' one doctor told him. 'One day, like aeroplanes, they eventually show metal fatigue.'

Basking in Broadway success Burton did a week's filming on the epic war drama *The Longest Day* (1962), a faithful re-creation of the D Day landings and a film as star-strewn as any other in history – John Wayne, Henry Fonda, Rod Steiger, Sean Connery, Robert Ryan, Richard Todd and Robert Mitchum among many others. Sadly Burton didn't share any scenes with his hellraising comrade Bob Mitchum.

After a lifetime of Mitchum's boozing his family persuaded him in the mid-80s to check into the Betty Ford Clinic and try to quit drinking. When he got out he met up with fellow actor Stuart Whitman who asked, 'What did you learn over there, Bob?' Mitchum replied, 'More ice.'

Defiant to the end, Mitchum died in 1997. 'The night he died,' his son recalled, 'he sat in his chair and there was a stubbed out Pall Mall and an empty glass that reeked of tequila. He got up during the night, knocked off a shot, smoked a cigarette, got in bed, and died in his sleep.'

* * *

Next for Richard Harris was a real blockbuster, *Mutiny on the Bounty* (1962). Director Carol Reed had been attracted by his Irish ruggedness and the actor said he'd lick the deck of the *Bounty* for the chance to appear opposite his acting hero Marlon Brando, but when the script arrived he rejected the role as too small. Friends told him of the risk he was taking but it worked because he was offered the much bigger part of chief mutineer alongside Brando's Fletcher Christian. Still not satisfied, Harris upped the ante even more by demanding star billing with Brando, a patent absurdity. Fearing he'd blown his chance Harris at last got the call from Hollywood; there'd be no equal billing, but more money. He agreed and flew out to Tahiti, clutching a bottle of bourbon. 'Good morning Mr Harris,' the clerk said at the check-in desk. 'How do you know me?' said a bemused Harris. 'I recognised you from your hand luggage,' replied the official.

What greeted Harris on that Pacific island was a production in utter chaos. Brando was unhappy with the script and new writers were being hired all the time, while the replica *Bounty*, built at huge cost, had been held up by storms. After weeks of delay and tens of thousands of dollars already wasted the film began. Brando was on edge the whole time, fluffing lines and dripping paranoia. Torrential rain hampered filming too and there were scorpions and rats to contend with. But Harris loved the primitive conditions; it was a chance to be like Robinson Crusoe.

When the production moved to Hollywood all hell broke loose. Brando's behaviour became ever more eccentric – when he deigned to show up on set at all – and he had Carol Reed fired and replaced by Lewis Milestone. 'It was shitsville,' said Harris, whose idolisation of Brando was battered to say the least. The constant rows with both directors and the star's absenteeism wore Harris out and his frustration erupted during the filming of the scene where Brando's Fletcher Christian strikes his character. Brando was absorbed with the method and mumbling away so his blow, when it finally came, was the dampest of squibs. Harris responded with a mock curtsy and waggled a limp wrist in the air. Brando didn't get the joke. Take two and again the blow was almost non-existent. Everyone waited to see how Harris would react. They weren't disappointed. Thrusting his chin forward he propositioned, 'Come on, big boy, why don't you fucking kiss me and be done with it!' Brando glared back, white with rage. Harris then kissed Brando on the cheek and hugged him. 'Shall we dance?' Angry and embarrassed Brando stormed off and afterwards the two men refused to appear on the set together. Brando played his scenes opposite Harris's stand-in, while Harris, adding insult to injury, used a packing case on which was drawn Brando's face. On the final day of shooting Brando sought reconciliation and requested Harris's presence on the set. The atmosphere was understandably tense. 'Would you mind giving me your lines?' commanded Brando. Harris refused, instead presenting him with the packing case. 'You'll probably get as much out of that as I got out of you.' The two men didn't speak to one another again for 25 years.

Production troubles resulted in *Bounty* going millions over budget and six months over schedule. Harris looked back on the film as 'nightmarish' and 'a total fucking disaster' and was conspicuously absent from the London premiere. But it did prove a commercial hit. Harris had finally arrived.

Playing the immortal role of Captain Bligh in *Bounty* was Trevor Howard, one of the great elbow-benders of movie history. Stories of his antics are legion. One tells of a dainty English theatrical visiting a New York bar when out of the gloom of a crowded corner booth came the sound of a familiar gruff voice. A closer look confirmed it was his friend Trevor Howard, red-eyed and unshaven, holding court amongst a group of young American actors. 'Trevor, what on Earth are you doing?' he said. 'Look at the state of you. How long have you been here?' An evil grin spread across Howard's face. 'Three days!' he roared.

Once, to relieve the boredom of a long theatrical run at Stratford, Howard and a fellow actor decided to attempt the ultimate pub-crawl. On market days in the town all 48 pubs stayed open from ten o'clock in the morning until ten at night. The plan was for both to drink a pint alternately in each of the pubs between opening and closing times. 48 pubs = 24 pints each. 'Can't be done,' said one landlord. 'Nonsense,' replied Howard. 'It's only one pint every 30 minutes; nothing to it.' 'Maybe,' continued the landlord, 'but you're forgetting something.' 'What's that?' 'You won't be on your feet for the last half of the trip.' 'Volunteers will pour it into us,' said Howard, revealing his contingency plan. 'We didn't say we'd be fucking conscious!'

In the 1940s a pint cost something like fivepence and when news spread of Howard's challenge there was no shortage of people eager to contribute towards the booze fund. On the day itself the gallant pair was given a rousing send off but alas failed to complete the circuit, only managing to sink 15 pints each before sliding into a gentle coma.

Whilst making the war film *Von Ryan's Express* Howard attended a lavish party thrown by its star Frank Sinatra. Upon leaving, Howard saw his hire car was blocked in the driveway by late arrivals. Undeterred, and unaware he was plastered, Howard attempted to extricate the car himself; a big mistake. First he accelerated forwards, ramming the vehicle parked in front, which in turn rammed the one ahead. Next he reversed gently, or so he thought, but the car thudded into the one behind, which shunted and damaged the car behind that. The noise brought other guests spilling out of the house to watch open-mouthed at the devastation. Luckily as the accident took place on private property the police weren't called, but the cost of replacing the damaged limos made it the most expensive night of Howard's life.

'On night shoots, waiting to be called,' says critic Barry Norman, 'sitting in a car just knocking back the booze,Trevor would get out, throw up, go onto the set and give an immaculate performance. He was almost thrown out of the Sydney cricket ground for bad behaviour, which I would have thought was nearly impossible. He was watching a test series there in the late 50s and he was so drunk and making so much noise that he was warned that if he didn't control his behaviour he would be asked to leave. You must be behaving pretty outrageously to get that kind of response at Sydney cricket ground.'

Right up until his final days Howard was a boozer. Just weeks before his death he fell over in his bedroom in a drunken state and knocked himself out. His wife called an ambulance and by the time they arrived Howard had regained consciousness and was busy grumbling over the unnecessary fuss as he was lifted onto a stretcher. As the ambulance men negotiated the stairway Howard called out suddenly to his wife. 'I'm here darling,' she loyally responded. 'What is it you want?' Howard looked at her and growled. 'I want another gin and tonic!'

Tony Palmer was one of the last people to work with Howard and, fully aware of the actor's habit of being regularly pickled, took the advice of fellow director Richard Loncraine, who'd just made the Michael Palin comedy *The Missionary* with Howard. 'Richard told me, the way to deal

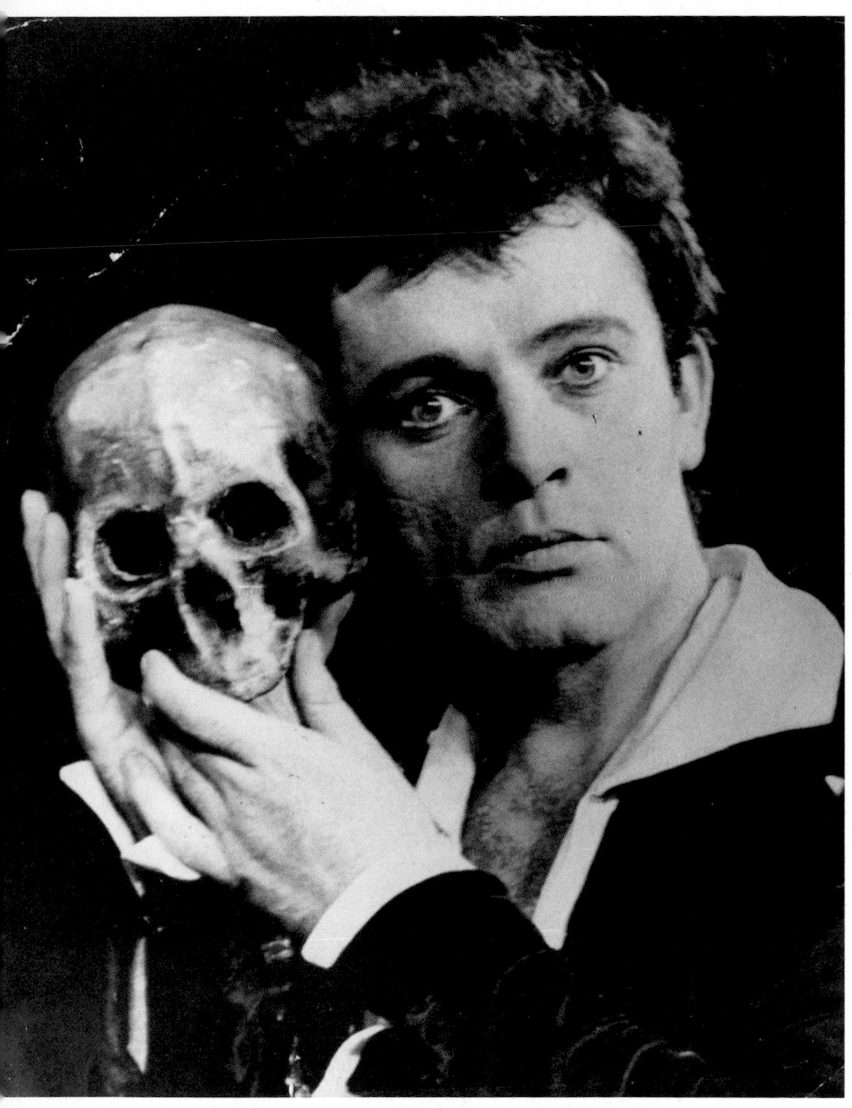

He might have been the greatest Shakespearean actor since Olivier but during one rehearsal Burton was refused permission to go to the bathroom, so he simply urinated on the stage.

Nicotine was another vice. He was a smoker by the age of eight spending most of his pocket money on packets of Woodbines.

And then there were women! Burton's legendary reputation was forged in his early Hollywood days. 'I knocked off everyone in sight.'

Burton regularly retired to bed paralytic. One night he crashed out with a lighted cigarette still in his hand and almost burned his house down.

Burton and O'Toole were booze soul mates, so much so that the crew on the set of *Becket* at Shepperton Studios spent more time getting them out of the local pub than they did filming them.

Burton and Taylor's marriage was like tying two cats in a bag. Once she caught him canoodling with a starlet and promptly attacked him with a broken bottle.

One day on the set of *The Night of the Iguana*, Burton drank 21 straight tequilas before casually wandering down to nearby shark infested waters and jumping in.

Portraying the marriage from hell in *Who's Afraid of Virginia Woolf?* took its toll on Burton and Liz's own relationship which crumbled still further.

Filming *Where Eagles Dare* in 1968, one evening in the bar a man whose wife Burton had had an affair with pulled a gun on him. Unfazed, Burton wandered off to the toilet and left Liz Taylor to deal with him.

After appearing in *Under Milk Wood*, Liz banned Burton from drinking and roistering with O'Toole. Burton chose his girl over his mate and their friendship foundered for years.

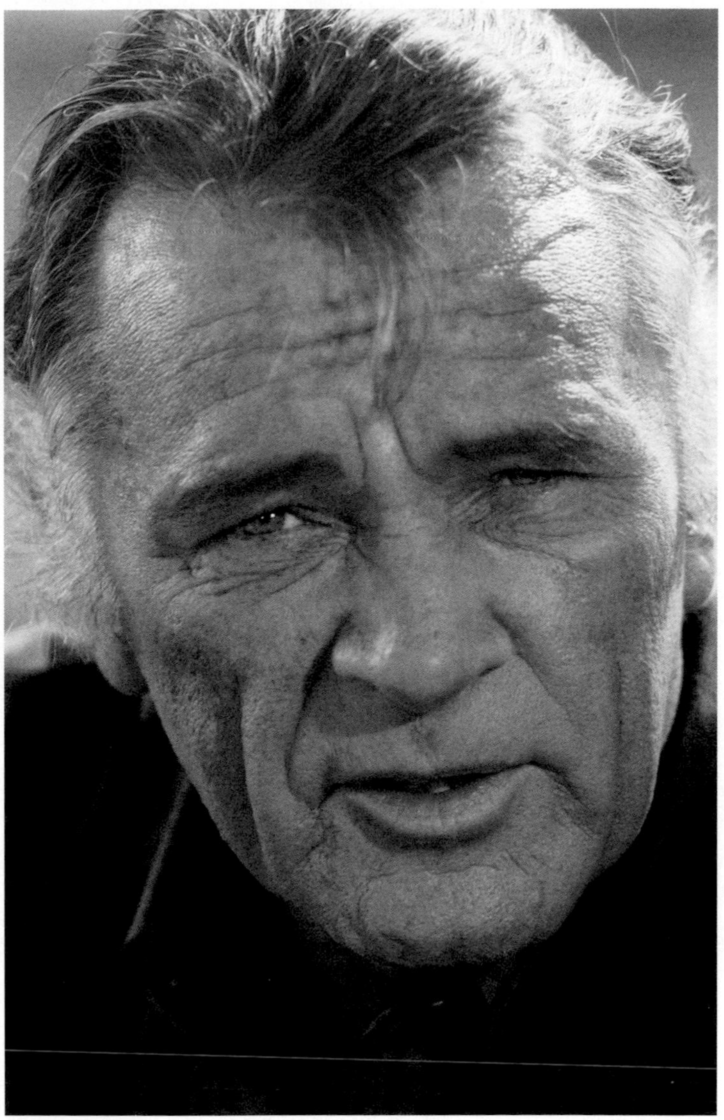

Burton was crippled by ill health in later life. In fact, during one operation surgeons were astonished to discover that Burton's entire spinal column was coated with crystallised alcohol.

Burton would go on the wagon for months, then dramatically fall off again.
'I like my reputation. That of a spoiled genius from the Welsh gutter.'

with Trevor is this: see if you can find a really, really sexy, pretty wardrobe girl. And we did, she was stunning, red hair, a very pretty girl. I said to her, "This is what you're going to do on day one. I'm told that Trevor will arrive with a brown paper bag, and in the brown paper bag is the booze, and you are going to appear, if not in your underwear, jolly close, and he'll go for you. I'm just warning you that this is what's going to happen. I'm sure you can deal with this. Now, the moment he is rebuffed by you he will head for the brown paper bag, but he's already been seduced by your flaming red hair, so you go across and you smack his hand and you say, naughty boy Trevor, and for the rest of the week he will behave impeccably." And it happened, and he did. Richard Loncraine told me that they discovered this very late, too late I think on *The Missionary*, that this was how to deal with him.'

Film history might have been very different had producer Sam Spiegel got his way and cast Marlon Brando as Lawrence of Arabia. His director, David Lean, wasn't so sure, anxious about the star's ego and that the film might turn into Brando of Arabia. Next on the list was Albert Finney, but after an expensive screen test Finney rejected the role on the grounds that he didn't want to be straitjacketed by a multi-film contract under Spiegel. Lean meanwhile was pushing for Peter O'Toole having seen him in *The Day They Robbed the Bank of England*. Spiegel, perhaps remembering the violin joke O'Toole had made, thought O'Toole's rowdy reputation was too much of a risk on so expensive a film. 'He thought I was a tearaway. He thought I lived up a tree. He didn't want to have to go looking for me every day with a net.' Finally a screen test was arranged and watching it even Spiegel had to admit that they'd found their Lawrence. The American producer called O'Toole with the news. 'I want you to play Lawrence.' 'Oh yes,' said O'Toole. 'Is it a speaking part?' Spiegel growled back, 'Don't make jokes.'

After signing for the role O'Toole was flown out to New York to meet the Columbia executives backing the project, an experience he didn't savour. 'When I look at you,' one of the suits said, 'I see six million dollars.' 'How'd you like a punch up the throat?' O'Toole replied. 'I hate that stuff,' he said later, 'it made me feel like a prize bull.'

With the role of Lawrence in his pocket O'Toole settled down to celebrate

Christmas with Siân. Then he suddenly went missing. O'Toole had a habit of vanishing for days on end without Siân knowing where or what he was up to. She'd almost gotten used to it. On Christmas morning he turned up with a brand new Morris Minor tied up with a huge ribbon. Of course Siân had a horror of cars by now after so many terror-stricken journeys with O'Toole at the wheel, but was thrilled by the gift. It didn't last long. O'Toole hastily commandeered the vehicle for a sentimental journey up to Bristol to bid the city farewell before leaving for Arabia. That night Siân received a phone call from the police. 'I'm very sorry,' said a voice, 'but I'm afraid we've had to lock Peter in the cells. We thought you ought to know.' O'Toole, rather the worse for wear, had driven the Morris Minor smack bang into the back of a squad car. After a night in the cells it was back to London. Sadly Siân never did see her Morris Minor again; it went to that great scrap heap in the sky of cars that O'Toole had wrecked.

Few actors have had more of a baptism of fire for their starring debut than O'Toole, not just a bugger of a role in one of the biggest pictures ever made, but having to appear opposite acting heavyweights like Alec Guinness and Anthony Quinn. Guinness admired O'Toole's talent and charm but as he watched him drink to excess on location his appreciation cooled. One day Guinness and O'Toole were invited to dinner at some local dignitary's house. O'Toole got plastered, quarrelled with his host and threw a glass of champagne in his face. 'O'Toole could have been killed – shot, or strangled,' Guinness wrote to a friend, 'and I'm beginning to think it's a pity he wasn't.'

A lot of O'Toole's scenes were played opposite another young, unknown actor, Omar Sharif. First introduced to the Egyptian O'Toole murmured, 'Omar Sharif! No one in the world is called Omar Sharif. Your name must be Fred.' Henceforth Sharif was known as Cairo Fred. The two have remained lifelong friends and on location for *Lawrence* behaved wildly, enjoying the flesh pots of Beirut, then known as the sin city of the east. Both were obliged to film non-stop for ten days, and then have three or four days off. 'We had the use of a private plane to Beirut and misbehaved ourselves appallingly!' recalled O'Toole. 'We'd just drink,' Sharif says. 'And try not to sleep too much so that we didn't waste any time.' Sharif also loved gambling, so they'd invariably lose all their money at the casino. 'We once did about nine months' wages in one night,' said O'Toole. 'And then got up to the usual things young men get up to.' Asked by a journalist if that entailed getting up to no good O'Toole gave a grin and replied. 'Oh, darling, do you consider it to be no good? We considered it very good indeed.'

Their revelries continued after filming. In Hollywood O'Toole took Sharif to see controversial stand-up comic Lenny Bruce and the trio enjoyed a night out on the town. In the early hours of the morning they staggered back to Bruce's home where the comedian shot up in front of his two guests. The next thing they knew the living room was full of cops and they were being bundled into vans and taken to the local station. Bruce's house had been under surveillance and it was a drugs bust. A sober Sharif decided to use his one phone call to ask Spiegel for help. It was three in the morning and the producer was fast asleep in his suite at the Beverly Hills Hotel. A groggy Spiegel took the call. 'Sam, it's Omar.' The producer was still half unconscious. 'Omar who?' Sharif identified himself and then dropped the bombshell that he and O'Toole had been arrested. 'You're nuts,' yelled Spiegel. 'You kids are going to ruin me.' The producer sent his lawyers to the precinct to bail the pair out but Peter was so taken with Lenny Bruce that he refused to leave the jail without him. 'Sam was going out of his mind,' Sharif recalled. 'And finally we got Lenny Bruce released with us.'

Lawrence of Arabia occupied O'Toole for the next two years, filming in seven different countries. His arrival in Jordan was accompanied by a massive hangover and he was warned that he was now in an Arab country and that if he got drunk the authorities would throw him out, film or no film. For the first three months he learned how to live as an Arab in the desert before a foot of film was exposed. He even visited Bethlehem, but was unmoved by the experience, calling it 'Christ commercialised'. Coming out of a holy shrine he noticed a cinema across the street that was showing a clunky British movie called *Circus of Horrors*. On a hoarding outside was a large picture of his acting chum Kenneth Griffith wearing a sweater he'd borrowed from O'Toole for the film and had failed to return. 'That was the reason that Bethlehem, I'm afraid, did not amount to a religious experience.'

O'Toole also had to learn how to ride a camel and after his first lesson blood oozed from the seat of his jeans. 'This is a very delicate Irish arse,' he warned his instructor. Eventually mastering the task O'Toole was almost killed during the spectacular sequence in which Lawrence's Arab army attacks the port of Aqaba. An effects gun loaded with small pellets went off too soon, hitting O'Toole in the eye, temporarily blinding him. Unable to control his camel, O'Toole was thrown in front of several hundred charging Bedouins on horseback. Luckily the camel stood guard over the prone actor, as they are trained to do, shielding him from serious injury and probably saving his life. Flown to hospital for treatment O'Toole was back on the camel the next day.

By the end of filming O'Toole had lost two stones in weight, received third-degree burns, sprained both ankles, torn ligaments in both his hip and thigh, dislocated his spine, broken his thumb, sprained his neck and been concussed twice. The conditions were such that some of the crew couldn't take it and left. At one point some feared O'Toole himself was close to a nervous breakdown, a combination of the harsh terrain and the pressure enforced on him by the tyrannical Lean. He begged Siân to come out and raise his spirits: 'Here, you have to be a little mad to stay sane.'

After six months in the desert O'Toole was allowed to go back to Britain for a few weeks' rest. He immediately checked into hospital to recuperate. Once out he went on the ultimate bender. 'After six months in the desert, I should think so.' But he was arrested for driving under the influence, jailed for the night, fined £75 and disqualified for a year. Spiegel was not happy. 'You're not supposed to get up to that kind of caper on a film like this,' he preached.

Eventually the desert filming closed and the unit moved to Spain, which O'Toole dubbed 'Pontefract with scorpions'. While there Sam Spiegel paid the production a visit on his yacht and summoned O'Toole to his cabin where he gave the actor a right bollocking. Whether this was meant to spur him on in the final stages of filming O'Toole never discovered. 'I left the yacht feeling dreadful,' he later recalled. 'Just as ever, destruction was Sam's game. I couldn't bear that man.' Pissed off he looked for a bar to drown his sorrows in and found one already propped up by the film's art director John Box, who'd got the same rough treatment from Spiegel. After consuming several bottles the pair decided to have their revenge, climbed up the anchor chain onto the tycoon's yacht, crept into his private quarters and stole all his prize cigars.

Lawrence of Arabia was a world-wide smash when it opened in 1962 and hailed as one of cinema's true masterpieces. O'Toole's extraordinary performance made him a star overnight. But during the American opening he behaved disgracefully, either turning up drunk for interviews or demanding outrageous sums for appearing on TV. 'You make a star,' said Spiegel, 'you make a monster.'

O'Toole was now a star. 'I woke up one morning to find I was famous. Bought a white Rolls-Royce and drove down Sunset Boulevard, wearing dark specs and a white suit, waving like the queen mum. Nobody took any fucking notice, but I thoroughly enjoyed it.'

After his stint as a werewolf more Hammer baddies followed for Oliver Reed: a scurvy bounder in *Pirates of Blood River* (1961) and then a vicious leader of a motorcycle gang in *The Damned* (1963), a performance and role that inspired novelist Anthony Burgess to later write *A Clockwork Orange*.

Work was coming in at a steady pace, including a lively appearance in the classic TV series *The Saint*. In the climactic scene Reed, inevitably cast as a villain, is gunned down by Roger Moore's Simon Templar and killed. As the blank cartridge was fired Reed dramatically hurled himself backwards and knocked himself out cold. 'It was the best example of method acting I have ever seen,' said the show's production manager Johnny Goodman.

Years later when the show was resurrected in the 70s as *Return of the Saint* with Ian Ogilvy stepping adroitly into Moore's shoes Reed was on holiday in the south of France and staying in the same hotel as the cast and crew. *The Saint*'s producer Robert Baker proudly introduced Ogilvy to Reed. 'This is the new Saint.' Ollie studied the young actor inquisitively then leaned forward to ask, 'You a poof?' *Saint* author Leslie Charteris was there too, unfortunately for him as Reed was so thrilled to meet the *The Saint*'s creator that he took a knife and ran it across his own wrist, drawing blood. 'You and I have got to be blood brothers,' he announced, grabbing out for Charteris's hand, which the author skilfully withdrew. Failing in his task Reed stumbled away from the table leaving a bloody trail on the carpet.

* * *

Cleopatra (1963), the most expensive film ever made, was in deep shit. Costs were spiralling out of control and filming had been halted in a rain sodden Britain and relocated to Rome, wasting millions. Burton was aware of the difficulties when he was drafted in to play Mark Antony, a decision that was to change his life and result in one of the all time great showbusiness scandals.

By the time Elizabeth Taylor met Burton she'd already been through four marriages and wasn't even in her thirties yet. Burton couldn't stand her to start with. 'I must don my armour once more to play against Miss Tits,' he said. So why did he go all out to seduce her? Was it Taylor's wealth and status that he lusted after, to win and ultimately own the most glamorous woman on earth? Not bad for a boy from the valleys. Or was it lust at first sight? Burton referred to Liz Taylor's tits as, 'Apocalyptic. They would topple empires before they withered.' Reportedly a sozzled Burton burst into Liz's rented villa during a cocktail party to confess his love for her at the top of his voice and demand that, 'If you're my girl, come over here and stick your tongue down my throat.' The guests watched dumbfounded as the Hollywood sex siren did exactly that.

Soon the rest of the world knew of the affair and the paparazzi followed the couple everywhere. Friends tried warning him off but Burton was in too deep; this time his affair with his leading lady would not end once the cameras stopped rolling. Burton had two children with Sybil, while Liz, then married to Eddie Fisher, had four, so there was enormous guilt on both sides about ripping the two sets of families apart. It eventually ended up being too much for Liz who attempted suicide. Not to be outdone, Sybil also tried to kill herself. Burton predictably hit the bottle.

The Burton/Taylor affair became the biggest news story on earth and everybody wanted a piece of the action. While filming an epic sea battle for *Cleopatra* in Ischia a producer invited the couple for lunch on his yacht and placed hidden cameras in their room in the hope of capturing and then selling exclusive pictures of them kissing. Liz, who'd been in front of cameras since she was a kid, sniffed them out and Burton had to be restrained from pulverizing their host.

Once *Cleopatra* was completed Burton and Liz tried desperately to end the affair, knowing how many people they'd hurt, but couldn't stop themselves;

their passion was just too intense. For the next two years the couple were literally on the run from the media while waiting for their respective divorces. 20th Century Fox, who'd bankrolled *Cleopatra* and were going bust because of it, tried suing the couple, claiming their conduct had prejudiced the film's box office chances. The case was dropped after Burton threatened to reveal the sordid private lives of certain top Fox executives. A US congressman introduced a bill to have Burton and Liz banned from entering the country; even the Vatican slagged off their public adultery. Lesser people might have been destroyed, but for Burton and Liz it merely enhanced their mythic status and helped turn them into the most glamorous couple of the 1960s. 'I have achieved a sort of diabolical fame,' Burton said, no doubt hiding a smile.

Glamorous they certainly were, but they were gloriously mismatched, too. He was a rough rugby playing Welsh working class hero, she a Hollywood starlet, pampered since childhood. It was the ultimate example of opposites attracting and the textbook case of can't live with her, can't live without her. There were endless rows, with Liz taunting Burton by calling him 'taffy', 'a burnt-out Welshman' or 'fatty'. He in return called Liz, 'my little Jewish tart'. Often the rows turned violent with Liz hitting out and receiving blows in return.

Battered by the public spotlight over his affair with Liz Taylor, Burton proceeded to give his body a good battering too. Drinking Bloody Marys at 10.30 in the morning, he'd be on to his second bottle of vodka by the afternoon. Throughout his 30s and early 40s Burton pushed his body almost to breaking point, but his powers of recovery seemed unimpaired. He always considered his acting talent a gift, so too his ability to withstand alcoholic punishment and the endless boozing.

Lindsay Anderson, a director at the forefront of British New Wave cinema, wanted Richard Harris to play the lead role in a gritty film about the cutthroat world of professional rugby, *This Sporting Life* (1963), based on a novel by David Storey, who also wrote the screenplay. 'We chose Richard,' Storey recalls, 'because of his emotional volatility, he was very accessible emotionally and had none of those traits of a conventional actor, or even a conventional leading actor. And his enthusiasm was total, he was completely committed, verging on the edge of insanity in some respects, and that became infused in the film itself. And then he had a very powerful effect on Lindsay in terms of a personal relationship.'

Some believed Anderson's interest in Harris was not entirely professional; Anderson was homosexual and when he flew out to the Tahitian location of *Mutiny on the Bounty* to meet Harris he felt himself falling madly in love with the Irishman. So began one of cinema's most bizarre partnerships. 'Really it was a combination of Richard's Celtic bravado and wildness and Lindsay's homosexuality which he never really came to terms with,' says Storey. 'And in *Sporting Life* it came to a climax in the sense that Richard became the epitome of everything that Lindsay desired, the very powerful physical and emotional presence that Richard generated was completely intoxicating to Lindsay and he really had to hang on by his fingernails at times.'

Harris knew it too and exploited the situation mercilessly. As filming began Harris quickly became master to Anderson's slave, resorting even to physical violence to show him who was boss. 'It was a relationship, a masochistic relationship in many respects,' says Storey, 'that exploded and went over the edge several times. And it was great credit to Lindsay's inner sturdiness that he managed to hold on to what he thought it might achieve for the film, but it very nearly broke him. We were offered several films after *Sporting Life* but I felt that the producer in each case wasn't powerful enough to control the wildness and ferocity of the relationship between Lindsay and Richard, which had become quite obsessional really on both their parts, particularly on Lindsay's.'

Years later Harris would be consumed by guilt over his behaviour towards Anderson and as late as 1990 would occasionally telephone the director, 'when I feel dreadful'.

To get into shape Harris trained hard, afraid he wouldn't measure up on the pitch to the professional rugby players hired as extras. On location in Wakefield, on the first day the local rugby league team congregated on the pitch while Harris was in his caravan. 'He was spending ages on his make-up,' recalls Storey, 'with his false nose, his dark eye lenses to make him look more mysterious, and his mascara. And then when he came out and saw all the players standing at the other end of the pitch going, "Oh Jesus, look at this flower coming out," he just took one look at them and ran down the whole pitch towards them. And as he ran he got faster and faster until they suddenly realised with horror that he was going to run right into them, which he eventually did. It was that initial gesture of total physical commitment, almost indifference and carelessness that caught the players' admiration and they really took to him in a major way.'

In the scene where Harris is roughed up behind the scrum, rugby league legend Derek Turner, who was playing the character doing the punching, was asked by Anderson to make the contact look real. So he did. He punched Harris square in the face and knocked him out. Shooting for the day had to be stopped while Harris recovered.

Harris was also up against a fiery co-star more fearsome than Brando and Mitchum put together, Rachel Roberts. A complete eccentric and bawdy beyond measure when drunk, Rachel Roberts was married to Rex Harrison. At the after-premiere party of one of their films the couple grew increasingly irritated that the paparazzi were ignoring them in favour of their guests, Burton and Liz Taylor. Finally Rachel, who'd been drinking all night, snapped and climbed atop her table screaming, 'We're the stars of this fucking film!' Not getting the desired response she lifted up her skirt and bawled, 'Here's my pussy. Take some pictures of that!' Poor Rex could do little to calm his wife down. 'Don't you talk to me,' she spat out at him. 'You can't get it up, you old fart.'

When really drunk Rachel took to impersonating a Welsh corgi; literally on all fours barking. At one all-star party Harris threw a few years later in Hollywood Rachel crawled over to a table where Robert Mitchum was sitting regaling colleagues with a story about how he'd caught and survived leprosy while working in the Congo. Suddenly he felt tugs at his trouser leg and some snarling growls. He ignored them and continued. Suddenly Rachel sank her teeth into Mitchum's leg and started chewing the expensive fabric of his made to measure trousers. When she got to his bare skin and was attempting to draw blood Mitchum stopped to pat her on the head. 'There, there,' he said, before returning to his story.

This Sporting Life opened to widespread critical acclaim and Harris was labelled 'Britain's Brando'. In America too critics favourably compared him to the method eccentric. Awards followed – an Oscar nomination and best actor at the Cannes Film Festival. Harris attended the ceremony, pissed as a newt, and when he heard his name called out as winner bounced onto the stage. But when actress Jeanne Moreau handed him his award, in the shape of a plain box, Harris barked, 'What's this?' Momentarily stunned Jeanne composed herself. 'Cufflinks,' she said. 'That's what the best actor gets.' Harris clearly thought, fuck that, so he grabbed the biggest trophy he could see, said thank you and darted off stage. Two gendarmes attempted to retrieve the statue but Harris barged them asunder and escaped into the night. The festival committee demanded the return of the statue, which was inscribed for best animation film, and Harris finally relented. The cufflinks were duly mailed to him. He kept them for years but the incident still pissed him off. 'Who gives cufflinks to an Olympic medallist,' he moaned.

With the success of *This Sporting Life* behind him Harris's drinking binges grew ever more legendary. On the American press tour for the film Harris got so bored with the endless interviews that he left his plush New York hotel to hang out with the bums and the tramps down in the Bowery. 'I spent four days down there while my studio was going crazy.' He even shared some of their awful gut-rot and was as sick as a dog afterwards. 'But it was wonderful.' Harris was near to being out of control. During another drinking binge he staggered back to his hotel room, undressed and climbed into bed, oblivious to the fact that it was occupied by a young couple. He was in the wrong room. 'Hi, what's the big idea,' said a voice. 'I don't have one,' replied Harris, 'but if one occurs to you by all means wake me up.'

Besides starting trouble Harris was also very good at attracting it. 'I never pick fights,' he once said. 'People pick fights with me.' In a New York bar a complete stranger came up to the actor and punched him square in the face. 'I got really mad.' Harris laid into the guy until he dropped like a stone to the floor. Ironically both men ended up in hospital in beds next to each other. Such incidents caused anxiety back at the boardroom of Associated British, where Harris was still under contract. They even sent him to counselling sessions in order to try and keep him from getting into fights. On a visit to Rome Harris persuaded one of the film executives to join him in order to witness first hand that it wasn't always the actor who started all the brawling. On their first night they went to a bar and listened as a drunken American tourist spelt out in a loud voice how he was going to do in Harris. The executive advised his client to take no notice. 'Do you want me to wait until I get a bottle across the face,' reasoned Harris, 'or go in and get it over with.' The executive could see only logic in this statement and Harris took the insulting Yank outside and flattened him. Amazingly the tourist came back inside the bar fists flailing and Harris had to fell him again. The executive reported back to his bosses that passive resistance on Harris's part simply did not work.

At home he was even more unpredictable. While he was drinking with friends late one night a sudden compulsion overtook Harris to burst into song, but not without piano accompaniment. Problem was he didn't own a piano, but the family upstairs did. He banged on the door and the poor man who answered had little choice but to let him in. Harris proceeded to raise a racket for the rest of the night. Another time Harris held a stag night at his flat and neighbours called for two police cars to be sent round to break it up. 'It was quite a small and quiet party,' said Harris. 'I know I stood on top of a car in the street and recited Dylan Thomas and Shakespeare, but really there was no cause for complaint.'

It was incidents like this that drove the residents of the apartment block Harris lived in to sign a petition demanding his removal. Luckily another tenant, who happened to be Harris's new drinking buddy, refused to sign and he was reprieved. Reaching the conclusion that all his neighbours were a snooty bunch of killjoys Harris paid a friend to march up and down outside the flats wearing a sandwich board declaring 'Love thy neighbour' – signed Harris. It only inflamed the situation. Luckily for everyone Elizabeth was pregnant again and the couple moved into larger dwellings. She then booked herself into a private nursing home where on the lawn outside Harris boozily serenaded her the night before the birth.

After the phenomenon that was *Lawrence of Arabia* Peter O'Toole was one of the world's leading stars and his lifestyle began to match it. His Hampstead home was lushly decorated with fine furniture and objets d'art. O'Toole was a keen collector of antiques. Filming *Lawrence* he smuggled some precious Greek earrings back through customs by hiding them in his foreskin, an act of daring that caused him pain for several weeks after.

In a bid to do something radically different after *Lawrence* O'Toole returned to the stage. *Baal* by Bertolt Brecht was certainly different, and it was a disaster. His dresser, on the night of the final rehearsal, screamed 'This show is cursed,' flung the clothes on the floor and fled into the night, never to return. The play itself, due to technical difficulties, ran almost five hours. People walked out rather than endure any more.

But O'Toole's star was rising and a hectic career schedule meant his children hardly ever saw him. O'Toole was not present at their births, and not around much afterwards either. Like all our hellraisers, he was something of a male chauvinist and had no intention of changing his ways now. 'If you don't like me, leave me,' he'd say to Siân. He'd grown up in a male dominated household and so expected the woman to be supportive, undemanding, do the house chores and look after the baby. Siân came to understand that, 'Clever women never nagged. Clever women dodged the flying crockery and went away to where they could get some peaceful sleep and never in the morning referred to the excesses of the night before.' She learnt to make meals and throw them away before going to bed, only for her returning husband to wake her at dawn, after a night on the piss, demanding food.

But O'Toole's absence from his children's lives led to one distressing incident. When his daughter was ill he paid her a visit in the nursery. Days later the child asked Siân, 'You know that man who came to see me mummy – who *is* he?' After that Siân made a point of putting up stills of O'Toole's current film or stage guises around the room to avoid any further misunderstandings.

It was also made clear to Siân that her husband's career would be the only one really tolerated in the O'Toole household. When O'Toole and Siân set up a company together, Keep Films, with the producer Jules Buck, Siân was 'mortified to realise that my work hardly figured'. The enterprise was totally geared to O'Toole's ascension to movie stardom; Siân was merely there to be the loyal wife. Buck once told her that it was all right for her to work in her spare time, 'or if I didn't get in Peter's way', Siân later recalled. In a joint interview when a reporter asked Siân how she combined her busy private life with a career O'Toole answered on her behalf. 'She doesn't have a career, she has jobs.'

Such was Peter O'Toole's reputation by the mid-60s that he was chosen to represent the new breed of British actor in the inaugural production of the National Theatre – *Hamlet* directed by Laurence Olivier. At first O'Toole didn't want to do it. 'But have you ever tried to argue with Olivier?' O'Toole confessed to the press after agreeing to the offer. 'He's the most charming, persuasive bastard ever to draw a breath.'

Actually the origin of O'Toole's *Hamlet* can be traced to an afternoon's boozing session with Richard Burton. 'We were neither of us entirely sober,' O'Toole later admitted. They got around to discussing *Hamlet*. Both had played it and agreed that they hated the damn thing. Then Burton said, 'Let's be masochists. Let's do *Hamlet* again and get it out of our systems.'

They discussed their common admiration of Laurence Olivier and John Gielgud, then fell to arguing which of the duo they would like to direct them. In the end, they tossed a coin. Fortunately, as O'Toole tells it, before they had recovered their sobriety, they telephoned the two old masters and O'Toole ended up playing Hamlet in London under Olivier's direction and Burton in New York under Gielgud's.

The stress of performing the five hour version, every night save Sunday, with two matinees, was punishing. Yet O'Toole still persisted in staying up late and drinking. He also downed three or four pints of beer prior to going on stage; although O'Toole once said he never drank while working. When he was at a party, and feeling depressed about performing the following day, a woman gave him a green pill from a fancy silver pillbox. 'I was on the ceiling for 48 hours. I was cuckooing and crowing from chimneys, hurtling about and gambolling and skipping – and I never stopped talking. I wept at weather forecasts.'

O'Toole's Hamlet was not well received and there were stories of numerous antics backstage, such as during one matinee when he forgot his lines and had to swat up on them between scenes in the wings only to re-emerge on stage with his glasses still on, causing the audience to snigger. But O'Toole's star name still guaranteed packed houses.

In 1962 Oliver Reed met a director who would become not just a friend but a big professional ally, Michael Winner. Winner was casting a film called *West Eleven* and wanted Reed for the lead role. 'But the producer thought he was a B picture actor, which in Oliver's case was true. The same producer also thought that Sean Connery was a B picture actor, we couldn't use him, Julie Christie was a useless blonde bimbo, we couldn't use her, and James Mason was a has-been.'

Winner's next film was called *The System* (1964), and tackled the thorny subject of young men mingling among the seasonal tourists at a seaside town in search of sexual conquests. Installed as producer this time Winner could cast whom he pleased, and he wanted Reed. 'And from then on we were very close. He and Burt Lancaster were my dearest friends in the industry. I absolutely loved Oliver. He was the kindest, the quietest and the gentlest man in the world, and the most polite and well behaved, except when he had a drink. But I very seldom saw him drunk on set because he knew I didn't like that. Once or twice he may have had a bit of a hangover from the night before, but nothing remotely serious; not like today where half of them are on drugs. But he was a menace at night, no question. He was very professional on the set – in the evening a disaster.'

Winner was never much enamoured of drunks so tended to stay away from Reed during social hours. 'Drunks on the whole are immensely quiet and dignified when they're sober. But when they're drunk, they're drunk. They're two people; they're Jekyll and Hyde. I remember once I met him in a restaurant and he went out and challenged someone to a fight; he was always doing that, and he always lost the fight. So he went out into Hyde Park in a beautiful Savile Row suit to fight this bloke and came back having been thrown in the round pond, he was soaking.'

One young actor making an early appearance in *The System* was David Hemmings, who made the mistake of going out boozing with Ollie and fell unconscious. When he woke up he was hanging upside down and 60 feet over a vicious set of spiked railings. Reed was holding him by his ankles, dangling the terrified actor from the sixth floor window of the Grand Hotel, Torquay. 'How do you like this, boy?' Ollie growled. 'Wanna come up, boy?' Hemmings did indeed and was hauled back in. But the memory of that incident haunted Hemmings for years and for the duration of his career he was terrified of Reed. 'He could drink 20 pints of lager with a gin or crème de menthe chaser and still run a mile for a wager,' said Hemmings of his old nemesis.

Reed was also starting to gain a reputation among journalists as being not the most orthodox of interview subjects. One such journo who had a close encounter with the young Reed was Barry Norman, showbiz reporter for the *Daily Mail* before his move to television. 'I went round to

Ollie's house in London,' recalls Norman. 'It was only about eleven o'clock in the morning but he was well into the beer already. And we talked for a bit and then he suggested that we go off and box each other. At that point I made an excuse and left because he was in much better shape than I was and I wasn't about to be knocked around by him.'

By 1964 Richard Burton and Liz Taylor still found themselves under severe media and public gaze over their scandalous affair. One night in London they went with O'Toole to the theatre, Liz sporting a particularly garish turquoise hat. In the interval Liz wanted to pop next door to the pub rather than enjoy drinks in the secluded privacy of the manager's office as pre-arranged. Outside the street was heaving with onlookers and she was instantly recognised. 'The bitch!' cried a woman. 'I'm so close I could spit on her.' Taylor ignored it, lamenting to O'Toole, 'It's so awful not being able to go anywhere in peace.' To which O'Toole replied, 'It might help a bit if you took off that fucking turquoise busby.'

As for Sybil, to escape the endless media intrusion about her being abandoned by her husband for the world's most glamorous female star, she left England and bought an apartment in New York, becoming the toast of the city's artistic fraternity. At one lavish party she bumped into the English actor Edward Woodward, in town with a play. Terrified of putting his foot in it he decided to steer clear of controversial subjects and talk about how hard it had been to find his character's very distinctive suit. 'Where did you get it in the end?' asked Sybil. 'Burton,' said Woodward, suddenly realising that he had said the word he had been at such pains to avoid. 'It's all right,' she said. 'It could have been worse. You could have said Burton the Tailor.'

Burton was still drinking very heavily. During the filming of *The VIPs* (1963), he allegedly drank half a gallon of cognac in one day. The publicist on his film *Becket* later said that he'd never seen anything comparable to Burton's boozing. 'It was something to behold.' Staying at the Dorchester Burton drank himself stupid one night and while reciting poetry in the foyer violently threw up. 'Oh my dear,' said an equally inebriated Liz. 'I think you have a fever.' The famous director Otto Preminger happened to be checking in and offered assistance. 'Fuck off!' Burton screamed at him. 'Just fuck off.' Preminger fled, never to forgive nor forget.

Leaving the hotel Burton went to record an interview for the influential *Ed Sullivan Show* in America to publicise *Becket*. He turned up at the TV studios hours late, still pissed out of his mind and struggling to put on medieval tights over his trousers, with Liz laughing uncontrollably nearby. He staggered onto the set, forgot where, when and why he was there, and promptly left again. A major publicity coup for the film was blown, and Burton never even knew it.

With his film career at unprecedented heights Burton returned to the stage, Broadway in fact, in Gielgud's production of *Hamlet* that broke box office records. To amuse himself during the long run he'd try out several off the wall interpretations of the role on the audience, sometimes even inserting bits of dialogue from other plays or speaking a few lines in German, just to see if anyone noticed. He even once drank a quart of brandy during a performance. 'The only visible effect was that he played the last two acts as a homosexual,' wrote one critic.

One night, however, Burton was shocked when a man in the stalls loudly booed him. Returning to his hotel suite he said to Liz, who was engrossed in a film on TV, 'I was booed tonight.' Hardly lifting her head up Liz said, 'Really?' Burton grew annoyed. 'Turn that bloody thing off,' he roared. 'Shh, I can't hear,' said Liz. 'Don't you understand,' Burton carried on. 'I was actually booed on stage.' Liz was still glued to the box. 'Yes dear, never mind.' Burton stormed out of the room, emerging minutes later in his pyjamas. Incensed to see the television still on he ran across and kicked it over with his bare foot. The set bounced off a wall and several of its knobs fell off. Seeing it lying defenceless on the floor Burton kicked it again for good measure. Unfortunately his foot struck an exposed metal screw that gashed his big toe. Burton let out an almighty scream as blood poured onto the carpet. Patching him up Liz could only see the funny side of it, which made Burton even madder. The next night he went on stage with a pronounced limp and grumbled, 'Some critics have said I play Hamlet like Richard the Third anyway, so what the hell is the difference.'

Richard Harris's success in *This Sporting Life* did much to turn him into something of an idol with teenagers, mainly those of a rebellious nature. Harris never had the matinee looks of an Errol Flynn; one journalist described him as being built 'like a beer truck, with the face of a thousand Irish navvies'. The film also brought him to the attention of one of the world's most fashionable directors, Michelangelo Antonioni. But relations between the two men on the set of *The Red Desert* (1964) were so strained that the film went three months behind schedule and at one point Harris punched Antonioni full in the mouth and knocked him out. Harris was constantly arguing about new script revisions and confusing direction from a man capable of speaking English but who preferred to communicate by wild gestures and the occasional guttural Italian expletive. It was getting desperate. Phoning his mate Ronnie Fraser Harris said, 'This may kill me, so keep an eye on the obits.'

It didn't help that in Italy Harris experimented with LSD, almost killing himself anyway in the process. 'I went berserk and was stopped at the last minute from jumping off a balcony. I never took it again.' Harris wanted out, despite the charms of his beautiful co-star Monica Vitti, and got his wish when Sam Peckinpah cast him in the western *Major Dundee* (1964). It was due to start filming in just a few weeks but Antonioni wouldn't let Harris leave insisting their movie wasn't finished. It was for Harris. 'I just thought he was having one long wank with Monica holding his balls. It went on forever, and he was enjoying it too much.' Harris worked frantically for the next few days, round the clock, even sleeping on the set, woken at five each morning with black coffee laced with brandy. At the end of the week he confronted Antonioni. 'Look, what you have is great, so – adios.' Grabbing a unit car he drove to Milan airport and headed for LA. Antonioni was forced to hire a Harris lookalike to finish the picture. The actor's passing remark on working with Antonioni was that if the director hadn't made a career in movies, he would surely have been head of the Mafia.

Harris missed his direct flight to LA so jet hopped there via London, New York and St Louis, desperate to make Peckinpah's rehearsal dates. In London he drank for six straight hours to stay awake. Arriving in LA 17 hours later, he was barely conscious and collapsed at the studio. Harris was hysterical when he came to, fearing he'd suffered a heart attack. Ever since his malnutrition-induced collapse at drama school he'd nervously awaited the next one. He underwent medical tests but the doctors found nothing and misleadingly gave him the all-clear. It would take 15 years and many more collapses until hyperglycaemia was finally diagnosed.

Major Dundee re-teamed Harris with old nemesis Chuck Heston. A family man with a legendary reputation for discipline, Heston did not approve of Harris's hellraising notoriety. Harris sensed that Heston looked down on him like a preacher, 'or some high-handed twat'. And although he tried to get on with the star most of Harris's time was spent figuring out how he could slip LSD into Heston's coffee to loosen him up a bit. Harris would sum up Heston as having 'issued from a cubic womb', for being so conservative.

With insurance cover of $4m riding on Harris and a unit doctor in constant attendance zapping him daily with vitamin injections, work began on location in Mexico. Heston started making a big deal out of the Irishman's tendency for lateness. 'He used to sit there in the mornings and clock us in with a stop-watch like some dreary great head mistress in enormous, gangling drawers.' Pissed-off Harris positioned dozens of alarm clocks around Heston's make-up trailer and set them all to go off at the same time in an explosion of noise. The star almost leapt out of his skin when he opened the door. 'Just clocking in,' Harris cracked, but Heston wasn't amused. 'He had no sense of humour, not a bit,' Harris later remarked.

Such incidents made an already fraught production even more tiresome. Harris argued with Heston and both actors argued with the director. Finally Peckinpah left the set and drove into the hills at night, declaring that he'd rather sleep with the snakes than with his stars. In his diary Heston wrote that Harris was, 'Something of a fuck up, no question.' Later he softened his position: 'If he was a fuck up, I was a hard-nosed son of a bitch.' Still, Harris decreed he'd never work with the American again. He didn't.

Some respite for Harris came from his friendship with co-star James Coburn; they'd frequently hang out together and booze in the local cantinas. 'When he wanted to, he could hit the liquor like no one I knew,' said Coburn. One afternoon the two men went to a bullfight but Harris got into a disagreement with someone seated nearby who'd knocked over his bag of sweets. Harris retaliated by smashing the stranger in the face, receiving howls of approval from fellow spectators. Even with Elizabeth's arrival in Mexico Harris remained in a state of despair. When Lindsay Anderson visited the set, he suggested they all make 8mm short films, each about Mexico: Coburn shot bulls, Anderson landscapes,

Elizabeth the locals. Harris recorded a child's funeral, to everyone's utter dismay.

When it came to booze Peter O'Toole rarely met his match. But he did in Richard Burton. O'Toole saw Burton immediately as a soul mate, someone who shared his love of booze. Both came to the film *Becket* (1964), a historical drama focusing on the relationship between Henry II and his archbishop, with notorious reputations, so the crew was surprised to see them both holding nothing but cups of tea for ten days. Finally Burton said to O'Toole, putting on an Irish accent, 'Peter, me boy, I think we deserve a little snifter.' They drank for two nights and a day and appeared quite blasted for the scene where the King places the ring on Becket's finger thus making him Chancellor of England. Luckily there was no dialogue, but O'Toole had a dreadful time putting the ring on. 'It was rather like trying to thread a needle wearing boxing gloves,' Burton later recalled.

After that it was non-stop drinking for the remainder of the shoot. The director Peter Glenville just about coped with his two stars periodically turning up for work pissed, but visiting executives from Hollywood were far from pleased with the spectacle. Obviously there to see how their investment was going the executives were horrified to see Burton and O'Toole reeling about pissed and slurring their speech on the set one morning; but when the cameras rolled the two stars instantly sobered up.

It was O'Toole who introduced Burton to the numerous pubs situated conveniently close to the studio in Shepperton village such as the Hovel, whose eccentric landlord displayed on the bar a shrunken head in a bottle, as well as a pickled penis. There was also the King's Head where the landlord, Archie, greeted the stars on their first visit with a steaming lunch and the words, 'Now is the winter of our discontent made glorious summer by this leg of pork.'

During another pub-crawl, this time in London, O'Toole and Burton got seriously sloshed. 'Richard was in a bad state,' O'Toole later recalled, 'worried about his career. "Oh Pedro, what am I doing?" That night he had fallen into a bottle of scotch and I wasn't far behind him.' Staggering home at three in the morning, O'Toole tried to carry his friend but he was too heavy and both men stumbled and fell into the gutter. Somebody stopped beside them on the pavement. It was Alan Bates, O'Toole's ex-RADA colleague. 'Peter,' he said, 'today I've just signed up for my first commercial picture.' 'We both looked up,' recalled O'Toole, 'and said, "You coming down to join us, then?" And we just lay there laughing.'

It was exactly this kind of going on a bender that Liz Taylor hoped to put an end to between her husband and O'Toole. For years the two actors had lived around the corner from each other in Hampstead – pre Liz. 'He'd come to my place or I'd go to his,' said O'Toole. 'And then we'd carry each other home. Elizabeth wasn't keen on that. She probably thought I led him astray. I don't know. She didn't approve. That was a bone of contention between me and Richard. I said, "If you now need permission to come and see me, then you go fuck yourself, you old git!"'

With the success of *The System* Oliver Reed's career seemed to be finally moving in the right direction but then it was almost tragically snuffed out after a West End brawl. In a nightclub Reed passed a table occupied by a group of rowdy young men and heard one of them shout, 'Look out, here comes Dracula,' a reference to his Hammer Horror roles. 'Watch it,' Reed said, 'or I'll bite your jugular vein out.'

Forgetting the incident Reed sat down with his drink. Half an hour later the same man approached him: 'Did you mean what you said?' Reed told him to fuck off and go play with himself. The next thing he knew a broken glass was in his face, followed by the rest of the gang jumping on top of him, punching and kicking. Reed stood no chance. Somehow he managed to get outside, blood spurting from his face, and hail a cab. Almost immediately one pulled up. 'St George's Hospital.' As Reed spoke he could feel shards of broken glass in his mouth. The driver took one look at his pummelled face and said, 'All that blood's going to fuck up my cab.' 'Fuck your cab,' snapped Reed, 'get me to hospital.'

During the journey Reed fainted twice and the driver had to stop in order to prop him up and stem the bleeding using a handkerchief. The glass had gone right through the side of Reed's cheek and shredded part of his tongue and he'd already lost several pints of blood by the time they reached casualty. Reed knew it was bad when a nurse caught sight of him and fainted.

Once he was back home Katie took one look at her husband's heavily bandaged face and hollered, 'You stupid bastard.' In the morning Reed looked at his appalling reflection in the mirror. 'Christ. That's it, there goes my career.' Except perhaps for more horror films, this time without the make-up. To drown his sorrows he went out and bought a bottle of whisky and drank half of it, through a straw because he could hardly move his mouth. But thanks to a young casualty doctor his face did heal except for a few scars that he carried for the rest of his life.

Fights in clubs, bars and restaurants unfortunately were to become a feature of Reed's life. After becoming famous he made much play in the press of the fact that he still drank in his local pub, despite the fact that people invariably wanted to pick a fight with him to see how tough he really was. 'It's impossible for me to go into a pub without having a few problems,' he'd complain. 'It's a bit like the gunfight at the OK Corral every time. There's always someone who wants to take me on.' And Reed was only too happy to oblige, unable to walk away because of his own fear of violence; he had to face it down. 'I'm a pacifist,' he once said, 'but I'm the most scarred, kicked and beat-up person I know.' Later in life Reed loved to show off the knuckles of his right hand, every one broken in fights.

Director John Hough, who worked with Reed three times in the 1980s, witnessed some of this first hand during a trip they undertook together to South Africa. 'When you met Ollie he was different to what one had imagined, he was quite a gentle person in real life. But he was a tough guy, no question about that. We were sitting at this bar in Johannesburg enjoying a drink when in walked this rugby team, 15 really big guys. One of them recognised Oliver and he came over and said, "You're Oliver Reed, aren't you?" Oliver, the perfect gentleman said, yes. And the guy then sat down and started to have a conversation and Oliver said, "Did I ask you to sit down?" And the guy was perplexed. He said, "Well, no.' Oliver said, "Fuck off then." And the guy stood there with all his mates waiting in the background to see what was going to happen, it was just like a western. I thought, oh no there's going to be chairs flying everywhere. There was a long silence and then the guy sort of shrugged his shoulders and went back to his rugby team. But Oliver was prepared to go the distance, he would never back down, he would have stood there fighting to the very end. He was a genuine tough guy.'

* * *

When they finally married in 1964 Richard Burton and Liz Taylor's fame grew even larger, if that were possible. When the couple flew into Boston after their honeymoon 500 fanatical fans broke through the barriers and surrounded the plane, peering in the windows and screaming. The aircraft was towed into a hangar and the Burtons finally escaped by sending their staff ahead in a decoy car. It was worse at the hotel where more than a thousand people crammed in the lobby, some tearing at Liz's hair, slamming her against a wall and clutching at her jewellery. Burton used his fists to fight his way through to his new bride. When they finally got into the lift Burton was bleeding from a cut face while Liz was crying hysterically. In such circumstances Burton usually resorted to using violence, shouting at fans to piss off and lashing out at intrusive photographers. Arriving at Los Angeles airport once Burton went to punch a man thrusting a microphone into his face, only to miss and instead knock out a very surprised policeman.

The couple were now the icons of their age; as Burton put it, 'We live in a blaze of floodlights all day long.' When Burton opened as Hamlet on Broadway the police had to block off the street after each performance so the couple could walk in safety to their limo. Fans would then swarm around them, some risking their lives by climbing on the roof. Inside Burton was agitated but Liz, ever the professional, sat there serenely smiling and waving like royalty while silently mouthing, 'Fuck you, and you, and you over there, and you too, dear.'

Soon they had to hire bodyguards and security men to ward off kidnap threats. They also began to build up an entourage of secretaries, dressers, nannies, tutors and hairdressers. 'Why do the Burtons have to be so filthily ostentatious?' asked Rex Harrison. Filming *The Taming of the Shrew* with the couple in Rome, Michael York recalls, 'They were Gods, Richard and Elizabeth; I think we've forgotten just what a big deal they were. Their dressing rooms, I've never seen anything like it, luxurious white carpets, butlers, maids, the lot.'

Siân Phillips knew that as a showbiz couple O'Toole and herself were no match for the Burton/Taylor roadshow, recalling one trip together to a film festival in Sicily where they drank champagne en route in first class. She later noted that it was impossible not to behave excessively in Burton and Liz's company. The benefits of such an existence were obvious and colossal, but such a lifestyle only served to close Burton off from reality as he bounced round the world with 93 suitcases, planes held up waiting for the couple and security guards for Liz's jewels.

Of course Burton revelled in this VIP treatment, travelling first class, getting the best table in the world's finest restaurants, or having home-grown food flown across the world to wherever he was filming. But he just as much enjoyed mixing it with his mates in a good old fashioned British boozer or stopping off at a fish and chip shop and eating it out of newspaper on the back seat of his Rolls-Royce. Occasionally the couple would also turn up unannounced at Burton's home town in a limo and go to the pub where he led the locals in song and drinks, but mostly it was the jet set life, swanning around Monte Carlo, shopping in Paris or New York.

The Burton/Taylor travelling circus next moved to Mexico City where Burton was due to start filming *The Night of the Iguana* (1964) for John Huston, playing a disbarred clergyman sexually desired by a teenage nymphomaniac. Hitting the tarmac they daren't even get off the plane due to the size of the crowds waiting for them. When they finally made a dash for it the mob turned into a riot. Liz was again manhandled while Burton punched anything that moved. At a press conference later that day he said, with utter sincerity, 'This is my first visit to Mexico. I trust it shall be my last.' It wasn't, they fell in love with the country and even purchased a home there. But it was a hellish location inhabited by scorpions, snakes, giant land crabs, poisonous lizards and mosquitoes.

Liz remained on location throughout filming, much to Burton's annoyance at times. One day she was fussing so much with his hair before a take that he grabbed a bottle of beer and poured it over his head. 'How do I bloody look now?' he roared. More than ever their passion could spill over into violent rows. Both were drinking heavily at this time and most nights propped up the local bar. Some snipers began joking that the recipe for a Burton cocktail began: 'First take 21 tequilas.' This apparently derived from the day he drank 21 straight tequilas and then dived fully clothed into the sea after a friend swore he'd spotted a shark.

Tom Shaw, Huston's assistant director, recalled Burton on the *Iguana* set. 'It used to amaze me seeing Burton at seven in the morning drinking beer, he'd drink beer all morning long. By the time we finished he would have had a case of beer. Then he'd shift into high gear! He started into that tequila and man you'd never have known he'd had a drink. He was a big league drinker. There was nobody in that league.'

On the odd evening when he didn't drink Liz was usually on the piss and egging him on to join her. One night she was on her fifth measure when she yelled, 'Richard, for Christ's sake have a drink. You're so dull when you don't have a glass in your hand.' Never needing much persuasion Burton obliged and after a dozen shots of tequila stood up and began reciting *Hamlet*, without slurring a single word. By the end of the evening he'd drunk 23 shots of tequila and five beer chasers. The next morning he arrived on set on time and word perfect.

In order to diffuse the tension prior to shooting (due mainly to the isolated location the stars would be working in together), John Huston made each lead actor a gold encrusted pistol with bullets – one with each actor's name on it. It was Huston's way of saying, if you want to kill each other, use the designated bullet. Bonkers, but the ploy worked, there were no problems between the cast and when *Iguana* wrapped Huston organized a party that few would ever forget – Ava Gardner water skiing in the dark with a glass of tequila in one hand and happy Mexicans shooting at everything in sight.

After his collapse on *Major Dundee* Richard Harris made a serious attempt to control his boozing. On doctor's orders he cut out spirits and confined himself to beer and champagne. He was ready to reform and to enjoy the taste of alcohol sensibly, without constantly pushing himself over the edge and getting in trouble. 'I don't drink for kicks,' he said. 'I drink when I'm happy, when I'm with friends. It's boredom and frustration, not drink, that makes me aggressive. But I do enjoy letting myself go once in a while and waking up in someone else's garden or in a police station.'

Next for Harris was the war film *Heroes of Telemark* (1965), shot in Norway with Kirk Douglas. Harris knew of Douglas's tough guy reputation and at first refused the offer. 'I kept turning down the film until the money got so high it seemed immoral to say no.' From the start both stars didn't hit it off. It was a clash of egos, of hard-nosed men who didn't compromise. Things got off to a bad start when Harris visited Douglas at his Hollywood home and saw that he'd hung all his film awards up in his hallway. 'Do you have to remind yourself how great you are?' Harris asked. 'Are you that sad?'

Inevitably there were rows on the set and fellow actors usually found themselves in the crossfire. 'It was a battle from beginning to end,' recalled co-star Ulla Jacobsson. 'They were both fighting for camera position and neither was prepared to give way to the other. I have never known anything quite like it before. Even when this battle for supremacy did not result in an explosion the tension remained.' One day on set Harris taunted Douglas that he was too old to start anything. 'Twenty years ago you could have handled me – maybe – but not now. So don't press your luck.' Douglas's constant bragging about his latest girlfriend also annoyed him. Upon the revelation that she'd once been Miss Norway Harris chided, 'Oh yeah, what year?' Director Anthony Mann later termed the eight weeks of shooting akin to 'working on the slopes of an angry volcano'.

As for Harris's own domestic situation, his marriage was still hanging together. He told reporters how lucky he was to have such an understanding partner in Elizabeth. Although in 1965 he summed up the perfect wife as 'a beautiful mute nymphomaniac who owns the local boozer'. Elizabeth certainly had the patience of a saint. For example, one Saturday lunchtime Harris went out with a pal to a football match. 'When will I see you?' Elizabeth asked. 'Tuesday,' Harris replied. 'And it might be in the police courts.' Another time he announced he was popping out for a drink. Only he forgot to say that the drink was in Dublin and he was gone for ten days. When things like that happened Liz would be anxious and start phoning hospitals and the police. 'But after a while I got used to it.'

It was really the kind of behaviour that no sane wife should have had to endure. One night Harris was thrown out of a pub at closing time, but still in need of a drink boarded a train just to make use of its open bar. With no idea where the train was headed he arrived in Leeds completely legless at one in the morning. With nowhere to go he walked down a nearby street and seeing a light on in a house chucked a stone at the window. The owner came storming out but upon recognizing Harris invited the star inside. Harris stayed there for four whole days and wasn't sober once. Eventually the man's wife phoned Elizabeth: 'I've got your husband.' She was shocked when Elizabeth replied, 'Good, keep him.'

Harris was now at the peak of his hellraising and enjoying his fame immensely. He was friends with Princess Margaret, even buying her old Rolls-Royce Phantom. Living in Kensington Harris's appearances at the local police station became so commonplace that on one occasion after a night on the town he dropped in at 4 am, demanding tea and toast. 'Oh, it's you again,' said the desk sergeant, ordering the kettle to be put on.

Not surprisingly his larger than life personality and domineering presence meant that he was easily hunted down by the fans and the paparazzi. He used to call himself 'the showcase fugitive'. He revelled in it and his notoriety. He was fully aware of his weaknesses, but the risk-taking buzz was too much to refuse. He couldn't say no to the forbidden fruit. 'I loved its taste. The illegal item was the best item. The wrong woman in my bed was the best woman. The rude comment far funnier than the nice remark.'

At the time Harris was a near neighbour and friend of film director Peter Medak. They'd often socialize together. Sammy Davis Jnr had just landed in town and was appearing at a top venue near Piccadilly. 'Richard called me and said, "I'll pick you up, we'll go and see Sammy Davis." He had an open top American car at the time and we drove down Piccadilly and it was getting late. Back in the 60s the Eros statue was in the middle of Piccadilly, not to the side as it is now, so it was a complete roundabout. We drove round in a circle looking for a parking space, then Richard suddenly pulled up in front of this big department store on the corner of Lower Regent Street and said. "Fuck it, let's just leave the car here." I said. "Richard you're insane, you can't leave the car here." Anyway we went to see Sammy Davis who Richard knew and we met the singer backstage.We returned and of course the car was gone. "Doesn't matter," he said. Richard was an amazing guy. He was one of the greats. But the drink affected him. He really was a bad drunk. He could turn really nasty and then not remember any of it the next day.'

On the closing night of *Hamlet* Peter O'Toole stayed up drinking until dawn and then raced out to the airport. Aching from 18 inoculations against tropical diseases, he caught the plane to Hong Kong, where he was to start shooting *Lord Jim* (1964). 'The next bloody day, I'm in a blazing small boat, wearing a funny hat and paddling like a man possessed.' In his six weeks there, O'Toole acquired an intense hatred for Hong Kong, which he called

'Manchester with slanted eyes', and proceeded to make his displeasure known. Staying in a sedate hotel, O'Toole horrified the management by personally pulling a rickshaw and its coolie driver into the elegant main lobby at 2 am and buying the fellow a drink.

Based on a Joseph Conrad novel, *Lord Jim* was another mammoth *Lawrence*-like epic and after Hong Kong the company moved on to Cambodia where the bulk of shooting was to take place. Producer-director Richard Brooks had managed to get permission to shoot location scenes in the jungle and around the ancient temple ruins of Angkor Wat. To accommodate his large cast and crew, Brooks had had to spend $600,000 to add a 47-room wing onto a little hotel near the location. 'That hotel!' raged O'Toole. 'More expensive than Claridges; ten flaming quid a night and a poxy room at that. Nicest thing you could say about the food was that it was grotesque.' Soon everyone was suffering from dysentery, set upon by giant stinging insects, and had contracted prickly heat rash that made clothing unbearable.

Then the snakes arrived. Walking down the middle of a jungle road, O'Toole came face to face with a huge black cobra. 'They say no snake can travel faster than a scared human,' he recalled, 'but I ain't so sure. The snake went like hell, but luckily away from me.' One dinner, O'Toole found a live snake in his soup. Another time a cobra slithered onto the set and dropped to the floor of the makeshift ladies' toilet. Of particular dread was a snake called the Two-Step. 'It bites you, you take two steps,' explained O'Toole, 'and then you die.'

What bothered O'Toole the most were the shipboard scenes. He had warned the director, 'I was in the Royal Navy two years and I was seasick every day we were at sea.' For the eight days the film crew shot on the ocean O'Toole was seasick every day. 'He'd rush to the side of the ship and heave, and then go before the camera as if nothing had happened,' said Brooks. 'In eight days he must have tried every known medical and non-medical remedy. Nothing worked.'

During filming there was a pulse of political violence beating just below the surface in the country. One day a mysterious Frenchman appeared on the location and darkly advised Brooks to get his company out of Cambodia by March 12th. With O'Toole's concurrence, the work schedule was doubled and the daily shooting went on from noon until nearly dawn. The scheduled

12 weeks was cut to nine and the company left the country on March 3rd. One week later the US and British embassies were attacked by mobs. O'Toole was convinced that some of the trouble-makers had worked on the film as extras. The country's ruler took to the national radio to denounce the movie company as 'Western imperialist invaders'.

'If I live to be a thousand I want nothing like Cambodia again,' O'Toole confessed on his return home. 'It was a bloody nightmare.' Cambodia's crowned prince took exception to this and banned O'Toole from the country. 'That is the sort of thing that tends to make tourists nervous,' was the royal quote.

Finishing in Cambodia O'Toole flew to New York for an appearance on the *Johnny Carson Show*, despite his aversion to planes. 'I can't believe all that tonnage can float in the air.' When he arrived on set he hadn't slept for over a day and was exhausted. Three minutes into the interview O'Toole, having been unable to put two words coherently together, collapsed, broke his glasses, excused himself and walked off. The effect was sensational. No one had ever walked off the *Johnny Carson Show* before.

With O'Toole in *Lord Jim* was his old *Lawrence* co-star Jack Hawkins and they enjoyed many a boozy night together. Hawkins was a fearsome drinker. One of his most famous roles was in *Zulu* as a fire and brimstone preacher with a soft spot for the bottle, one of the greatest instances of playing to type in movie history. According to one of the cast Hawkins was pissed all the time on location in South Africa and they couldn't get him up in the morning. It wasn't the booze, though, that ultimately led to the downfall of this popular and respected actor, but fags. Hawkins was a chain smoker and not long after *Lord Jim* was found to be suffering cancer of the throat and was forced to undergo an operation to remove his larynx. It was O'Toole who gave Hawkins his first post-op role in *The Great Catherine* in 1968, the only film in which he used his new voice, produced in the oesophagus by belching wind from the stomach. For the remainder of his films Hawkins's voice was dubbed, usually by Charles Gray. Desperately seeking a way to restore his distinctive voice Hawkins underwent an operation in 1973 to install an artificial voice box, which would allow him to speak normally. Tragically the incision in his throat developed an infection and kept haemorrhaging, resulting in his premature death.

O'Toole's next film appearance was in the cult sex comedy *What's New*

Pussycat? (1965). He'd won the part of a sex-crazed Parisian fashion designer after Warren Beatty pulled out and was delighted at last to have lots of glamorous babes like Capucine and Ursula Andress about the place. 'Usually in a movie I'm in love with Richard Burton or camels.' Also sharing the screen were comedy giants Peter Sellers and Woody Allen. O'Toole first met Sellers in the company of mutual friend Kenneth Griffith. They'd arranged to meet Sellers in the foyer of the theatre he was appearing in after curtain down but instead spent the evening waiting in the pub next door entertained by a busker who had a pram with a dog sitting bolt upright inside. 'I bet that dog is nailed down,' O'Toole said to Griffith. 'Look carefully at its paws. Can you see the nails?' When the pair remembered their rendezvous with Sellers the comedian was nowhere in sight and they spent an age crawling around the empty auditorium on their hands and knees searching underneath the seats shouting, 'Come out Peter, come out, come out, wherever you are.'

O'Toole adored Sellers and cherished their time working together. On the set he met the comedian's pregnant new wife Britt Ekland and said, 'Isn't it shocking? You've only known him a short while and he's got you into trouble already.'

While in Paris O'Toole demonstrated that he still harboured a grudge against figures of authority when, returning to his hotel from filming one night, he saw two policemen roughing up a prostitute. One had the helpless girl by the hair while his mate whacked her with his truncheon. The outraged O'Toole was in a nightclub a few nights later when he noticed another policeman, not connected to the incident, but a policeman all the same, and under the cover of a packed dance floor took the opportunity to take revenge. 'By the time I'd finished with him I don't think he was in any condition to whack any poor old whore around the head for a night or two.'

By coincidence Burton and Taylor were also in Paris, shooting interiors for their dreary romance *The Sandpiper* in the same studio and O'Toole decided to play a prank on his drinking pal. In one of Burton and Liz's interminable love scenes two drunks appear and disturb them. O'Toole did a deal with one of the actors, smuggled himself onto the set and as the cameras rolled exploded into bad Welsh, cursing the bewildered Burton. Not to be outdone Burton had a small cameo role in *Pussycat*. 'How's what's her name?' O'Toole asks Burton as they pass each other in, where else, a bar.

For about a year Oliver Reed carried the red angry scars of his close encounter with a smashed bottle and no producer would hire him. Strapped for cash, with a wife and young kid to support, Reed had no choice but to find a 'normal' job. He'd just passed his driving test and owned a red mini so took up employment as a minicab driver. A big mistake since he quickly became convinced his mini was jinxed. On the day he passed his test he executed an emergency stop only for the car behind him to plough right into his arse and for a police car to ram the other man up his boot. Reed naturally got the blame. Weeks later he picked up a hitchhiker and just avoided a head-on collision with a car which was on the wrong side of the road by throwing the mini into a ditch. The hitchhiker called Reed a fucking maniac and refused to get back inside. Then during his first fare as a cab driver proper he hit a milk float in Earls Court Road and was threatened with court action.

Then as now minicab drivers were mistrusted and unpopular, especially with black-cab drivers who hated them for taking away their fares. 'We'd drop off old ladies at Victoria Station,' said Reed, 'and the black-cab drivers used to be very grumpy with us – in fact they used to punch you very hard in the mouth. So when I used to drop the old ladies off, I'd always give them a kiss goodbye – then the other drivers would think they were my granny.'

An Australian pal of Reed's called Roddy often accompanied him on his taxi jobs. He was there one night when Reed drove at 90 mph to London airport with a client who was late for his flight. Driving back Reed was cut up by another vehicle and flashed his headlights at the offending driver who replied with a two finger salute. Pissed off Reed chased after him and forced the car off the road. He yanked open the door to thump the driver in the face and announce that he was making a citizen's arrest when the stranger suddenly sped off down the road again shouting, 'Bollocks!' This served only to incense Reed further who followed the car to a house at which point the man's wife bailed out to call the police. 'I amused myself by jamming the man's head against a rising main while we waited for them to arrive,' said Reed. Sure enough two constables turned up. 'Arrest this man,' said Reed. 'He has been driving dangerously and nearly killed me.' The driver protested, declaring Reed to be the madman. The copper tried to calm the situation by suggesting it was all a storm in a teacup. Meanwhile Roddy scrambled out of the mini smelling like a sewage works. 'Storm in a teacup!' he blasted. 'What about you Ollie, you crazy bastard, driving to the airport at a hundred miles an hour, no wonder I shit myself.' Reed put his head in his hands, wishing it was Roddy's head he'd jammed against the rising main.

Again it was Michael Winner who came to Reed's rescue casting him in a couple of movies, principally *The Jokers* (1967), a swinging 60s comedy about two brothers out to steal the crown jewels. Playing Reed's brother was Michael Crawford, who in just a few years time created the immortal television comic character, Frank Spencer. Crawford thoroughly enjoyed his time working with Ollie. The only sticky moment between them came during the filming of a scene where the script called for Reed to half-strangle Crawford's character. (In the story, his brother had supposedly betrayed him.) 'I was really dreading it,' recalled Crawford, who'd seen first-hand how Reed often 'lived' the role he was playing. 'Quite rightly, because as we shot the scene Oliver took my "betrayal" as something entirely real and completely personal and suddenly my life wasn't worth tuppence. His hands were fastened so tightly round my neck, I felt the end of my life was imminent. It took four people to get him off me.'

Fifteen years later the pair worked together again on the insipid comedy adventure *Condorman* (1981) for Disney. Crawford was the butt of numerous practical jokes perpetrated by Reed on location. One night Crawford woke up to see Ollie in his hotel room silently turning every piece of furniture upside down. He then quietly crept out again. 'Thank you, Oliver,' Crawford whispered.

There was also a strange film Reed made in Canada called *The Trap* (1966), in which he played a sullen, brutish trapper who bought a young mute girl (Rita Tushingham) for a wife. It remained one of Ollie's personal favourites. 'It was the first time I'd ever come into contact with Indians. In actual fact a very drunken Indian once said to me, "White man taught the Indian to drink so now he must pay the price." He wanted to scalp me, but he was hit on the back of the head with a stool by a rather large

Canadian called Moose. I didn't meet him again until they gave a party and it was there that I saw this same young Indian, with a rather large bruise on his head, pretending to be an eagle. Still pissed.'

After the turgid *The Sandpiper* (1965) that made money but did little for Richard Burton's reputation, his next film role was a real challenge, that of a down at heel spy in the gritty John Le Carré thriller *The Spy Who Came in From the Cold* (1966). But it was not a happy film to make. Director Martin Ritt clashed with Burton over his drinking habit and co-star Claire Bloom was still smarting from their love affair. It didn't help that at their first meeting off the set, Burton snubbed her with such callousness that she never forgave him. Claire noticed that Burton was still drinking hard and that he had a slight tremor in his hands early in the morning that was lessened by an early cup of coffee sipped from a mug emitting a whiff of the hard stuff. This was nine o'clock. By midday he was drinking champagne in his dressing room followed by several bottles of wine. 'By late afternoon Richard was pretty well out of commission,' recalled Claire.

During one particular scene Burton was required to down a whisky. The props department brought in flat ginger ale, the movies' usual substitute for scotch, but Burton waved it away. 'It's only a short scene, won't need more than a couple of takes. Bring me some real whisky.' In fact the scene needed 47 takes. 'Imagine it, luv,' Burton bragged to a journalist later, '47 whiskies!'

Burton on his own could match anyone for the sheer quantity he drank; he and Liz together were a formidable team. In 1967 they attended the wedding reception of Richard's close friend Brook Williams. The small gathering of a dozen people consumed 36 bottles of Dom Perignon champagne and 14 magnums. In their suite the Burtons continued drinking, then Ivor, Richard's brother, fell over in the bathroom and cracked his head open. When Liz got down on her hands and knees to clean up the blood she dropped one of her diamond earrings down the toilet bowl. Finally at 4 am the party drew to a close and Burton was urged to help send poor Ivor home in a car. 'Yes, when I finish this drink we'll be off.' He wasn't holding a glass, though, but a bottle of brandy.

Another evening, Burton got so drunk in a restaurant that after the meal he fell down the steps on his way out. Liz, having had every bit as much

Actor for hire. So there would be no confusion, at one private audition with a gay director Reed's wife scrawled 'This is mine' on her husband's cock.

Playing a werewolf for Hammer, Reed enjoyed keeping his make-up on at the end of the day and terrifying fellow motorists at traffic lights.

Off-set during the filming of *Oliver!* At one party Reed got child stars Mark Lester and Jack Wild violently drunk on vodka by spiking their cokes.

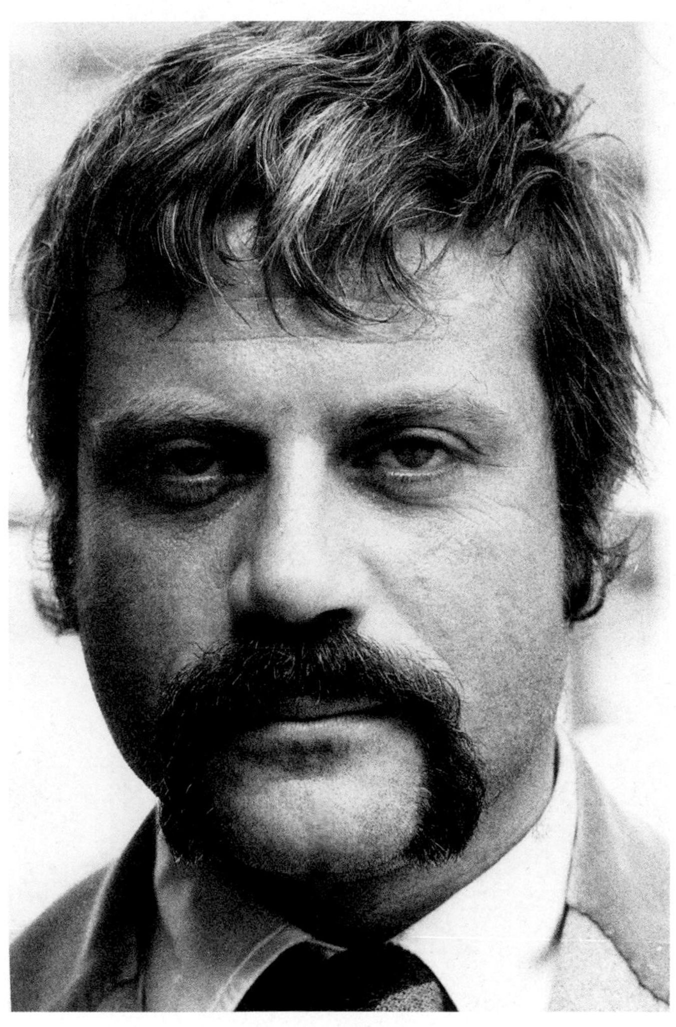

Reed made a habit of dropping his trousers in public to show off his 'wand of lust. My mighty mallet.'

Reed, the country gent, at his 18th century mansion Broome Hall, scene of many drunken rampages and wild parties.

Filming *The Three Musketeers*, even the stuntmen were terrified of fencing with Reed, who often lost control during fight scenes: 'He was a menace,' says co-star Christopher Lee.

A 1970s sex symbol, Reed never made it big in Hollywood.
Throwing up over Steve McQueen probably didn't help.

Reed was banned from all his local pubs. His most spectacular eviction came when he clambered up the chimney at the Bull's Head shouting 'Ho! Ho! Ho! I'm Santa Claus.' He was naked at the time.

Reed celebrates knocking back 126 pints in just 24 hours – about 12 minutes per pint.

At nightclubs Reed played his own game of 'head butting'. The rules required each player to repeatedly smash his head against his opponent until one collapsed or surrendered.

Snooker ace Alex Higgins foolishly dozed off in Reed's presence. Reed took this as a personal insult and Higgins woke to find Reed brandishing an axe at him.

Filming *Gladiator* in Malta Reed caroused with and arm-wrestled a gang of sailors. Not long later, he collapsed and died. 'His death was a total nonsense,' said film director Ken Russell.

to drink, fell about laughing. Burton was enraged and snatched off the wig she frequently wore. Furious, Liz refused to share the marital bed that night, instead pouring out her woes to Burton's buddy Stanley Baker. In truth, Elizabeth could be every bit as uncontrollable as Burton. Many friends attest to the fact that she was the heavier drinker. Burton enjoyed boasting that he could drink any man under the table, but not necessarily every woman, meaning Elizabeth. Both being drinkers inevitably led to rows in public, usually about who could drink the most. Like Burton, Elizabeth never showed any ill-effects from her boozing. Around this time it was usual for her to start every morning with Bloody Marys, made with special salt and pepper flown in from America to wherever she was currently in the world. At noon she moved on to Jack Daniels whiskey. 'I had a hollow leg,' Liz said once about those days. 'I could drink everyone under the table and not get drunk. My capacity was terrifying.'

Their drunken antics sometimes ensnared the most innocent of parties, including on one occasion the noted theatre critic Kenneth Tynan, who was filming an interview with Burton. The star drank wine steadily all day (around five bottles) and after wrapping invited Tynan to the villa he was renting outside Rome. Liz Taylor was shooting *Reflections in a Golden Eye* at the time with Marlon Brando, who a day earlier had presented the couple with two memorial antique silver goblets. The first was engraved: 'Richard: Christ, I've pissed in my pants.' And the second: 'Elizabeth: That's not piss, that's come.'

At the villa Tynan continued the interview when suddenly Burton, with a wolfish grin on his face, asked, 'How do you think Elizabeth is looking, Ken?' 'Fine,' said the critic, inwardly thinking, Fat. A pause, then, 'How would you like to go to bed with her?' Tynan panicked; to answer in the positive meant one had the hots for the host's wife, to answer in the negative meant she must be a dog. Tynan tried to get out of it with self-deprecating wit: 'To be quite candid Richard, I doubt whether I'd be capable of making it with Elizabeth.' Burton leapt on this: 'You mean you couldn't get it up.' 'Something like that,' Tynan apologised. 'Elizabeth!' Burton bellowed across the room. Breaking away from the other guests Cleopatra herself walked over. 'Yes Richard,' she said. 'Do you know what our friend Ken just said about you,' went Burton. 'No dear,' Liz replied. 'He said he didn't think he'd be able to get it up for you in bed.' Elizabeth's eyes blazed right through Tynan's soul. 'That,' she yelled, 'is the most insulting thing that has ever been said to me. Leave my house!' Tynan was now even more confused; here he was being thrown out for *not* making a pass at the hostess. The next morning the phone rang at his hotel. It was Liz apologising profusely for their behaviour. Flowers were also sent to his room. But as Tynan later wrote in his diary: 'The scene sticks in memory, not inspiring affection.'

Richard Harris's promise to curb his boozing hit the dust on location for his new film, *Hawaii* (1966), when he discovered the local cocktail Mai Tai – rum, cointreau and grenadine. It was as seductive as neat brandy and he devoured it, paying no heed to the intensified warning symptoms. Elizabeth arrived on the island to see first hand the horrendous after effects, notably his violent outbursts. Sometimes Harris would rush into fast moving traffic on the local main road and mindlessly attack passing cars with his bare fists. He was also barred from a nearby hotel when he took a swing at the manager for having the impertinence to suggest that he'd had enough to drink.

Hawaii's director, George Roy Hill, found Harris 'an interesting force of nature'. But his co-star Julie Andrews took a dim view of his rabble-rousing and Harris reciprocated in kind after filming. 'When I worked with Julie Andrews I think I experienced the greatest hate I ever had for any human being.'

When filming was completed Harris had trouble getting off the island when a clerk at the check-out desk wouldn't let him on the flight home. 'They said I was drunk. I'd have to come back next morning. I said, you might as well let me on now because I'll be drunker tomorrow.' But it was no good. Harris picked up his luggage and headed for the nearest bar and kept it open all night. In the morning a different clerk was on duty and let him on.

So bad was Harris's drinking at this stage – sometimes he'd booze for days on end without even eating and make himself really ill – that a group of friends bet him $25,000 that he'd not survive into the 1970s. 'I never thought of my health, never worried about what drink was doing to me.' Harris would walk into a bar and never ask for just one vodka and tonic, he'd ask for four and line them all up, 'because by the time the bar tender had taken my money

I'd want another.' Harris did, of course, make it to the new decade, surprising himself probably, and happily collected his winnings.

In America Harris became pally with Frank Sinatra and his rat pack gang and hit the nightspots of Sunset Boulevard with a vengeance. He was determined to live for every moment, 'grabbing life by the balls' as he hedonistically put it, and having fun. 'People spend the first half of their lives being cautious and the second half regretting it.' He was also highly promiscuous, getting involved with swingers and daylong orgies. He behaved like a married bachelor.

One Hollywood party Harris attended was hosted by fading star Merle Oberon. She was then in her 50s, but Harris didn't care; as a kid back in Limerick he'd fallen in love with her, watching her movies at his local fleapit. 'I'd masturbate about her all night. With the lights off, so God couldn't see me.' Summoning up the courage to approach her Harris stared into her eyes and spoke. 'Merle, I have fantasised about you, kissed every part of you and made love to you in every position that man has conceived.' The startled actress said nothing and walked away. But deep down Harris knew he'd have her that night. Sure enough when all the other guests were leaving Harris was invited to stay. 'These fantasies of yours,' enquired Merle, 'do you think you would like to make them come true?' Harris, in a trance of utter disbelief, followed his dream goddess into the bedroom. Undressed he waited breathlessly for Merle to appear from the bathroom. She came out in a see-through nightgown, 'with nothing on underneath and all I could see were these fabulous tits and a gorgeous black bush.' In bed she went to turn off the light but Harris stopped her. 'Merle, if you are going to turn the lights off I might as well be back in Limerick.' Smiling she put them back on. 'The fantasy was better, though,' Harris later sighed, disappointedly. 'Fantasies always are.'

Peter O'Toole's next film appearance was as no less a personage than God himself in John Huston's *The Bible* (1965), one of the most ironic casting decisions in movie history. Richard Harris was in the film too playing Cain and O'Toole joked that Huston ought to re-title his picture 'The Gospel According to Mick'. O'Toole struck up a close friendship with Huston, helped no doubt by the fact that the Hollywood director lived the life of Riley in a stately pad in Ireland. During one visit the pair planned a hunting trip on horseback but come the morning it was pouring with rain. Huston crept into O'Toole's room, wrapped in a garish green kimono, to announce, 'Pete, this is a day for getting drunk!' For breakfast they shared a bottle of whiskey and ended up on the horses anyway, still in their pyjamas, tearing through the countryside. 'John in his green kimono, me in my nightie in the pissing rain, carrying rifles, rough-shooting it – but with a shitzu dog and an Irish wolfhound, who are of course incapable of doing anything. John eventually fell off the horse and broke his leg! And I was accused by his wife of corrupting him!'

The Bible's impressive cast also included George C. Scott who had the hots for co-star Ava Gardner. Their affair was dominated by heated rows that usually ended in violence. One day on the set a pissed Scott went to hit Ava and it took Huston and six other crew members to hold him back. When O'Toole heard about the incident it was only Huston's intervention that prevented the Irishman and his bodyguard from beating the crap out of the Hollywood actor. Ava later said it was impossible to keep Scott sober during this period and to get him off the booze he had to be sedated and then locked up in, as she described it, 'a nuthouse with bars on the windows'. When the film wrapped Scott followed Ava to London and the Savoy hotel, breaking down a door to get at her only to be arrested and banged up overnight in the cells. When Scott later went out of control in the Beverly Hills Hotel Ava left him for good and sought the protection of her previous lover, Frank Sinatra.

While staying in Rome O'Toole hit the bars with Albert Finney and horror actress Barbara Steele, despite being warned about the paparazzi. The next day O'Toole was resting in his hotel suite when the door suddenly flew open and a gorgeous blonde fell at his feet. Quick as a flash he darted into the next room before two photographers entered. As he came out of a café later in the afternoon the paparazzi descended once again and during a scuffle a photographer was smashed in the face. O'Toole and Steele were taken to the police station and questioned for two hours. The next day the police arrived at O'Toole's hotel informing him that they were going to press charges of assault and that he wasn't to leave before the trial. When the police returned to confiscate his passport and luggage O'Toole got his stunt double to wear his cap and spectacles as a decoy while he smuggled himself out of the back door wearing the beard he used to play

God. 'And nobody spotted me.' Vowing never to work in Rome again O'Toole recruited other stars who had also suffered at the hands of the paparazzi, the likes of Burton, Liz Taylor and Sinatra, to follow suit until the problem had been eradicated.

After the success of *What's New Pussycat?* Peter O'Toole looked for another frothy 60s caper movie and found it in *How To Steal a Million* (1966), a romantic/heist comedy again set in Paris and starring Audrey Hepburn. With Siân in London and Hepburn's husband Mel Ferrer at home in Switzerland, inevitable rumours surfaced of an affair between the two stars. In truth nothing went on, though the two became fast friends. Audrey loved O'Toole's zany antics, which included the Irishman getting the actress plastered on set for the first and only time in her career. It was a cold morning and the scene required Audrey to drive down a street in a car. O'Toole suggested a shot of brandy to stave off the chill, but one glass became two glasses which became three until finally when she was required on set Audrey bounded out of her trailer, tottered towards the car, got in and drove straight into five huge arc lights, totally demolishing them.

Playing Audrey's father in the film was notorious boozer and general mad old bastard, Hugh Griffith. During production he was actually fired for persistent bad behaviour, culminating in a naked stroll down the corridors of the ultra posh George V hotel holding a 'Do not disturb' sign over his privates, which he'd altered to read 'Do disturb'. Years later when Griffith was nominated for a Tony award on Broadway he was asked by a reporter if he was a method actor. 'No, no. But I *am* a Methodist.'

Perhaps best known for his role in *Ben Hur*, in which he won an Oscar as the mock-sinister Sheik Ilderim, whose fine white horses won the chariot race, Hugh Griffith was a close drinking friend of Dylan Thomas and thought nothing of boozing away on film sets. He was reportedly drunk through much of the production of *Tom Jones*. The scene in which his horse falls on him was not planned and many believe he was saved by virtue of his inebriated condition. The film incorporated every frame of the footage before rescuers rushed in to save him.

For lunch he downed double brandies and when asked to perform drunken scenes invariably warmed up with bolt after bolt of black velvet (champagne and stout). 'Do they think I can fake it with bloody tea?' he asked.

But perhaps the most bizarre tale involving Griffith was a 1962 London stage production of Brecht's *Caucasian Chalk Circle*, during which the world was nearly deprived of his future services when, during the hanging scene, he slipped off the box he was standing on and hanged himself in full view of the audience. After gurgling and turning black, he passed out. The curtain fell and he was cut down by his fellow actors. Coming to, Griffith took a shot of brandy and got on with the show.

After Paris, O'Toole's next port of call was Warsaw to play a nasty SS general and serial killer in a film that reunited him with Omar Sharif, *Night of the Generals* (1967). En route he visited Siân in London who was appearing in a play, only to pass out drunk backstage. For the entire performance the cast were forced to step over him in order to make their entrances.

After years of false dawns and crushing disappointments, what Oliver Reed termed as the turning point of his career arrived when he made the acquaintance of a director later christened the enfant terrible of British film and dubbed 'an appalling talent', Ken Russell. For years Reed had been battling against his villainous looks to escape typecasting as teddy boys, thugs and Hammer monsters. 'I had the misfortune to look like a prizefighter and speak like a public schoolboy. When I started, the only jobs I got were as teddy boys in leather jackets who whipped old ladies around the head with a bicycle chain and stole their handbags.' Ken Russell changed all that and proved Reed's artistic saviour when he cast the actor in his television film about Debussy.

The pair immediately took to each other while filming in France, going out to restaurants and getting pissed on the local plonk. In one fish speciality restaurant Russell took pity on the intended dinner, displayed live in a tank, and handed them through a window to Reed who then released them in a local stream. Alas they were discovered and made to pay for the lot.

Another evening, this time back in England, Russell walked into a pub and ordered a bottle of wine and a plate of whelks. 'I'm sorry sir,' said the landlord, motioning his head across the saloon bar. 'We've just sold the last whelks to Mr Reed.' Ollie raised his glass, a big soppy grin on his face. Annoyed Russell left and got back into his car. As he made to drive off an object hurled itself on the bonnet – it was Ollie. Undeterred

Russell revved up the engine and manoeuvred his way onto the main road, Ollie still lying spread-eagled on the bonnet, his feet braced on the wing mirrors and his hands clamped on the windscreen wipers. 'Since when do you refuse to take a drink with me?' Reed screamed through the glass. 'Since you ate all the whelks,' Russell shouted back, nursing the car up to 70mph. 'You want whelks.' Ollie roared, 'I'll give you whelks. Turn back.'

Russell was approaching a roundabout, swung the car round and headed back to the pub. In the car park Russell hit the brakes and watched as Ollie shot off the bonnet, flew through the air and landed in a heap on the gravel. 'You want whelks,' said Ollie, dusting himself down and marching to an estuary that adjoined the pub. Open-mouthed Russell watched as his leading man dived into the water, fully clothed, emerging seconds later with a fistful of seaweed and undetermined gunk. 'Here's your fucking whelks,' Reed said, throwing what he'd found onto the car bonnet. 'Thank you Oliver,' said Russell as he examined the rather unappetizing shellfish. 'Now, what'll you have?' asked Reed. 'Half a shandy,' said Russell. Inside the bar Russell borrowed a knife and prised open the shellfish. 'It was worse than swallowing two globs of phlegm soaked in sump oil,' he recalled.

Reed was growing increasingly eccentric in his behaviour. At home he had amassed an impressive collection of antique weapons and one night after the pubs had closed equipped seven of his drinking pals with various swords, blunderbusses and pikes, forming them all up in the garden. 'Right lads,' he said, sergeant-major style. 'We're going to take over the police station.' Out of his front gate the gang marched and down Wimbledon High Road towards their local Cop shop. Once there they all lined up in front of the building and Ollie marched inside, only to emerge a few seconds later with a stern-faced police officer. 'Attention!' Reed commanded his troops. 'Left turn, quick march.' In the police station yard a constable was holding open the doors of a van and herded Ollie and his mates inside. They were then driven back home like a bunch of naughty schoolboys. 'If I see you lot out again with those weapons,' said an officer, 'I'll have them confiscated.'

Reed continued to showcase his weapons at home, pride of place going to a pair of broad swords and when he'd had a few drinks, out they'd come. After dinner with Ken Russell one evening Reed lifted the swords off the wall and proposed they have a duel. 'I had this six foot sword,' Russell recalled years later. 'And he said, "Now you've got to try and kill me." I said, "Fine." I raised it up and I knew I had to try and kill him. As he came up I pulled the sword down, it ripped his shirt open, blood poured out and he stood there and said, "Great!"'

Despite the overblown rubbish of *The Sandpiper*, Richard Burton and Liz Taylor continued to look for suitable projects to make together, finding their best ever vehicle in the film version of Edward Albee's disturbing play, *Who's Afraid of Virginia Woolf?* (1966). It focused on a married couple who delight in destroying one another in a hail of insults and invective. Liz as Martha, a fat, vicious, domineering bitch, gave her greatest screen performance, though Burton is equally outstanding as the put upon husband. According to some, though, Liz is masterful as the wife only because she was that person in real life. 'That role was more or less her, really,' confirms Waris Hussein, who directed the husband and wife team in the 70s. 'It is one of her best performances because she was actually playing herself. That was absolutely their relationship.'

Friends warned the couple that it was a mistake to appear in the film together, that no marriage, however feisty, could withstand the sheer hatred of Albee's dialogue. Sure enough after a few months the play was beginning to spill over into their private lives. Having spent the day fighting viciously with each other in character in the studio, they'd return home, share a bottle of vodka and fight all over again.

The fighting continued on their next film, when Franco Zeffirelli invited them to appear in Shakespeare's battle of the sexes, *The Taming of the Shrew* (1967). It was to be filmed in Rome, the city where Burton had seduced Taylor and where their lives were so horrendously intruded upon by the paparazzi, to such an extent that both had sworn they would never go back to the city. However here they were and when asked what had happened to his resolve, Burton answered, 'We got plastered and middle-aged, I suppose, and forgot.'

One evening senator Robert Kennedy, who'd befriended Burton during the Broadway run of *Camelot* after discovering their mutual love of poetry, visited the set. Well oiled, both men began to compete over recitals of the

Shakespeare sonnets. Burton eventually won by employing his old party trick of reciting the 15th sonnet word for word, backwards.

For the film's Royal London opening Burton invited all his Welsh relations up to London for the weekend to see it, taking over 14 double rooms at the Dorchester hotel. Not surprisingly there was a massive party held for everyone the night before the premiere that went on until dawn. Then after the premiere Burton held another one. The Dorchester complained that the Burton family had drained every bottle of booze in the hotel.

The star couple continued to make movies together with such alarming regularity that one day Burton grumbled to Liz that, 'We'll soon end up like Laurel and Hardy.' Next up was *The Comedians* (1967), based on Graham Greene's controversial novel about political dictatorship in Haiti. Amongst the cast was Alec Guinness, who'd first made Burton's acquaintance in the late 40s. Since then he'd been an occasional guest at Burton's home, but hadn't seen him for a while and now saw in his appearance a marked change. 'I hardly find him the same person,' he wrote in his diary. 'Drink has taken a bit of a toll, I fear.'

This was followed by a real curate's egg of a movie, *Boom* (1968), directed by Joseph Losey and co-starring Noel Coward. In it Liz played a dying millionairess who as her last lover takes a wandering poet who happens to be the angel of death. Losey was hardly enamoured of the Burtons at their first meeting. 'They arrived both screaming, drunk and abusive, it was unimaginably awful.' At breakfast the next morning Burton turned to Losey. 'I understand that I behaved rather badly last night.' Losey looked up from his coffee and said, 'I don't know whether you do or not.' Burton replied, 'Well, this is as much of an apology as you're ever going to get.' Actually the two ended up on rather friendly terms.

Burton drank for most of the filming, which took place in Sardinia. One evening he disappeared, despite having promised to meet Elizabeth for dinner. Kidnapping was rife in Sardinia at that time and Liz was desperately worried. The police were called, hospitals alerted, but of Burton there was no sign. He was finally found by the police at ten o'clock at night outside a bar, standing on a table reciting Shakespeare to an audience of bemused locals, and promising a drink to anyone who could tell him which play the speeches came from.

* * *

When Richard Harris heard that Warner Brothers intended to film the stage musical *Camelot*, in which Burton had scored such a hit, he set out to claim the role of King Arthur more obsessively than any other in his career. The only drawback was Julie Andrews, who'd been the stage Guinevere. If it's her, Harris thought, forget it. For six months studio head Jack Warner and composer Alan Jay Lerner pursued Burton, until the star finally priced himself out of the deal. The role of King Arthur was up for grabs and so began a four-month campaign of Harris chasing Lerner, Warner and director Joshua Logan. It started with handwritten letters and 'I love you' cards. When Logan attended a party in Palm Springs Harris gatecrashed and delivered a note describing himself as 'The out of work actor, King Richard Harris'. Logan ignored him and moved on to casting sessions in London where he was inundated with telegrams like ONLY HARRIS FOR ARTHUR and HARRIS WORKS CHEAPER. When these were ignored Harris flew to London and burst into Logan's hotel suite, as the director was about to tuck into breakfast, demanding an audition. 'I don't want you,' blasted Logan. 'You wouldn't be right, so please go away.' 'Never!' cried Harris.

The next evening Harris dressed up as a waiter to gatecrash a private party at the Dorchester hotel. As Logan reached out for a drink the Irishman was standing there. 'Jesus,' shrieked the director. 'Will you leave me alone, for Christ's sake?' 'Never,' said Harris, handing him the drink. 'Wherever you go, I'll be there. If you go to the toilet, I'll pop out of the bowl. If you catch a plane, I'll be in the next seat. Just give me a test.' Finally Logan could take it no more after returning to his hotel from a morning jog only to see Harris waiting in the lobby looking as if he'd been there all night. 'Look, I'll even pay for my own test,' Harris pleaded. 'OK,' conceded Logan. 'Now please go away.'

Harris hired top cameraman and future cult director Nicolas Roeg to shoot the screen test. When Logan and Warner saw it they had to agree that they'd found their King Arthur and Harris was finally awarded the role for which he would become most identified in the public's mind. But this obsession cost Harris one of his closest friendships. Laurence Harvey, his old drinking buddy, was currently a success in the London stage version of *Camelot* and assumed he'd be first in line for the film. One evening there was a knock at his dressing room door and Harris stormed in and warned

Harvey that King Arthur was his and his alone. 'I didn't know you were interested,' queried Harvey. 'Well I am,' snapped Harris. 'So keep your fucking hands off. King Arthur's mine.' It would be the last time the two men spoke to each other and Harvey's career faded into obscurity until his untimely death in 1973 from cancer aged only 45.

Having won the role Harris decided to sail to New York in style on the Cunard liner *Queen Mary*, and then fly on to Hollywood. Elizabeth came along, as did Patrick Walker, whose astrology newspaper column would soon be read by millions. Harris had just hired Walker as his personal astrologer after he'd predicted the *Camelot* role would indeed be his. One evening over dinner Harris was drinking to excess and brooding over his wife's recent admission that she'd been unfaithful. Walker, sensing Harris was about to erupt, excused himself and headed for his private cabin. Harris duly self-combusted and hurled every abuse imaginable in his wife's face, shocking fellow passengers. One member of staff later called Harris, 'Probably the most dangerous drunk I have encountered in 40 years on passenger liners.' Elizabeth fled to Walker's room and as he began consoling her Harris suddenly stormed in, grabbed the astrologer by his lapels and flung him against the far wall. He then slowly and deliberately proceeded to destroy every item in the room. Walker later confessed that it was the most frightening experience of his life.

While in Hollywood waiting for *Camelot*'s start date Harris quickly made the spy spoof *Caprice* (1967) with Doris Day, something he later deeply regretted; getting onto an aircraft once, when he heard *Caprice* was the in-flight movie, Harris walked off. Elizabeth was also regretting travelling out to Hollywood with her husband. His drinking was reckless and their arguments were rousing neighbours nightly. During the filming of *Caprice* Harris collapsed on set, excusing it by explaining that he had been on the tiles with actor Jason Robards the night before. After another long booze session Harris drank vodka diluted with water from his swimming pool, full of chlorine, bees, ants and spit. He collapsed again on the set and was rushed to hospital, everyone fearing it was a heart attack. The doctors ruled that out but were baffled as to the actual cause. After two days of tests they said it was an inflamed gullet and that recovery was dependent on a sensible stress-free lifestyle and a drastic reduction in alcohol. Harris celebrated his near death escape by getting pissed.

This endless drinking – at the time Harris was consuming two bottles of vodka a day as well as a bottle of port and brandy – and mad behaviour was finally too much for Elizabeth. Drunken rows were growing more and more violent. 'Richard had success and fame,' she later said. 'We had money, we had three healthy kids. Yet my only thought was how I could keep out of his way.' Driving back from one Hollywood party Harris began hurling abuse at some invisible demon in the night. He then set about destroying the inside of the car, tearing up the upholstery, ripping his hands until they bled. Finally Elizabeth flew back to London and filed for divorce.

It was the height of irony that just when Harris had cracked Hollywood and was earning the big bucks there was no one to share it all with. In July 1966 a *Daily Mirror* headline screamed, 'Star's wife says: I am scared of him.' Elizabeth had gone to the extraordinary lengths of putting out injunctions to stop Harris molesting her and to stay away from his own children. 'I am frightened of him,' she declared in her sworn statement. 'I seek the protection of the court from him.' Her solicitor said it was a matter of grave urgency. Yes he acknowledged Harris was a man of success and talent. 'Unfortunately his wife alleges he drinks regularly to excess and when he is drunk he goes berserk with whoever is in sight, and she is the victim.' When the court agreed to the injunction Harris was devastated. Later he came to accept the situation. 'I gave Liz hell and I'm glad she gave me the boot. Life is strewn with compromises and scars. In Elizabeth's and my case we needed more Band-aids than most people.'

After their divorce Elizabeth sent Harris a bird in a silver cage, with the message: 'Here's one bird that will never get away.' In turn, he sent her an antique cowbell saying: 'Wherever you go, I'll now be able to hear you.' They maintained this fond bantering right up until Harris's death, developing probably a more meaningful and closer relationship as friends than they ever managed as man and wife. At one get together in the late 80s Harris, in a candid moment, asked his ex-wife, 'What was it like being married to me?' Elizabeth thought for a while before replying, 'It was magic until you had that one drink too many and then a veil dropped over your face.'

After a couple of frothy comedies O'Toole took on the more testing role of Henry II in the literate historical drama *The Lion in Winter* (1968). He also took on the challenge of a quite formidable co-star in Katharine Hepburn. Many felt that O'Toole had met his match in the Hollywood legend. She'd boss him about and he'd meekly obey, much to the crew's amazement and amusement, more used to his tyrannical, mad ways on a film set. 'She is terrifying,' he told the press. 'She has been sent by some dark force to nag and torment me.' Hepburn relished sparring with O'Toole, 24 years her junior, and their relationship quickly developed into a kind of bantering, affectionate warfare. 'Peter and Kate had a wonderfully funny relationship,' recalls the film's director Anthony Harvey. 'Kate would jokingly call him "Pig" and he'd call her "Nags". One afternoon I was doing a scene with Katie and she needed the make-up man, but he was away playing poker with Peter. "I bloody need him!" she yelled. So off we went looking for this guy and found him with Peter and Kate got in a right rage. "We're supposed to be making a film," she hollered at O'Toole and brought out her handbag and swiped him; she was really furious. We went back to the set and about an hour later O'Toole arrived, in the most enormously dramatic entrance, wrapped up in bandages and carrying crutches. "Look what you've done to me." Of course, everybody fell about. That's the sort of thing that happened between them. She had huge affection for him, and he for her. And the chemistry on a film is so important and they had real chemistry as people.' O'Toole told friends that he simply adored Hepburn, 'Even if she does hit me.' Katharine was quick to defend herself: 'I only hit people I love.'

The filming of *The Lion in Winter* was notable for a number of bizarre accidents involving O'Toole. Shooting a scene on a lake Katharine was on a boat and O'Toole paddled out towards her to talk about the scene but caught his finger between both vessels. 'Bloody agony it was, took the top right off.' There were no doctors around so O'Toole carried the tip of his finger back to shore, dipped it into a glass of brandy for safe keeping and then stuffed it back on, wrapping it in a poultice. Three weeks later he unwrapped it and there it was, all crooked and bent and frankly disgusting. 'I'd put it back the wrong way, probably because of the brandy which I drank.'

Another time he awoke at four in the morning to discover his bed was on fire. For a moment he thought it was all a dream, then reality kicked in. 'At first I tried to put the thing out myself, but I couldn't read the small print on the fire extinguisher. By the time the first fireman arrived I was so glad to see him I kissed him.' But fires and O'Toole were no strangers. As well as burning down the kitchen in the Welsh cottage when making toast for Siân, during his season at Stratford he managed to set fire to his dressing room – twice.

Amongst the cast of *The Lion in Winter* were a couple of young actors making their film debuts, Anthony Hopkins and Timothy Dalton. For the first time O'Toole no longer felt part of the new breed of British acting talent and was aware of a fresh and hungry new generation coming up fast behind him. Ironically he became something of a father figure to the younger members of the cast, once remonstrating with them about a crackpot dare to swim across a river. 'The problem was keeping a straight face. I'd done exactly the same thing when I was their age. Playing *Man and Superman* in Switzerland I'd swum across one of the lakes. In evening dress, as I remember.'

Dalton, of course, was destined to become James Bond, while Hopkins went on to achieve massive fame, but not before a drink problem that almost cost him his life. Hopkins's drinking spiralled out of control when he walked out of a National Theatre production of *Macbeth* in 1973. After his move to Hollywood his drinking increased and peaked when he was putting away a bottle of tequila every day. 'I went around for years thinking I was some kind of fiery, Celtic soul,' Hopkins explained, 'but I wasn't – I was just drinking too much.'

For years Hopkins feared that his heavy drinking would one day cause some disastrous consequences. 'I used to space out and hallucinate. I was a lunatic, very hyper and manic.' He'd go on long car journeys, driving over the prairies and canyons of the mid-west, and black out, not knowing where he was going. 'In the mornings I would wonder – did I kill somebody? – and would check the front of the car.'

After waking up in a Phoenix hotel room with no recollection of how he got there, Hopkins realized that his destructive lifestyle would eventually cost him his career and his wife. In 1975, he quit drinking.

O'Toole had high hopes for *The Lion in Winter*. 'If this one doesn't come off, then I shall hang up my jockstrap and retire.' The film turned out to be a success both critically and commercially, although he had to sue producer Joseph E. Levine when his full fee wasn't forthcoming. Levine retaliated by claiming that O'Toole's 'disgraceful conduct' had added to the film's costs and that he'd been booted out of two hotels on location when he became 'excessively drunk'. O'Toole won his case.

The Lion in Winter made quite an impression on a young would-be director, Roger Young, who would cast O'Toole in 2003 as Augustus Caesar in an epic TV movie. 'It was an amazing performance. I asked Peter how he arrived at that character because it flies all over the emotional map but never for one second is it melodramatic or overdone. Peter replied to my question: "It was in the script, my boy, in the script." I doubt that any script could be that good. Peter made that film into something beyond film; beyond theatre. It was a combination of the best of both. Peter is the only actor I can think of who has the ability to combine the best qualities of theatre and film into one performance. Richard Burton came close, but he always had a feeling of arrogance about him. Peter is always swallowed up by the character. Sometimes, as in *Venus*, the character is Peter, but even then there is vulnerability in the character which Peter O'Toole the man never unveils. Peter is truly one of the very, very few great treasures of film and theatre we have ever seen in either art.'

In 1968 Oliver Reed landed his breakthrough role, that of Bill Sikes in the musical *Oliver!* It might have been a case of nepotism, since his uncle Carol Reed was directing, but his moody and disturbing performance brought him plaudits and recognition and frightened the kids in the cast half to death. Cast as the Artful Dodger Jack Wild's abiding memory of Reed was one of total intimidation. 'As kids we were all terrified of him because he was this giant of a man and the only time we ever saw him was when he was in costume and made up for the part.'

Reed didn't truly let his hair down until the end of filming party, as Oliver himself, Mark Lester, recalls. 'He got Jack Wild and me completely drunk on vodka by spiking our Cokes. I remember getting home and my mother put me in the bath with all my clothes on. I think I was violently ill, but other than that, yes, it was quite amusing looking back on it.'

While working on *Oliver!* Reed met Jacquie Daryl, one of the dancers, and by the end of the film they were lovers. Reed had indulged in casual affairs before but this was different and was the death nail in his marriage to Kate. It was a marriage already close to collapse; Kate could put up with her husband's perpetual boozing, but not his perpetual womanizing. When she learnt that Jacqueline was pregnant with Reed's child Kate walked out, angry and bitter that after years of living together almost as paupers when Reed was an out-of-work actor, he'd now taken up with a 'younger and prettier' model once fame had arrived. They divorced in 1970.

Reed's womanizing was quite staggering; he truly loved women, certain parts of their anatomy more than others. Surprisingly breasts were only his second favourite part of a woman. His main preference was eyes, not the shape, but the expression. 'Eyes and what they say are a constant surprise. Breasts have expression, too, not as much as eyes perhaps, though I have never suckled an eyeball.'

Reed also happily proclaimed himself to be a male chauvinist pig. By his own admission he liked to see women in their proper place, and that was on their hands and knees scrubbing the kitchen or dusting the house. 'In return I feed them, wine them, make them laugh and give them a punch on the nose and a good kicking when they need it. A woman should behave like a lady – a nun by day in the kitchen and a whore at night in bed.' When Reed espoused similar thoughts on womankind on an American TV chat show fellow guest Shelley Winters emptied a jug of bourbon over his head. Later quizzed about the incident, Reed stated: 'My row with Shelley Winters was caused by her abominable lack of manners. She is getting old now and I think she is quite crazy.' On another occasion, with his gob on full chauvinistic mode, and sounding uncannily like Richard Harris on the same subject, he described his ideal woman as 'a deaf and dumb nymphomaniac whose father owns a chain of off-licences'.

Reed enjoyed working with his uncle on *Oliver!*, remained close to him until his death and happily attended a celebration of the director's life at the National Film Theatre. A prior meeting with a film producer took Reed to the Dorchester where he liberally partook of the bar, so by the time he arrived at the tribute, loaded as he was with gin and tonic, he was quite unprepared when the presenter asked him to say a few words. Bounding upon the stage, standing in front of a packed audience comprising the director's relatives, friends and admirers, Reed dried. He managed to garble some words about how humble he was and then fell off the stage. He was upset at the thought of ruining the evening, but friends said, 'Don't worry, Oliver, they all loved it because that's what they expected you to do.'

By the late 60s Richard Burton and Liz Taylor were still the most glamorous couple on earth and boy did they flaunt it. Burton bought her diamonds, only for her to wear them once and then dump them. Liz's fourth husband, Eddie Fisher, said that a $50,000 diamond could keep her happy for approximately four days. They owned a jet, houses around the world, his and her minks and a luxury yacht that frequently cruised around the Mediterranean with friends visiting all the time. One trip included Rex Harrison and his wife Rachel Roberts as guests. One night everyone got drunk, but Rachel uncontrollably so. She lay on the floor barking like a dog, her usual pissed as a fart party trick, but it reached new sordid heights this time when she started to masturbate her basset hound, a sloppy old thing called Omar. How poor old Harrison put up with her Burton for one couldn't imagine. 'She wouldn't last 48 hours with me,' he noted.

The Burtons also had their own canine troubles. On these yacht trips the couple were always accompanied by several pet dogs, but they were incontinent and Burton had to fork out close to a thousand dollars a month for new carpets. Visiting London the dogs couldn't come ashore because of the quarantine laws so while Liz and Burton Rolls-Royced it to their usual suite at the Dorchester the dogs were kept on board. Tour guides on river cruises, aside from pointing out the Tower of London and Big Ben, would also say, 'And on your right ladies and gentlemen is the most expensive bleeding floating dog kennel in the world. It belongs to Elizabeth Taylor.' One day Burton was on deck and on about his fifth vodka when he stood up and bellowed back, 'It bloody well does not. It belongs to me.'

The Burtons were also mixing with the cream of high society: the Rainiers, the Rothschilds, and the Duke and Duchess of Windsor. At one party Burton, quite sloshed, told the Duchess, 'You are, without any question, the most vulgar woman I've ever met.' Hours later he picked her up and swung her round to such an extent that Liz thought he might drop and kill her.

In between all this jetting about Burton found time to make the odd movie, though sometimes he really shouldn't have bothered, like *Staircase* (1969) in which, bizarrely, he along with Rex Harrison, the two most heterosexual men one could meet, played a gay couple living in Brixton. Harrison later admitted he should never have made the film, 'even to pay for my villa and vineyards'. It was done almost as a dare after Burton phoned Harrison saying, 'I'll do it if you do it.'

Adding to the surreal nature of the project was the fact that although set in London the whole film was made in Paris to protect the tax position of the two stars. In the studio next door Liz Taylor was shooting *The Only Game in Town* and Burton paid intrusive set visits, threatening to punch her co-star Warren Beatty for getting too familiar with his missus in their love scenes.

The director of *Staircase* was Stanley Donen, infuriated by Burton's habit of not learning his lines. The crew ended up pinning his dialogue on pieces of paper littered about the furniture. 'Then at six o'clock he would start to drink,' Donen later recalled. 'After that, you could forget about working with him.'

At the end of one week Donen cornered Burton. 'Richard, your big scene is coming up, it's a long speech, and you've got to learn it.' Burton left for the weekend and on Monday morning strutted onto the sound stage towards Donen. 'I've learnt it,' he said proudly. 'Stanley, do you want to come into my dressing room to hear it?' Donen did and Burton performed the scene. Donen couldn't believe it. 'Richard, you learnt the wrong fucking scene. We shot that weeks ago.'

At last for Richard Harris *Camelot* was ready to go before the cameras, but it didn't take long for the production to descend into arguments and difficulties. Richard Harris insisted on cutting Lancelot and Guinevere's love scene, played by Franco Nero and Vanessa Redgrave, real life lovers at the time, as he felt it reduced the dignified aspects of the King. Jack Warner refused to comply so Harris burst into the mogul's office and started pounding on his desk. Unfazed Warner stood up, took Harris by the arm and led him towards the studio gates. Harris panicked, thinking he was about to be thrown off the lot. 'What does that say?' said Warner pointing to the sign above the entrance. 'Warner Brothers,' Harris meekly replied. 'Right,' said big Jack. 'And when it reads Harris Brothers, you can rewrite *Camelot* any way you want. But not till then.'

But Harris's boisterous behaviour continued. At a celebrity bash *Camelot* co-star David Hemmings began playful sparring with his fellow guests. Harris took exception to this and, demonstrating his own boxing prowess, landed a punch on Hemmings's jaw that split his lip. Watching the fracas Vanessa Redgrave burst into tears and announced she'd never act with Harris again. She didn't.

Actually Harris and Hemmings got on rather well, boozers both of them. With Warner being a dry studio the two actors resorted to smuggling in alcohol in the prop van. The problem was getting rid of the empties. As luck would have it two portaloos had been installed outside their dressing rooms and it didn't take long for one of them to fill up with discarded bottles. One afternoon Jack Warner was personally showing a group of distinguished Japanese visitors around the studio when one lady was suddenly caught short and rushed to Harris's portaloo. As she opened the door the sound of crashing bottles echoed around the sound stage. Harris grabbed the woman and hurriedly carried her over to the other toilet leaving Hemmings alone with a suitably embarrassed Jack Warner. When Harris returned, Warner ordered the crew to clean the mess up and as he left with his guests whispered out of the corner of his mouth towards the two actors, 'This bar is now closed.'

Harris remained friends with Hemmings and never forgot the day he saved his life. The filming of *Camelot* had hit a rocky patch for Harris, and Hemmings had come to collect him one morning from his house up in the Hollywood Hills. When Hemmings arrived he found his friend had clambered out of a window and shuffled along a very narrow balcony which overhung the swimming pool. 'I'm going to jump,' Harris announced. 'You can't do that,' Hemmings pointed out. 'There's no water in the pool.' Harris looked down to see the evidence for himself. 'I don't give a fuck. I hate fucking Warner Brothers and fucking Hollywood, the people here are all fucking assholes.' By now Hemmings had managed to climb up onto the balcony and edge his way towards Harris. 'Do you really want to do this?' he asked. Harris's face fell. 'No I don't. Let's have a fucking drink.'

Camelot represented a career peak for Harris but the actor had still not reconciled himself to the collapse of his marriage and as a result channelled his energy and rage into boozing and whoring. He embraced the party scene in LA, dancing and singing most of his nights away, the oldest hippie in town. Yet he always managed to get to the studio on time every morning. Franco Nero sometimes joined Harris on the party circuit but always left at eleven, 'which for Richard would have been the equivalent of lunchtime'. Nero saw the amount of booze Harris was throwing down his neck and remained incredulous how he withstood it, let alone how he was able to turn up coherent the following morning for filming. One night a *Life* magazine reporter ventured out into Harris's nocturnal party world, noting that the star was, 'never happy without women at his feet. But, in truth, Harris's lust is for life.'

Such was Harris's drinking during this period that in an interview he boasted that whenever he landed in New York he'd make a beeline to one particular bar on Third Avenue where Vinny, the regular barman, would see him walk in and line up six double vodkas. 'That's a load of bull,' said the journalist. 'It's got to be one of your bullshit stories.' Harris stood up. 'Right,' he said. 'Call me a taxi.' The pair got in and drove to Third Avenue and the bar in question. As soon as Harris walked in through the door he caught the barman's eye: 'Vinny, my usual.' Seconds later six double vodkas appeared on the bar.

Camelot was a success around the world when it opened at the end of 1967. At the London premiere Harris bumped into his wife, now dating Christopher Plummer. Princess Margaret was the royal guest and asked Harris if he and Plummer were acquainted. 'We share something in common,' he said.

Harris's career as a film musical star might have continued post-*Camelot* had he accepted an offer to appear alongside Barbra Streisand in *On a Clear Day You Can See Forever*. He said he'd do it on condition he got to sing as much as the female diva. Composer Alan Jay Lerner invited Harris to his home to listen to the full score. 'I knew immediately something was afoot because Streisand wasn't there.' Harris sat at the bar and listened intently. Lerner played five songs intended for Babs. 'And now here's one for you,'

Lerner said, before then playing another five Streisand numbers. 'Fuck this,' said Harris and walked out.

After a slew of mainstream pictures Peter O'Toole's next few films were commercial clangers. There was *The Great Catherine* (1968), a moribund historical effort that hardly got a cinema run. During filming O'Toole's habit was to go back to his dressing room when not required, ostensibly to rest and perfect his dialogue. In reality he opened a bottle of champagne and chatted to his minder, whose job it was to drive the star everywhere and get him home safely after a night on the sauce. One particular afternoon the director, Gordon Fleming, needed O'Toole for a scene and dispatched his first assistant to fetch him from his dressing room. The assistant knocked on the door. No reply. He knocked again, still no reply. Opening the door the assistant discovered the room devoid of O'Toole; there was just a TV in the corner showing horse racing from Sandown Park, not far from the studio. Suddenly the TV camera zoomed in and amongst the crowd was O'Toole gamely cheering on the nags. The assistant rushed over to Fleming. 'Peter's not in his dressing room. He's at Sandown races.' Fleming looked puzzled. 'How do you know that?' he asked. 'I've just seen him on television.' A car was dispatched to bring the errant actor back to the studio. O'Toole arrived all smiles, thinking it was one big joke.

Then there was a musical version of the sentimental school drama *Goodbye Mr. Chips* (1969). Before shooting he announced his intention not to drink during the production, except for Dom Perignon champagne, which he didn't count as alcohol. In fact behind closed doors he was swigging away at the hard stuff as liberally as ever.

Lastly there was the little seen (and plainly ignored) *Country Dance* (1969), about a love triangle, focusing on a woman and the two men in her life: her husband and her brother. Filming in Ireland O'Toole took some of the crew out on one of his customary pub-crawls through Dublin which ended in a restaurant at 3.30 in the morning. When the group became too boisterous for comfort the owner asked them to leave and when they refused brought out his Alsatian dog to reinforce the point. O'Toole demanded he be allowed to stay and was bitten for his trouble. Meekly everyone left, but when the front door was slammed behind them O'Toole spun round in anger and started kicking it in. The owner burst out screaming and yelling only to come into contact with O'Toole's fist. A policeman observed the whole incident and O'Toole was arrested, humbly accepting a fine of £30 the next morning in the magistrate's court.

O'Toole was drinking heavily during this period. Monday morning shooting schedules were arranged without his participation because it was a foregone conclusion that he wouldn't have recovered from his weekend boozing. After another monster pub-crawl O'Toole invited the crew up to his cottage in Connemara at the dead of night, leading them all to the edge of his property, which during the day looked out across the sea. O'Toole pointed and asked his guests if they'd ever seen a more beautiful sight. The drinking party gazed into the pitch-blackness and after a pause agreed that the view was indeed a splendid one.

Poor Siân had now become exasperated by her husband's hellraising image. 'All those newspaper articles which begin "O'Toole poured a bottle of whisky down his throat and said, let's have another one." It's not him at all . . .' Journalists weren't really convinced and nor quite frankly was Siân, adding, '. . . though it may be part of him.' O'Toole once arrived late for a ferry back to Ireland, the gangplank having just been raised. When the captain refused him entry O'Toole seized the ship's papers, without which it couldn't sail. He was only persuaded to hand them over by the arrival of a policeman. O'Toole then chartered a plane to Dublin, hired a taxi upon landing and raced from the airport to the harbour. When the ferry arrived there was O'Toole waiting on the dock to challenge the officer to a fistfight.

Now a household name thanks to his performance as Bill Sikes, Oliver Reed went back to work with the director who'd been championing his talents since the mid-60s, Michael Winner. The film was a wartime drama with a difference, *Hannibal Brooks* (1968), in which Reed was cast as a POW working in Munich Zoo who escapes with a bull elephant after a bombing raid and makes a dash for neutral Switzerland. Filming on location in Austria, Reed understandably upset the locals when after a drinking binge he tore down the Austrian flag from outside the crew's hotel and urinated on it. 'In Austria we had to change the hotel every half an hour because Oliver was always throwing flour over people, running up and down the corridor or pissing on the Austrian flag,' lamented Winner.

In the end Winner had to apologize in order to restore the townsfolk's goodwill towards the film unit, but later got into hot water himself when a stunt driver careered into a group of German tourists injuring a 19-year-old boy who had to be hospitalized. 'That's one back for the six million,' was the director's only response.

Reed himself was a rabid patriot. Filming in Germany he entered a bar only to be dismayed to find it festooned with every national flag in the world save for Britain. He grabbed hold of the startled manager and menacingly threatened, 'I'm coming back tomorrow night. If you haven't got a Union Jack by then I'm going to trash this place.' The next evening Reed walked in and still no Union Jack fluttered over the bar. Within seconds he was hurling chairs through the window.

In *Hannibal Brooks*, American actor Michael J. Pollard, hot after his appearance in *Bonnie and Clyde*, had been cast as WWII's most unlikely resistance fighter. At the time Pollard was heavily into drink and drugs. One day on the set Winner confronted the actor and told him he ought to clean himself up. 'Why is it you have to keep taking drugs and keep taking pills? There's no reason for that.' Pollard looked at the director and said, 'You don't share a hotel with Oliver Reed.' Winner said, 'Michael, you just won the argument.' Winner himself had wisely booked into a hotel at least ten miles away from Oliver's.

Reed's other co-star in the film was several tons of elephant whom the actor insisted on sleeping with for three nights in order to build up a relationship, and vice versa one presumes. 'Oliver,' said Winner, 'the elephant won't give a fuck that you're sleeping with him.' But Reed insisted, and according to Winner the elephant tried its level best to kill Ollie during filming. One scene had them both walking along a narrow mountain path with a 2,000-foot sheer drop on one side and hard rock the other, and the elephant would try either to squash Reed against the rock or flip him with his heavy tail over the edge.

Back in London friends became concerned about just how much booze Reed was consuming. Many feared he was plunging headfirst into alcoholism. After one party at a friend's house it was discovered he'd swallowed the contents of every perfume and scent bottle on the host's wife's dressing table. Whenever Reed checked into a hotel he'd immediately drink the minibar then complain to the management that it was empty and demand a new room with a fresh stock of booze. This ruse was ultimately uncovered when he was banned from a hotel for changing rooms five times in one night. 'I do not live in the world of sobriety,' Reed once confessed.

After a string of box office clangers Richard Burton returned to paydirt with the classic 'boy's own' war film *Where Eagles Dare* (1969) based on the bestseller by Alistair MacLean. Burton was a Swiss neighbour of MacLean but the author disliked him intensely. The two men fell out big time at the film's post production party at The Dorchester when a fierce argument led to a fistfight in which MacLean, in his own version, landed a punch on Burton that put the Welshman on his arse. They never spoke to each other again.

The action-packed script required the use of so many stunt doubles for the actors that co-star Clint Eastwood quipped, 'They ought to change the title to Where Doubles Dare.' Stunt veteran Alf Joint was Burton's double and loved the experience of working with the Welshman. 'He was a fantastic raconteur. One Friday he was in his dressing room from about four in the afternoon and he never left until five the following morning! Everybody was enthralled by his stories.'

Numerous old friends popped by the studio, including Trevor Howard, O'Toole and Harris. Burton and his drinking buddies helped give producer Elliott Kastner a few hairy moments. Alf Joint recalls one of them. 'It was really hysterical. One time they left on the Friday night on a plane for Paris. Harris and Howard were there – all the Alcoholics Anonymous – and Kastner was a bit worried. He said, "Well, you will be back Monday?" Richard said, "Oh, don't worry." They turned up on the Wednesday.'

Bizarrely, on location in Austria, Burton was drinking with Eastwood and Liz Taylor in the hotel bar when a man came up and pressed a revolver against his stomach. 'I thought with Clint there and Liz, who's tough enough for two men, I'd leave them to deal with him. So I stood up, excused myself politely and went off to have a slash.' When Burton returned the man was gone and Liz sat purring in triumph.

This wasn't the first time Burton had stared a gun straight in the face; twice before, angry husbands had brandished firearms at him for indiscretions with their wives. The first time happened on location in Africa when a man came at him with an elephant gun. 'And you know what sort of damage that can do. I had to give him several large bottles of booze to persuade him to go away.'

Next for Burton came a very different role, that of Henry VIII in the historical drama *Anne of the Thousand Days* (1969). For Charles Jarrott, a prolific TV director, this was his first feature and the prospect of working with Burton was a daunting one. Their first meeting was in the star's trailer on the set of a film that he was making with Tony Richardson; Burton naturally had director approval. 'We began a little hesitatingly,' recalls Jarrott. 'But as I had been an actor, we had a common bond on discussing the theatre. I remember him talking about how the theatre made you respond to discipline, that it was the backbone for an actor, that it made you punctual and made you learn your lines. I agreed and we got on well.' Two weeks later Jarrott read in the paper that Richardson had fired Burton because he was always late on the set. 'I think that fact reassured me in a funny sort of way,' says Jarrott. 'Richard Burton, star extraordinaire, was a human being after all.'

Of course Jarrott was fully aware of Burton's reputation, that he was often very late back on the set after lunch. But for the whole duration of the shoot Jarrott can recall only one moment of lapse. 'I had a two day shoot on a scene when Henry tells the councillors that he is going to form a Church of England. They all sat on benches around long tables while he sat in a throne, giving them the news at some length. On the first day he came in, and said, "Can you shoot around me today, love. I feel a bit hung-over." And indeed he looked it. So I spent the whole of that day shooting over his shoulder. I think he felt a bit embarrassed, just giving lines to the others, while he swayed a little now and again. The next day I was scheduled to put the camera on to him the whole day. I felt a little nervous that he would be the same. Not a bit of it. He asked to speak to the cast and crew, apologized for his condition the day before, and said to me, "OK, let's go." And his performance was as sharp as a razor blade. I never had a problem again.'

It seemed appropriate that here was Burton making a film about royalty, while he and Elizabeth arrived at the studio with an entourage fit for a king. So many were their staff and collective hangers-on that several dressing rooms were knocked down at Shepperton Studios to make one big suite to house them all. Despite this show of ostentation Jarrott found Burton a pleasure to work with. 'He had a great sense of humour and was wont to tell a few too many stories to the other actors and they were great stories. They were so good, it was hard for me to break it up to work! He was a trifle lazy. Sometimes he would come down on to the set at the end of a day, dressed in his Henry costume, but only the top piece. The lower half was a pair of immaculate trousers and brilliantly shined shoes. He was looking for a fast away after the wrap.'

On the whole, though, Burton conducted himself with supreme professionalism, happy to carry out Jarrott's wishes to perform some of Henry's long speeches in a single take. 'In one scene opposite Anthony Quayle as Wolsey, Henry has an explosive speech when he says he will split the world in two like an apple if he can't have his way. For some reason, Burton began to get a little tangled up. As I was doing the whole scene in one shot, it demanded another take. We went to Take 18, and I suggested to him that I could break the scene up, so that he could do it in pieces. The whole stage, including myself, was a little tense. He refused. He was determined to do it – and he did – in Take 22.'

So good was Burton's performance as Henry in *Anne of the Thousand Days* that he was Oscar nominated for Best Actor: the sixth time, and for the sixth time he lost out. Some have theorised that the reason Burton never won an Oscar was that the long list of women he'd shagged over the years were either the wives or mistresses of Hollywood's bigwigs. No one was going to vote for a man who'd shagged his wife, however many years ago it was. Burton's infidelities had perhaps returned to haunt him.

The winner in 1969 was John Wayne for *True Grit*, a popular choice and Burton left the ceremony to go back to his hotel in no mean spirit. Just as he was about to have a cup of tea in his suite the door burst open and there stood Wayne holding his toupee in one hand and his Oscar in the other. 'Why, you limey son of a bitch,' he bellowed, 'why don't we both have a real drink?' They started on the hard stuff and later in the evening Wayne turned to Burton's companion Brook Williams and snarled, 'That's a really lousy rug you're wearing.' Brook replied rather stiffly, 'This happens to be my own hair.' Wayne didn't believe him and tried pulling it off. A female guest of the Burtons, who'd joined them in their drinking, felt suddenly groggy, made her excuses and left for one of the bedrooms. Later Wayne got up desperate for a piss and went in search of the bathroom only to fall over her sleeping form. When Burton told the woman the next day she was mortified. 'That's the trouble,' she said. 'When one drinks one misses such a lot.'

By the late 1960s Richard Harris claimed to have mellowed. 'I found it better to wake up feeling a success than clawing, hung-over, through a fog of self-disgust wondering whether I, or some other fella, still had the same number of teeth he went to bed with.' The 60s had been Harris's decade for punch-ups; evenings out in pubs or restaurants invariably ended in an argument or a kerbside brawl. Like Ollie Reed, he seemed to be a magnet for the wrong kind of person who, with a couple of pints inside him, wanted to test his manhood against the screen tough guy. Harris confessed that he probably lost more fights than he won. 'I was dangerous; you'd have to knock me out to beat me. I'd whack you with a glass if it was necessary. But fighting wasn't about winning; it was about having some fun.'

Harris once admitted that it sometimes seemed as if he were two people. One was quiet and gentle, a lover of literature, serious theatre and writing poetry; the other was the hellraiser. What most worried him was that the two separate parts of his personality hated each other.

The violence that spilled out of him when the booze took over alienated friends and lost him sympathy, even his own staff, not least chauffeurs. Some drivers told of how Harris might kiss them goodnight of an evening, while in the morning they might be on the end of a torrent of abuse. If they weren't quick enough in opening the door they might also receive a swift boot up the arse. Many handed in their notice after just a month.

But the playful side of Harris was never far away. Appearing on a TV chat show, when his name was announced he walked though the curtains on to the set, straight down the aisle, out of the studio and into the street where he hailed a cab to take him back to his hotel where he went to sleep. 'It's different,' he explained.

But his barnstorming antics and cavalier lifestyle came with a price and by the end of the 60s Harris was bankrupt. Little wonder really, when he used to rent Lear jets to take parties of mates to Paris for the weekend and pick up the tab for 18 suites at the swankiest hotels. But never for a second did he ever regret the excesses of the decade. 'I have an unrepentant past,' he once claimed. 'I loved the excitement of my drinking days. Life is made from memories, which is a pity because I don't remember much; but we entertained the world.'

Essentially a private man, Peter O'Toole rarely gave interviews and when he did he usually insisted they take place in a pub or at home where he could drink in comfort. Inviting one journalist round he showed him a bottle of mountain-brewed Calvados that an artist friend had sent over. 'You drink it?' enquired the reporter. 'You must be raving mad,' said O'Toole. 'This is for taking the rust off car bumpers.' He told the journalist that his friend washed his brushes in the stuff, then with a wry smirk said, 'Great though, don't you think?'

O'Toole knew the amount of drink he was consuming was not doing his body any good, even joking that the only thing he got from booze was a hangover and a grim look from the wife. But he resented the general impression given by newspaper articles and the like that he was a falling down drunk. 'Too many people make me out to be some kind of drunken sot,' he complained, 'but I'm not at the meths stage yet. I like booze because it anaesthetizes pain and makes everything a little less nightmarish. Another thing, I've only ever met decent men at the barrel-head.'

During the course of the 60s O'Toole blazed a mighty trail of hell-raising, but as the decade came to a close he was approaching his forties and some wondered if he was now getting tired of lugging around his reputation as a piss artist and general crank. 'The damage has been done,' he lamented. 'There is a legend: there is a myth: to protest is daft.'

He still enjoyed getting up to mischief, causing chaos and general lunacy. There was a period of time when, drunk, he'd wander around buying the same book. 'My life is littered with copies of *Moby Dick*.' Or take his two young daughters into pubs under his coat just as his father had done with him. Such eccentricity is charming in itself, and however bad O'Toole's behaviour was, few could fail to forgive him completely. But at home things were different. Siân still felt a second-class citizen within the O'Toole household, expected to cook, clean and iron. She was also living, essentially, with two people. Whenever O'Toole was preparing for a job he was 'a hard working, moderate, benevolent presence'. It was just that when the work was over, 'He became a different person, erratic and unpredictable.'

More often than not he'd lose himself in drink, but O'Toole always insisted that he never needed booze as a stimulant to have fun. 'But what could be better than waking up and asking yourself, how the hell did I get to Marseilles? I used to cry with laughter.'

Women in Love (1969), director Ken Russell's screen adaptation of the D. H. Lawrence novel, is notorious for cinema's first ever full-frontal male nude scene between Oliver Reed and Alan Bates. Both actors were nervous about doing it. 'I was scared stiff,' Reed admitted. 'And that's definitely not the right word as anyone who has seen the film will confirm.'

Russell originally set the wrestling scene at night in a meadow by a river so the audience wouldn't see much, the actors ending up in the water anyway where you'd see even less, but it could still look very beautiful and evocative. 'And then one night I was having dinner at home and Oliver came in with a girlfriend I'd never seen before and announced, "She says they wrestle in his house not in a poofy meadow, in the poofy moonlight." I started to argue the point with Oliver and then suddenly I was hurtling through the air in a Japanese wrestling throw and crashing to the ground. "You've convinced me Oliver."'

But when the day arrived to shoot the scene both actors wanted to chicken out. 'Oliver said he had a cold and Alan said he'd sprained his ankle. They said, "You should do another scene tomorrow because we ain't gonna turn up because we've got doctor's certificates to prove our illness." Oh yeah, I thought, because they'd just done one scene perfectly without limping or coughing. Then much to my surprise the next morning they turned up on the set in their dressing gowns, cast them off and set to. At lunchtime Oliver's stand-in came up to me and said, "Ken, gonna buy me a drink?" I said, "I always buy you a drink, what's it for this time?" And he said, "Well I got 'em wrestling, didn't I?" I said, "*You* did it." He said, "Yeah, they're not the best of friends but they ganged up on you and went to the local pub to drown their sorrows and they drank pint after pint as I knew they would. I encouraged them. Sure enough the time came when they had to go to the outside loo which was beautifully moonlit and they stood side by side and they pissed and they glanced to the left and right and saw there wasn't much in it." It was all a question of ego, each was afraid his manhood would be outdone by the other's. But in the event Ollie cheated: before every take he disappeared behind a screen and gave nature a helping hand. In a way they made history.'

On the morning of the shoot Reed had knocked up the landlord of his local pub and got him to sell him two bottles of vodka which he then took to Bates's caravan where the actor sat looking deathly pale. 'Drink some of this,' said Reed and they polished off a bottle each. The scene took three days to complete, during which time the continuity girl, sitting on a low stool, had a bird's eye view of Reed's cock. Giving it a towel down between takes, 'Trying to get a semi on so that it would look more purposeful and stop all my girlfriends saying "why bother" and deserting me,' Reed noticed the continuity girl watching him with mounting interest. She broke out in embarrassment when Reed returned her gaze and went even redder when he suggested she go fetch a ruler to measure it. 'Just for continuity, of course,' he joked.

It's difficult today to appreciate just what impact that scene had on audiences. Now of course it's terribly tame, quaint even. Russell described how a friend of his went to see the film again at a revival screening a few years ago in a small town. He was the only person in the auditorium save for two old dears in front of him. When Reed and Bates stripped off and started throwing each other round the room one of the pensioners said to the other, 'Nice carpet.'

Reed remained pretty philosophical about that scene, relishing the honour of becoming the legitimate cinema's first full-frontal male nude. 'It will be something to tell my grandchildren, that I was once seen stark naked by millions of women all over the world.' He expected to run the gauntlet of insults and mickey-taking wherever he went after the film opened. 'In fact, the only embarrassment I suffered was when an old fruit wolf-whistled me in the King's Road.'

Reed was flown over to attend the Paris opening of *Women in Love* and arrived at his hotel with a bunch of roses for Russell's wife, only to be informed that he wasn't staying in the building proper but the annexe. 'No I'm not. I'm staying here,' blasted Reed, who lay down in the middle of reception, using the flowers as a pillow, and started drinking champagne. The manager arrived. 'Will you please desist from bedding down here for the night.' Reed refused: 'If this hotel was good enough for Oscar Wilde to die in, it's certainly good enough for me to sleep in.' The manager finally relented and a room was found.

Walking up the grand staircase Reed spotted associate producer Roy Baird ahead of him. Manhandling him from behind Reed pulled down the man's trousers, causing him to fall backwards down the stairs. Like a big soppy dog Reed bounded down after him, pulled him up and started landing soggy wet kisses on each cheek. Only then did Reed discover the man wasn't Roy Baird at all but a lookalike, a lookalike who just happened to be an important French businessman. Reed tried to explain that he hadn't pulled the gentleman's trousers down because he fancied him, but this proved rather difficult as he knew not one word of French. Suddenly the real Roy Baird walked in and Reed gesticulated frantically to the Frenchman that this was the man he'd mistaken him for. The businessman finally twigged and broke out in laughter.

After the premiere Reed got really quite dreadfully pissed and, being driven back to the hotel by Alan Bates and his fiancée, started to sing bawdy rugby songs. Bates took great offence to this, 'not in front of my fiancée Ollie if you don't mind', and in the end chucked him out into the street. 'So I ended up singing to a crate of horse's heads in a French market.'

Back in London Reed made headlines when he landed in a fight with the new James Bond, George Lazenby. Reed was in a party of friends that included Lazenby at a posh West End restaurant when the Australian began to get quite offensive in his language. 'Come off it, George, ladies present,' said Reed. But Lazenby ignored the advice and continued to profane so Reed leant across the table and slapped him gently on the face. Ten minutes later, wham, Lazenby threw a surprise punch and knocked Reed to the floor. Momentarily dazed, Reed then swung into action and the two men demolished what was left of their meals. The headwaiter rushed in. 'Please, Mr Reed, not here!' Finally they were pulled apart and Lazenby made his exit. Covered in custard, Reed wanted to finish the job but his friends refused to divulge Lazenby's address. Instead Reed sought medical attention for a badly cut lip. Somebody knew a doctor in nearby Eaton Square so off they went at three in the morning. The doctor himself had only just got back from a cocktail party and emerged at the top of the stairs equally intoxicated; a fact confirmed when he fell head-first over the last dozen steps to land in a pile at their feet. Reed, patched up and walking back home, visited a string of pubs, for the second time in his life having to drink his beer through a straw. As for Lazenby he understandably went to ground, fearing reprisals.

The Sozzled Seventies

Throughout the late 60s and into the 70s Richard Burton drank like a fish. In one interview he said, 'I was fairly sloshed for five years. I was up there with John Barrymore and Robert Newton. The ghosts of them were looking over my shoulder.' Liz Taylor was drinking too and the rows were getting worse. They'd fly off the handle at each other, arguing just for the hell of it sometimes, she blasting him for being a talentless son of a bitch, and he calling her an ugly, fat dwarf. In his diary Burton wrote, 'I have always been a heavy drinker but during the last 15 months I've nearly killed myself with the stuff, and so has Elizabeth.'

But Burton still couldn't help showering his wife with gifts, most notably the famous ring. Burton was determined to claim the world's most fabulous piece of jewellery and bid a cool million dollars for it, beating Aristotle Onassis who bailed out at $700,000. Then Cartier topped Burton's bid by $50,000. 'The bugger,' yelled Burton, who upped his price to $1.1m and won the day; the whole transaction conducted on a pay phone outside a pub with Burton reversing the charges. Not surprisingly the ring was shipped over by security guards armed with machine guns. After all that ballyhoo John Gielgud was visiting the Burtons one day and was amused while helping with the washing up to find the ring lying on the draining board next to a saucer. Years later Liz auctioned off her diamond ring from Burton to raise money for an AIDS charity.

In 1970 Burton was told by doctors to stop drinking for three months because at his present rate of boozing he'd have sclerosis of the liver within five years. Later he liked to joke, 'I don't have much liver left and very little bacon to go with it.' An appearance on television also disturbed him. 'I looked at myself and was appalled, horrified. Could this bloated, corpulent, puffy-faced monstrosity be me?' He hit the wagon for three months, and then fell off. 'You're lucky I'm sober,' Burton said one day to director Andrew Sinclair on the set of *Under Milk Wood*. 'Define sober,' asked Sinclair. 'Never more than one bottle of vodka a day,' replied Burton. He wasn't joking.

Making *Villain* (1971), a brutal London gangland film, he was knocking back two, maybe even three bottles of vodka a day. But his sheer presence was still enough to leave a lasting impression on a young stunt man working on the film, Vic Armstrong. 'Burton was so aloof, like this God-like figure. He'd only come out of his trailer every now and again to sit in the car and say his lines and then go back leaving his stunt double to do the rest. I'll never forget lunchtimes; Elizabeth Taylor would turn up with the Rolls-Royce and the boot would open and there'd be a Harrods hamper with champagne and old Richard would get hammered and be unable to work any more.'

Burton's drinking was also evident on the set of Liz's film *Zee & Co*. Burton was permanently at the studio, spending most days dozing in his wife's dressing room. At the wrap party Liz's co-star Michael Caine bumped into Burton and wished him a merry Christmas. 'Why don't you go and fuck yourself,' said Burton. 'With less than the usual festive spirit,' Caine recalled. Years later the two men became friends, though Caine never did ask the cause of Burton's hostility to him that day. Caine was also taken aback by the sheer scale of the Burton/Taylor entourage: hairdressers, make-up artist, secretary. On the set the studio joke was that if the retinue alone went to see *Zee & Co* the film would have to make money.

The Burton and Taylor entourage had grown so large by this stage that old friends found it increasingly impossible to get in touch with them. One day, however, Burton's old Oxford chum and now successful actor Robert Hardy got a call out of the blue inviting him to lunch at The Dorchester. Hardy hadn't seen Burton for some time and had always previously refused such offers, unable to cope with the multitude of hangers-on that flitted around the Burton/Taylor honey pot. 'Don't worry,' Burton assured him. 'There'll just be us and the children.' It was agreed and Hardy arrived at the private suite only to discover it overflowing with around a hundred people. In the middle of the room was the largest mound of caviar he had ever seen; it stood some five feet high. As the evening grew old and the crowd whittled down Burton jumped to his feet.

'Right, that's it.' It was now four o'clock. 'The rest of you can go now; I'm going to fuck my wife.'

The next day Hardy wrote a brief note to his old colleague thanking him for a memorable evening. 'But getting to see you nowadays is rather like getting through the protocol of a mid-eighteenth century minor German court.'

There was one positive about the travelling road show that surrounded the Burtons: many of them were from his own family. 'At one point Richard was supporting 30 people on the payroll, 20 of whom were members of his family,' says director Tony Palmer, who made a documentary on the star shortly after his death. 'All surviving 12 brothers and sisters had benefited, had been brought out of the mines and poverty, had been looked after and set up, and all the nieces and nephews, by Richard's largesse.'

Since *Camelot* in 1967 Richard Harris hadn't made another film, although he'd found unlikely fame as a pop singer with the top five hit 'Macarthur Park' (one critic referring to his voice as sounding like 'coal being shovelled'). He did accept a part opposite Michael Caine, an actor he didn't particularly care for, in the war drama *Play Dirty*. Harris's contract stipulated that his role could not be tampered with once he'd agreed to appear, but arriving on the set he discovered four of his major scenes cut to ribbons. No way was he going to play second fiddle to Caine. Outraged, Harris confronted producer Harry Saltzman, blasted 'You are a contemptible, low life fucker,' and caught a plane home.

More bad news arrived when his divorce from Elizabeth became official. He'd later admit that his first marriage was, 'An absolute, catastrophic fuck up because of my behaviour.' Harris acknowledged his freedom by touring the brothels of Amsterdam and Hamburg 'fucking for Ireland'. As for Elizabeth, she did temporarily mourn the loss of Harris. 'This is a dull bore,' she declared at one party. 'What it needs is Harris to liven things up.' Another time she was dining in a restaurant when she heard a commotion on another table. It was a drunken Oliver Reed who had somehow fallen into an American tourist's tomato soup while reciting poetry to anybody who would listen. 'I'm terribly sorry,' said Reed, but the American's wife was not amused. 'Don't be sorry. Just pay for the cleaning bills.' So Reed took out some money, put it on the dining cloth, then stood on the table and clapped his hands to demand the attention of the whole restaurant. 'Excuse me. Not only would I like to apologize to this man but, seemingly' – he picked up the American's wine bottle and looked at the label – 'if he doesn't facilitate himself of the opportunity of having his clothes cleaned at least he'll be able to afford a better bottle of wine. Good night, sir,' and walked out. As Reed reached the door a waiter handed him a note from Elizabeth who had scribbled, 'Thank you for the show. It's very good, but it's not as good as Richard.'

Dumping Christopher Plummer Elizabeth had found solace in the arms of Rex Harrison, despite the fact he was still married to Rachel Roberts. One day Rachel confronted the lovers determined to resolve things one way or the other. The three of them stood for a while in silence in the lounge of Elizabeth's flat, her dog Dodger sniffing excitedly round their feet. 'All right Rex,' said Rachel, breaking the uneasy silence. 'Make up your mind. Which one of us do you want? You must make a choice, now!' Rex looked at both women in turn, paused, then pointed to the dog and said, 'I'll take Dodger,' and made a run for it.

It was only a matter of time before Harrison left Rachel and Elizabeth became the fifth Mrs Rex Harrison. Harris joked that at least his ex-wife didn't have to change the initials on her luggage. He also kept in touch and when he read in the papers that Harrison had slapped her in a restaurant he phoned the man up in a rage. 'If you ever do that again I'll come round and knock off your hairpiece.'

Alone, and without the addictive and combative relationship she'd shared with Harrison, Rachel Roberts took her own life by drinking weed killer, ensuring a lingering and agonising death. Hours after drinking the stuff she was still alive and in her torment broke through a glass door in her flat, butchering herself in the process. It was loss of blood that finally killed her.

Harris hit the new decade with a sudden spate of films, but his first was a disaster. *The Molly Maguires* (1970) focused on Irish immigrant miners in Pennsylvania and co-starred Sean Connery. It bombed. Harris was livid that Robert Evans, the mercurial head of Paramount, had tossed out the movie with no fanfare whatsoever. A big New York premiere was promised and Harris had agreed to the promotional gimmick of going on a glorious bender and getting his pissed mugshot in the papers. 'I was willing to lie in the gutter for those fuckers,' roared Harris, when the premiere was cancelled.

One good thing to come out of the film though was a lifelong friendship with Connery who became one of Harris's very few showbiz pals. On the whole Harris didn't have much time for actors. 'I don't like them,' he once said. 'I find them fucking boring. Connery is my only genuine friend. I'd spend an evening with O'Toole, Roger Moore and Burton, but I can't be bothered with the rest of them.' Oliver Reed felt much the same when it came to friendships with his fellow thespians. 'I'm more interested in my barman and the scotch he's got for me than some actor rambling on about his next film.'

After the dismal showing of *Maguires* much more popular was *A Man Called Horse* (1970), even though Harris was fifth choice after the likes of Robert Redford had turned it down. The role of an English aristocrat who becomes a Sioux Indian ranks alongside King Arthur as the film character audiences will always remember him for. But his overwhelming public image was still that of a brawling hellraiser; Harris made the papers once again after a fistfight at the Talk of the Town nightclub. He was watching Sammy Davis Jr in cabaret when a heckler started to chant anti-Jewish remarks. In court Harris told the magistrate that he asked the heckler twice to shut up but he refused, 'So I hit him.' Unfortunately Harris also hit two detective constables who intervened in the resulting brawl. He was fined £12. Two weeks later he was in court again, this time charged with harassing a female traffic warden by embracing and dancing with her after being given a ticket. 'You must not think that everyone enjoys being hugged and jigged around by a film star,' the magistrate cautioned.

Peter O'Toole's first film of the 70s, *Murphy's War* (1971), was another gruelling location shoot, this time on a stretch of the Orinoco River that was polluted from countless oil drills and sewage from nearby villages, notwithstanding piranha fish, alligators and water snakes whose poison had no known cure. 'We are all dead,' one crewmember was heard to mutter, 'and this is our hell.'

Not surprisingly O'Toole, playing a torpedoed British merchant seaman obsessed with destroying a German U-boat, was in a foul mood for the duration, not helped by the fact that he and the rest of the cast had to live for seven weeks in cramped conditions on a former Belfast ferry. He was drinking heavily too, knocking back spirits early in the morning, and lived almost in isolation, hardly talking to anybody. One crewmember described the atmosphere on set as 'picnicking on Vesuvius'. Making matters worse was a recent upsurge in terrorist activity in the area with various foreigners being kidnapped by guerrilla types. Taking no chances the Venezuelan government sent 75 soldiers to surround the set. O'Toole had to suffer three personal bodyguards armed with Smith and Wesson .38 revolvers.

To escape the drudgery of movie making O'Toole took to exploring the region: taking a helicopter and tracking down lost tribes. He even convinced the pilot to land next to the top of an enormous waterfall where no one had ever landed before. Later he chartered a tiny open boat to go up the Orinoco, managing to get 400 miles further upstream than a BBC film crew complete with hovercraft and armed guards.

On one expedition he met Hank, a missionary, and was invited back to his hotel room for a drink. Hank grabbed a bottle that had a worm floating in its neck. 'I'm going to lock all the doors now,' he said after they'd shared a couple of swigs. 'Why?' asked O'Toole. 'Because funny things happen with this stuff, it's mescal.' O'Toole had never tried mescal before, nor would he ever forget the experience. Both men killed off the bottle and then Hank sent O'Toole to walk back to the cabin he was staying at nearby. It was near dawn and O'Toole sensed that he wasn't alone. 'I turned around and looked; and it was me – only very small. It didn't disturb me in any way. We kept each other company for about 24 hours.'

On his return from Brazil O'Toole was exhausted and recuperated in hospital near his Hampstead home. Hungarian director Peter Medak visited him in his room to talk about doing a movie. 'I went to see Peter and he was not supposed to drink, but he was sitting up eating caviar and having vodkas.'

Medak had wanted to film Peter Barnes's satirical play *The Ruling Class* for some time and saw O'Toole as the perfect candidate for the lead role, that of an English Lord who believes himself to be God. O'Toole saw the play and was so entranced by it that he literally bought the film rights to it that very evening. Alas this initial burst of enthusiasm was followed by a period of inactivity while O'Toole was busy on other projects. 'Then one night we came back from the theatre,' recalls Medak. 'And to go home with Peter meant stopping at every pub between Soho and Hampstead, and it didn't matter that it was after closing hour because he would knock on the door and just say, "Peter's here," and every door opened for him. So about three o'clock in the morning we staggered into his house and he said to me, "Come on, let's do *Ruling Class*." And I said, "You say you're going to do it but then nothing happens." And he picked up the phone and called his manager and said. "I'm with the crazy Hungarian and I know I'm drunk but I give you 24 hours to set this movie up." And the next day I got a call from United Artists and the deal was made.'

A comrade of Richard Harris, Medak naturally knew all about O'Toole's reputation as a drinker. 'But the problem with Peter was because he used to drink so much, he just needed a little touch to put him over the edge. I've been in situations with him which are kind of unbelievable. I took Peter Barnes up to Ireland to meet Peter and we had lunch in this restaurant in Dublin that had a steep staircase leading up to it from the street. During the meal Peter didn't touch a drop, but afterwards the chef came over to our table with a bottle of champagne saying, "With the compliments of the restaurant." He opened it and Peter just took a sip. I turned away to pay the bill and when I turned back he wasn't there any more. I looked down and he'd fallen all the way down the stairs, he just went, whoops!'

Filming at Twickenham Studios O'Toole installed his own bar in his dressing room, which was for after-shooting parties. 'But in those days everybody was drinking,' says Medak. 'Each of us used to drink a bottle of wine at lunchtime at the studio and I don't know how we went on working after that, but that was nothing, everybody drank, it was the culture. But it was a wonderful experience working with Peter. He was incredibly intelligent and bright, on a genius level. He also had a photographic memory, so it took him only one reading to remember a script, and everybody else's lines. Yes, he was very demanding, but all those great actors were demanding, but once they knew the person that was directing them was not a total idiot then you could get anything done.'

The Ruling Class (1972) is rightly regarded as one of O'Toole's best films, and it's remained something of a cult hit ever since. The supporting cast was also extraordinary, full of great English character actors like Alastair Sim, Arthur Lowe and Nigel Green. Most famous for his role as a gruff sergeant major in the film *Zulu* Green was a complex man and a tortured soul who suffered from depression. He was also a hellraiser. When drunk he could be aggressive and rudely intolerant. At a party held by the then biggest theatrical agency HM Tenant, Green, at the height of the festivities, bellowed, 'You're all a load of poofs.' Binkie Beaumont, head of the company, went over to fill his glass and with a smile said, 'Are you enjoying yourself, Nigel?' It was the end of Green's career with HM Tenant.

When he married, Green left his weeping wife at the wedding reception after a massive row and went on a monumental drinking binge that lasted two days. That was the end of a marriage that never truly began. In 1972 Green was found dead in his flat in Brighton after the collapse of his second marriage. The coroner's verdict was accidental overdose of sleeping pills. He was only 47.

Oliver Reed consolidated his fine work for Ken Russell in *Women in Love* by appearing in the director's even more controversial *The Devils* (1970). Its story of devil worship in the 17th century really got everybody frothing at the mouth, with its scenes of masturbating nuns, torture and full frontal nudity. None of that bothered Ollie, or the fact that in his role as a persecuted priest who is tortured and burnt at the stake he had to shave his head and legs, but he balked at Russell's suggestion that his eyebrows also had to go. Russell flew into a rage. 'We might as well not make the film at all.' 'Don't be bloody silly. It can't make all that much difference,' said Reed. 'Of course it's important,' blasted Russell. 'They shaved off all his bodily hair and then stuck red hot pokers up his arse.' Reed finally relented but only on the condition that his eyebrows were insured for half a million pounds in case they didn't grow back properly.

Co-star Brian Murphy saw the volatile and often playful nature of Reed's relationship with Russell first hand. 'He was a great practical joker Oliver and it seemed to me that he and Ken played games with each other. I remember one particular scene: Oliver had done several takes but Ken wanted more and in the end Ollie stormed off the set. Everything ground to a halt. Then word was sent to me, Max Adrian and Murray Melvin, who were also appearing in the scene, would we all go to Oliver's dressing room. So we did and we all sat down and Ollie was grinning from ear to ear. "We'll have a drink in a minute," he said. "Have you got something?" I asked. "No," he replied, "but we will have." There was a knock at the door and this assistant came in with a bottle of champagne and said, "This is from Mr Russell and when you feel ready for it Mr Reed, we'll see you back on the set." I think he was up to those kinds of things all the time.'

The film when it opened drew howls of outrage from critics; the distinguished film critic Alexander Walker called it 'the masturbation fantasies of a Roman Catholic boyhood'. Russell got his revenge on Walker on live TV, by thwacking the pompous critic over the head with a rolled up newspaper.

Ignoring the fact that Reed gave an outstanding performance in *The Devils* the press still revelled in his image as a mad, boozy loon, which to be honest Reed did very little to dispel. He told one astonished reporter that he believed in leprechauns and searched for the little beggars on Wimbledon Common. He even engaged in conversation with some of them, on the way back from the local no doubt. Then there was an appearance on the radio show *Desert Island Discs*, in which the guest is cast adrift on a fictional island and to pass the time must choose his favourite records and one luxury item. It proved to be a troublesome recording, with Ollie choosing an inflatable woman as his luxury item, and afterwards the normally placid host Roy Plomley was heard to mutter, 'The only island that man should be cast away on is Devil's Island.'

Most interviews with Reed were either conducted in pubs or hotel bars and the journalist was under an obligation not just to drink, but drink to excess. 'A small glass of wine please,' one reporter said when asked by Reed what he wanted to drink. The actor returned with a pint pot of wine slopping over the brim. At another interview Reed, drinking sangria with wild abandon, suddenly stood up and pulled open his shirt to display his stomach at the reporter. 'Look at that! Do you know what I am? I'm successful, that's what. Destroy me and you destroy your British film industry. I'm the biggest star you've got.' He then began pointing accusingly at the bewildered hack. 'But it took years for it to dawn on you that I was worth writing about, pig, didn't it. I'm Mr England.' Getting increasingly agitated Reed knocked into the table sending the reporter's glass crashing over. Reed's brother Simon was on hand though to expertly field it, getting a crotch full of sangria for his pains. Reed darted off into the pub and returned with a bottle of whisky, which he handed to Simon. 'That's for saving the glass.' He then turned on the terrified reporter again.

'Do you know who my grandfather was? He was Sir Herbert Tree. Sir Carol Reed is my uncle. And I'm Oliver Reed – Mr England!'

Of course much of this bluster and bad behaviour was put on. 'I do like to clown around. Christ, life would be pretty boring without it.' Filming *Dirty Weekend* (1973) on location in Italy Reed showed up on set unshaven, dishevelled and fell out of his car and lay motionless, apparently unconscious, on the road. No one noticed, or cared, so he got up and went and had a coffee. His co-star Marcello Mastroianni and the Italian crew did become a little perplexed with Reed's behaviour as filming went on. One night in his hotel Reed playfully scuffled with some mates but too boisterously for the barman who fled in fear of his life.

There were inevitably more incidents on location in Italy. Reed was drinking in the bar of his hotel with Reg Prince, his stand in, a tall, burly ex-Navy man and former junior boxing champion. After a few bottles they wandered outside to be greeted by a huge looking bastard who was known locally as 'Jesus' because he used to think he was God's gift to women. He didn't speak a word of English, and was approaching Ollie with his arms outstretched. Fearing he was going to be attacked Ollie pounced on him and bit his nose.

Just then two cars pulled up and some sinister looking chaps got out. 'I think there's going to be a little bit of trouble here, Reg,' said Reed. 'It's the local syndicate.' Suddenly the two men heard gun shots and hit the dirt. When they realized it was only a radio programme on one of the car radios Ollie and Reg tore into the mob and everyone started chasing each other around the cars. One of the Italians did happen to be the local heavy of the Mafia and felt very indignant that he had lost face against two true blue Englishmen. Luckily for Ollie a contract wasn't put out on him: the gang ended up buying him and Reg drinks and spaghetti.

Probably the biggest example of Reed's shock tactics and playing to the gallery was his habit of removing his trousers, or worse, showing his cock in public: 'My snake of desire, my wand of lust, my mighty mallet.' The first recorded instance of this was at a press conference for his film *Triple Echo* in 1972. The questioning turned to Burt Reynolds's recent decision to pose totally naked in *Cosmopolitan* magazine. Reed had turned down a similar opportunity. 'I love the thought of a lot of girls masturbating over a nude picture of me,' he'd said, but coming so soon after *Women in Love* he didn't want to get stuck in that particular rut. At the press conference he was asked why he'd declined the offer and replied it was because his dick was too big to fit on the page. 'Prove it,' demanded an elderly female journalist on the front row. Without pause Reed dropped his pants and flashed the end of his knob. 'Is that it?' said the woman. 'Why have you stopped?' 'Madam,' replied Ollie. 'If I'd pulled it out in its entirety, I'd have knocked your hat off.'

Reed's dick would make periodic appearances over the years in the most unlikely places. Michael Parkinson was hosting a radio chat show with American actress Elaine Stritch and Reed was late arriving. 'I was talking to Elaine,' Parky recalled, 'when the door burst open and there he stood, Oliver Reed, absolutely drunk, naked except for a pair of green wellies. Elaine Stritch looked at him and said, "My dear Oliver, I've seen bigger and better quite frankly."'

Richard Burton's career had never been in so much trouble, from the dizzy heights of the late 60s he was making interminable rubbish like *Raid on Rommell* (1971), a war film patched together wholesale from action sequences 'borrowed' from the much better *Tobruk*. There was also *Hammersmith is Out* (1972) in which he played an escaped mental patient in a film that probably only appealed to escaped mental patients. He knew he was slumming it but how else could he afford to live in the style to which he and Liz Taylor had grown accustomed. 'I find it ludicrous, learning some idiot's lines in the small hours of the night so I can stay a millionaire.' It's a quote fairly indicative of Burton's attitude to his profession. 'Actors are poor, abject, disagreeable, perverse, ill-minded, slightly malicious creatures,' he once confessed. 'And of that august company of idiots, I'm afraid I'm a member.'

At least *The Assassination of Trotsky* (1972) had at the helm the distinguished Joseph Losey, but it failed to ignite. For much of the filming Burton was on the wagon, although strangely some of the crew noticed that Burton sober was sometimes not as good an actor as Burton the drunk: he was tense and hesitant on dialogue. One evening Norman Priggen, the assistant director, received a call from Liz Taylor explaining that Burton would not be working tomorrow. 'Why's that?' asked Priggen. 'Well you'd better get back to our hotel and look in the bar and see for yourself.' Priggen drove quickly to the hotel and found Burton and Peter O'Toole, both as drunk as lords, lying on the floor, fondly embracing each other and singing 'Happy Birthday'. They had been there since lunchtime. Burton was furious at being interrupted and it took a number of staff to carry him to his suite. Priggen was certain the actor would be in no state to work the following day. Yet, the next morning Burton gave what many considered to be his best performance and best day's work during the whole shoot.

Burton's next turkey, *Bluebeard* (1972), a tale of a lecherous aristocrat who can't keep his hands off nubile young women and then stuffs their corpses in his wine cellar, inevitably led to the set in Budapest being awash with drop dead gorgeous co-stars. When one young actress romped too intensely with Burton and the poor bastard couldn't help but respond Liz Taylor stormed over and gave her a vicious punch in the face. As for her husband, Liz told the press, 'I don't know how many plates I broke over his head.'

Burton did eventually sow his oats when Liz flew out of Hungary. On a night shoot Burton and Nathalie Delon were obliged to walk serenely down a street and then disappear round a corner. Action shouted the director. All went well. OK and cut. Everyone waited for them to re-appear. They didn't. The director sent his assistant to find out what had happened only for him to run back and report that there was no sign of either of them. Craftily Burton had arranged for his chauffeur to be waiting nearby with the Rolls so both he and Nathalie could hop in and speed off to the nearest hotel. When the couple also failed to turn up the next morning, shooting was cancelled for the day. Liz took her revenge by having a very public dinner with Aristotle Onassis, minus Jackie, which turned into a brawl between 25 paparazzi, the restaurant staff and local police.

Burton was drinking heavily on the set too. Invited to the British embassy in Budapest for an official dinner he insulted two ambassadors and their wives, swore at his hosts, condemned the privileged classes and walked out. He was a loose cannon, enjoying his booze, too, describing its charms to one reporter in the following manner: 'If you drink it straight down, you can feel it going into each individual intestine.'

Filming on *Bluebeard* coincided with Elizabeth's 40th birthday and Burton laid on the birthday party to end all birthday parties. Family, friends and colleagues were flown in from all over the world, including Princess Grace of Monaco, Michael Caine, Ringo Starr, Frankie Howerd and Raquel Welch. The festivities lasted the whole weekend; it really was the most ostentatious display of wealth and over indulgence. A few spoilsports whined about the insensitivity of such grandeur taking place in so poor a country as Hungary. Burton hit back at the complaints by donating a hefty sum of money to a children's charity.

Many an eyebrow was raised when Richard Harris, an Irishman and nationalist, agreed to appear in a film dramatisation of Oliver Cromwell, the man who had attempted genocide in his country. The paradox was intriguing, but it bagged Harris one of his biggest paycheques yet – $500,000.

Filming in Spain, Harris had to hire a private jet to get him out there when he missed his scheduled flight. No wonder, since the previous evening he was completely sloshed and wandering the streets of Kensington in his dressing gown. He was almost run down by Bruce Forsyth, returning home in his Rolls-Royce. Harris staggered towards the car, gripped hold of its iconic mascot and stood there looking vacantly into the windscreen. 'What shall I do?' asked Forsyth's chauffeur, Robbie, nervously. 'Don't worry,' said Forsyth, climbing out of the car and confronting Harris.

'Hello, Richard. Who's a naughty boy, then. What are you up to and where are you going in your dressing gown?' 'Ah Bruce,' said the rambling Harris, who'd met the entertainer at numerous showbiz dos. 'It's lovely to see you, lovely to see you.' 'Richard,' said Bruce, pointing to Robbie at the wheel of the Rolls. 'This man is just driving me back to my flat. Is that all right with you?' 'Of course, of course, away you go. But I'm going to have some fun tonight!' I can imagine, thought Forsyth.

Depositing the great entertainer home Robbie turned the Rolls back into Kensington High Street where he came face to face once again with Harris. The Irishman stood in front of the car, blocking its passage forward. Robbie got out and said, 'I'm with Bruce.' A spark of recognition animated

Harris's face. 'Ah,' he said, 'Bruce's friend, fine, on your way . . . on your way . . .'

Logistically *Cromwell* (1970) was a huge film, and the pressure of playing such a controversial and complex character, plus all the boozing combined with gruelling temperatures, meant Harris came close to a total breakdown. When the time came to shoot the execution of Charles I, played by Alec Guinness, Harris flipped. He woke up in his hotel room at dawn in a cold sweat convinced that they were actually about to cut off the King's head. 'We must give him another chance!' Harris yelled down the phone to the director. 'We must think twice about this!' The production nurse was summoned, as was a psychiatrist. Harris's hysteria was uncontrollable and he had to be held down by people kneeling on his chest. Harris was tranquillized and slept non-stop for 18 hours. 'It was that bad, I had finally crossed the line from sanity to madness.' He knew at last that the drinking had to stop. Alas, in order to help cope with the absence of booze Harris started to take drugs, first cocaine, then heroin and LSD. Harris eventually overdosed on cocaine and woke up in hospital with a priest administering the last rites. He decided then that he'd rather die of booze than drugs.

In a bid to stave off the demons Harris sank himself into a personal project, a film called *Bloomfield* (1970). Filmed in Israel it was the story of a 12-year-old soccer fan who hitchhikes across the country to see his hero, an ageing footballer (Harris), play his last game. Granted a gala charity premiere in his hometown of Limerick, this promised to be the ultimate homecoming, but instead it turned into a disaster. 'A cross between a religious visitation and the Keystone Kops,' is the way Harris later described it. At Heathrow his party of star guests, which included Roger Moore, Bee Gee Maurice Gibb and his wife Lulu, were delayed by a bomb scare. When they finally got to the cinema the streets were cordoned off because of sheer weight of numbers. Once seated the luckless audience then heard a voice come over the tannoy to say that the police had been warned about a bomb inside the cinema. There was a mass evacuation as 100 policemen combed the auditorium before the all-clear was given. 'I can think of 50 fuckers who might have made that call,' Harris said, 'and none of them had anything to do with the IRA or the UVF.'

Bloomfield turned out to be a miss with critics and public alike. At the

Berlin Film Festival it was booed off the screen. Harris responded by gamely booing back. Despite such bravado the film's failure hit him hard. Ironically his singing career was proving much more popular than his films. After the success of 'MacArthur Park' and a series of singles and albums, Harris embarked on a world tour, playing the UK and the States. With a full entourage, parties and boozing, the Harris roadshow was just like any other rock tour. Predictably groupies were in evidence at every venue and Harris took full advantage. At one concert the orchestra struck up the intro to 'MacArthur Park' but where Harris should have been standing the spotlight illuminated instead an empty stage. The director sent an urgent call to 'find Harris, for chrissake!' as the orchestra started the intro again. Eventually he was located in his dressing room, stark bollock naked with a black beauty on her hands and knees giving him a blow job. A stagehand grabbed hold of Harris and got him dressed fast. As the orchestra struck up the opening bars of 'MacArthur Park' for the umpteenth time Harris bounced onto the stage, gamely pulling up his flies.

For years Peter O'Toole and Richard Burton had wanted to make a film record of Dylan Thomas's play *Under Milk Wood*. Both men had known and idolised the poet, Burton especially who had a love of great drinkers generally. 'I have to think hard to name an interesting man who does not drink,' he once claimed. Another of Burton's heroes was a Lancastrian he met in a Westminster pub who could down 12 pints of beer while Big Ben was tolling midnight.

There was the Dylan Thomas of the magical phrase and the mellifluous voice, the darkly seductive bard of the Celtic twilight. Then there was the unkempt, slightly bloated Dylan Thomas with the haystack hairstyle and odious dentures who would get drunk, vomit and fall down the stairs. This was the same Dylan Thomas who pissed on Charlie Chaplin's door as he made an early exit from a party in his honour.

Dylan was his own worst enemy. He learned to drink copiously as a young journalist in Swansea and his poetry, beautifully crafted though it was, came second to his image as a pissed man of letters. Much of his later writing consisted of begging letters to friends. Burton often lent the poet money and invariably he'd use it to buy drink. On one occasion

Thomas was on the scrounge and phoned Burton asking for £200. It was for the education of his children, he claimed, but Burton knew better, and besides didn't have the money readily at hand. Thomas offered him the rights to a play he had not yet written in return for the cash. Burton refused. They never spoke again. Thomas left for America and at one party the glamorous starlet Shelley Winters asked why he'd come to Hollywood. Very solemnly Thomas said, 'To touch a starlet's tits.' 'OK,' Winters said, 'but only one finger.'

Sadly within the month Thomas was dead. His final immortal words were, 'I have seen the gates of hell' after drinking 18 straight whiskies and keeling over in a gutter. 'We all wanted to imitate that,' said O'Toole.

A clash of filming schedules and Burton's elaborate tax dodging itinerary had always scuppered the plans to film Thomas's most famous work. Unlike O'Toole, Burton had to ration the amount of time he spent in Britain in order to avoid the taxman. In 1971 his schedule finally allowed him a few spare days so he rang O'Toole, roped in his wife Liz Taylor and *Under Milk Wood* went before cameras on location in Wales. All three stars claimed only £10,000 in expenses, plus a share of any profits.

During filming Burton arranged a quiet evening meal at a local restaurant with an actress friend, stipulating a table in the corner away from prying eyes. Suddenly O'Toole burst in, making something of a grand entrance. Not to be outdone Burton leapt onto a table and broke into a song in Gaelic. O'Toole leapt atop another table and sang the second verse, and so on; so much for a quiet, unobtrusive meal.

Much ribbing also went on. When he heard that Burton had just played a queer gangster in *Villain*, having previously essayed a gay hairdresser in *Staircase*, O'Toole quipped, 'It looks as though you've cornered the limp wrist market, ducky.'

O'Toole continued to be pally with Burton and didn't realize anything was wrong in their friendship until, visiting Rome sometime in 1972, he discovered that he was in the same hotel as Burton and Liz Taylor. O'Toole tried telephoning Burton but couldn't get beyond the bodyguard or the secretary who invariably answered the phone. For two days Burton didn't return his call, and then one of his staff came with a message and led O'Toole to a clandestine meeting in the corner of a dark bar tucked in the back of the hotel. 'Elizabeth does not approve of our racing around

Perfect day: drink himself insensible, rampage all night and then read all about it in the newspapers the following morning.

In *This Sporting Life*, Harris' relationship with director Lindsay Anderson was masochistic, obsessional and ferocious, often flaring up into violence.

Harris' attitude to women was cavalier to say the least. He told his wife that he was popping out for a drink and was gone for ten days.

When pissed Harris' behaviour could be eccentric and violent. It was not unknown for him to run into traffic and attack passing cars.

In his favourite New York b
the barman would see Harri
walking in and immediately
line up six double vodkas.

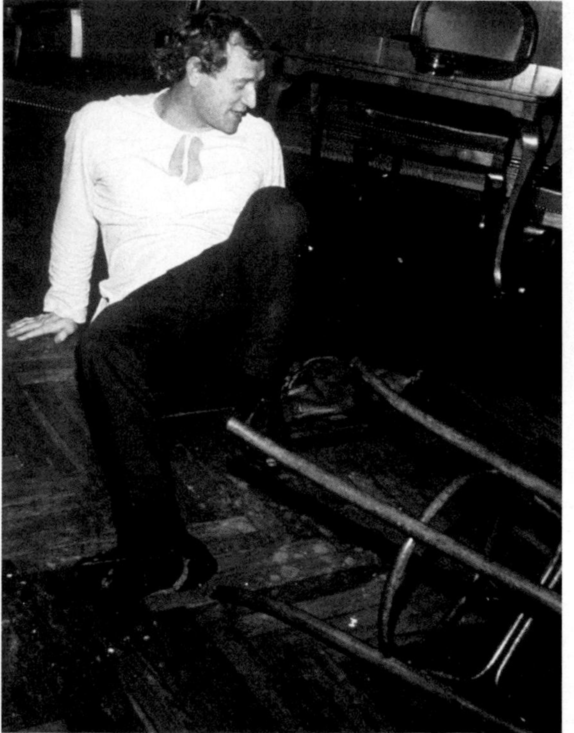

Harris' drinking became so chronic in the 1960s that friends bet him $25,000 he'd be dead by the 70s.

ing Arthur in Joshua Logan's 967 film *Camelot* is perhaps Iarris' most famous role. But uring one particularly rocky atch, co-star David Hemmings ad to persuade a depressed Iarris not to jump off a ledge nd kill himself. They went for drink instead.

Iarris often had no recollection f his hellraising. One morning, e was bemused to find stitches n his face, totally unaware that e'd wrecked a restaurant the ight before.

The ultimate hellraiser's movie, *The Wild Geese*. Harris and Burton had promised faithfully not to drink, so indulged prolifically in the local ganja instead.

A lifelong rugby fan, Harris played as a kid and broke his nose. Subsequent encounters with walls and fists busted it a further eight times.

Ann Turkel, Harris' second wife: 'The stories I could tell would make every other Hollywood exposé look like a Disney movie.'

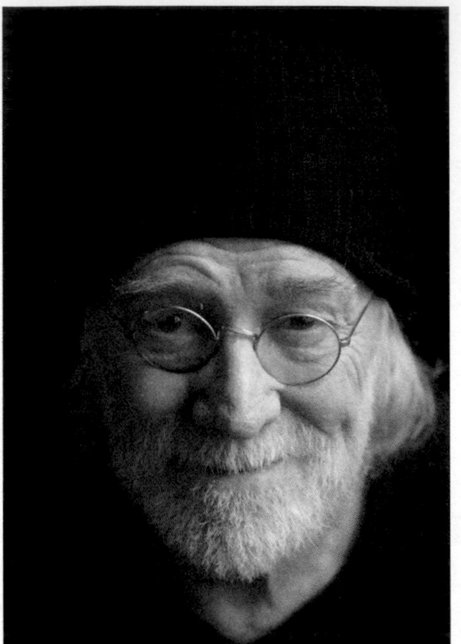

Well into his 60s Harris remained a womaniser. He invariably answered the phone in his hotel suite not with 'Hello' but 'Come straight up and take your knickers off.'

One of his last roles in *Gladiator*. Shortly before he died, Harris collapsed at the Savoy hotel. As he was stretchered out in front of horrified fellow guests, he yelled 'It was the food!'

together,' Burton announced. 'That was it,' said O'Toole. 'Goodbye. I didn't see him again for many years; poor soul.'

Alexandre Dumas's classic swashbuckling tale *The Three Musketeers* has often been filmed, but never so wonderfully as Richard Lester's 1973 version. It began life as a possible film vehicle for The Beatles; instead it turned into an all-star epic featuring the likes of Charlton Heston, Faye Dunaway, Michael York, Christopher Lee and Raquel Welch. Oliver Reed was perfect casting as Athos but his extreme nature caused problems when it came to the numerous sword fight sequences. Reed didn't bother much with rehearsals and went hell for leather when the cameras rolled, so much so that the 40-strong stunt team drew lots to determine who would fight him. Such exuberance impinged on his co-stars, too. 'Oliver did nothing by halves,' notes Christopher Lee. 'I remember during a fight scene he came at me with both hands on the sword, like an axe, and I parried it and stopped totally. I said, "I think we'd better get the routine right." Then I said to Oliver, "Do you remember who taught you how to use a sword?" He said, "You did." And I said, "Don't forget it." You see I made *Devil Ship Pirates* with him for Hammer and he was a bit of a menace in that, quite frankly. People leapt out of the way when he had a fight, because he went at it absolutely flat out.'

The Spanish fight arranger on the film was so unprepared to be charged at the moment Lester shouted 'Action' that he came close to throwing up with fear and refused to go near Reed again. 'Oliver sometimes would go totally berserk and start to really fight – 100 per cent real,' recalls producer Ilya Salkind. 'And we'd have to say, "Oliver, it's just a movie." Finally Oliver got a sword through his wrist. I guess one of the stunt men wasn't happy with him, because he was always going at them like a maniac.' Unfortunately this 'accidental' stab wound landed Ollie in hospital for four days with blood poisoning. He lay in bed receiving blood transfusions as the ever-dependable Reg Prince smuggled spaghetti dinners in at night through the window.

Ollie's madcap sword fighting style was later to bring praise from an unlikely source, that of director Quentin Tarantino. 'Oliver Reed is just fucking GOD in this movie. During the fight training Reed threw himself into the fighting so much he made all the other musketeers work twice as hard. They knew if they didn't, Reed was going to own the movie completely. He was that good. You've never seen sword fights the way Reed fights them in this movie.'

It wasn't just Lee and the sword masters who were unnerved about Reed; his other co-stars reacted coolly to the star as well. 'Oliver Reed was a terrifying presence, an extremely dangerous man,' recalled Richard Chamberlain. 'He could be very sweet, but if he turned on you, he could make life terrible for you. He was up all night, drinking, then coming to work the next day and being fine.'

Along with the rest of the cast Reed stayed in a plush hotel in Madrid. As a practical joke Reed removed the goldfish from the ornamental pond in the dining room at the dead of night, keeping them in his bath, and replaced them with fish-shaped carrots. The following morning at breakfast he dived in and began devouring what his horror-struck fellow guests presumed were the helpless 'live' fish. The manager called the police and Reed was hauled off the premises bellowing, 'You can't touch me! I'm one of the musketeers!'

'Oliver was a real character,' recalls Michael York, 'but nobody mentions the fact that he would turn up fully prepared to work, knowing his lines. The tragedy was that everyone expected him to be this hellraiser, and he often obliged; the press wouldn't allow him to be this very serious actor. But he did have this larger than life side to him. He was brought up in good schools, with good manners; there's a residue of that as well. Oliver wasn't run of the mill. He was like an aristocratic ruffian, a complete contradiction in terms.'

More problems followed. Drinking one night in the hotel bar Reed started challenging his fellow guests to tests of strength. 'I am the greatest,' he pronounced. 'I'm a British true blue and will take on anyone.' When no one obliged he started overturning tables and smashing glasses. Again the police were called and he was dragged away. It took five officers to bundle him into the interrogation room. 'Oliver, God bless his soul, was incredible,' recalls Salkind. 'He could go out and get totally smashed until six in the morning and show up on the set at seven and be ready to go. That was pretty fantastic.'

Reed claimed this latest arrest was all a misunderstanding, that he'd been Indian wrestling with a Finn who was seven foot two. 'I thought he seemed like a good fellow to wrestle with,' Reed revealed on the Russell Harty TV show. 'Unfortunately, the table broke and we fell into the ice cream trolley. The ice cream went over an American lady's dress, so the husband picked up a bun and threw it at me. So I picked up the glacé cherry and threw it at him. Then all of a sudden 15 boys came in dressed as policemen, with machine guns, and they dragged me off.'

The hotel manager revealed in court that this skirmish wasn't the first problem he'd had with Signor Reed; he'd previously insulted guests, broken chairs and punched a hole through a bathroom door. In the end the judge ordered Reed to leave the hotel, 'So I was thrown out on to the streets with my bags.' Russell Harty, not quite believing his guest's tale, offered this gem: 'All life seems to be a kind of adventure to you, doesn't it?' Reed smiled. 'I think it should be. I think that everybody would like that. It's just that very few people have the opportunity.'

By this time Reed was developing a reputation as something of a sex symbol, with his dark, dangerous looks. He described himself as having the appearance of a Bedford truck, with the promise of a V8 engine. One critic was rather crueller, writing that he had a face that reminded him of a neglected part of Stonehenge. In any case Reed was now starting to win Hollywood offers. Steve McQueen came to London to meet him with the express intention of their making a film together. Ollie invited McQueen to Tramp's nightclub where he got dreadfully drunk and vomited over the American superstar. The nightclub's staff managed to find some new jeans for McQueen to wear but couldn't offer him any replacement shoes. 'So I had to go round for the rest of the evening smelling of Oliver Reed's sick,' McQueen complained. Needless to say Ollie didn't get the part.

Considering the combustible nature of Richard Burton and Liz Taylor's relationship, it surprised many when they agreed to make a pair of TV movies about the break-up of a marriage seen from each partner's viewpoint: *Divorce His* and *Divorce Hers*. At the time Burton was once again trying very hard to give up booze and made a very big show of drinking only Perrier water during his first meeting with director Waris Hussein. 'This unfortunately did not last once Elizabeth Taylor turned up on the scene,' recalls Hussein. 'This is the key to what happened in their relationship. She certainly triggered off his alcoholism. We started filming in Rome and for the first week Elizabeth wasn't there and he was fine, very much on the straight and narrow. Then she turned up and on that first night he disappeared and drank a whole bottle of vodka.'

It went pretty much downhill from then on, much to Hussein's dismay; he came to the project with a great deal of respect for Burton and at the start of filming was made to feel very much at ease by the star. 'Unfortunately when the drink hit, it was a Jekyll and Hyde situation. He just became a roaring mass of anger and frustration and he would shout and scream. One day he couldn't remember his lines and was swaying so much that we couldn't take close ups of him, so I went up to him and said, "Can I help you?" And he just said, in an incredible bellow, "FUCK OFF!" and the whole place shook. Then he stood up and yelled, "I could be Lear, I could play Lear." It was really pathetic, because he was self-aware, he saw what was going on but couldn't control it. He came to me the next day and apologized profusely; he always apologized afterwards; it was terrible really.'

The project was the brainchild of acclaimed scriptwriter John Hopkins, and on paper at least looked an interesting concept that was ultimately scuppered by the Burtons according to Hussein. 'In the hands of a more conscientious, competent couple it would have been absolutely riveting, but they didn't even look at the script until they came on the set, because they wouldn't rehearse. Liz would arrive and say, "What's this crap I'm saying? Who wrote these crappy lines?" I'd say, "Elizabeth they're not crappy, and by the way this scene here refers to something that is in Richard's story." She'd suddenly interrupt, "Oh fuck that. I don't care about Richard's story. I'm talking about mine." I'd say, "Yes Elizabeth, but it's all tied in together." Now, with that atmosphere going on the result was absolutely barmy. It was a ship out of control, and I was trying to keep it afloat; unfortunately it sank.'

Things got even worse when they moved to a German studio to shoot interiors. For a scene in a hotel a group of eager young American women, recruited from a nearby air base, were hired as extras. The next day Hussein was informed the women were no longer available. 'It turned out that the night before Richard had taken one of them up to his dressing room and Elizabeth jumped out from behind the sofa, smashed a bottle of vodka and chased him around with a broken bottle. They also trashed their hotel room in Munich to the tune of £20,000.'

It was quite ironic that Burton and Liz were making a film about the disintegration of a marriage when their own was hurtling down a very similar path. Their fights were growing increasingly ugly and spilling out into the public domain for all to see. In Hollywood they quarrelled outside a nightclub, resulting in Elizabeth spending the night with a friend. The next day she turned up at the Beverly Hills Hotel, walked up to Burton in the bar and punched him in the face.

Finally early in July 1973 Liz Taylor announced to the world that she and Richard Burton had officially separated: a story that knocked Nixon and Watergate off the front pages. Burton drowned his sorrows in copious amounts of drink in Italy where he was shooting *The Voyage* (1974). Barry Norman went out to interview him for his BBC film programme and was told that Burton's daily ritual consisted of getting pissed and then getting extremely horny whereupon he'd take a young actress to his hotel room. The next morning, full of post-coital remorse, he'd ask the girl to leave. But the guilt only started him drinking again, the horniness would return and he'd shag the same actress. When Norman arrived to conduct the prearranged interview he could see that Burton was sozzled and offered to reschedule it. No, Burton was adamant that it had to take place then and there. The crew quickly set up the cameras and Norman asked his first question which was answered by a burst of snoring. Burton had fallen asleep, on camera. Annoyed, Norman gave the star a swift kick in the shin. 'Richard, wake up!' But he just shook himself slightly and snored again. 'Let's go and have dinner,' said the director after a while. Norman nodded in agreement and packed up, leaving Burton to his dreams.

Outside the room Norman spotted the film's publicist and explained what had happened. He laughed. Norman asked if they could reschedule the interview for tomorrow. The publicist laughed even louder. 'No, that's it. You only get one shot; tough luck.' Seething, Norman hit back. 'OK then I'll tell you what's going to happen. Listen carefully. In my programme next week I will use the stuff we have just recorded and I will explain to the viewers how it came about. You think Richard will like that, do you – five minutes of him, pissed out of his head, on national television?' The publicist visibly cowered. 'You wouldn't.' 'I bloody would,' barked Norman. 'And I will.' A second interview was hastily arranged.

For the whole of the next day Norman watched Burton like a hawk, even standing next to him between takes to see that he sipped nothing stronger than coffee. When shooting finished Burton wanted to change prior to the interview and went to his dressing room, Norman followed. As he feared, one of Burton's acolytes was waiting with a large Bloody Mary so pale that Norman wondered if it contained any tomato juice at all. Unlike his old hellraising days when a stiff drink wouldn't have affected him at all, now just one Bloody Mary was enough to make Burton drunk and when the interview began he was hardly more coherent than he'd been the previous night. At least he didn't pass out this time. The interview went out on air and it must have been obvious to viewers that the man was pissed. When Norman ran into Burton again some years later the actor recalled that infamous interview by saying, 'I think I was sloshed at the time, was I?'

After the disastrous *Bloomfield* Richard Harris's choice of movies didn't get much better.

There was *Man in the Wilderness* (1971), a rather piss-poor *Man Called Horse* rip-off. Next was a crappy western that he made in Mexico called *The Deadly Trackers* (1973). Cult director Samuel Fuller was at the helm but fierce clashes with Harris resulted in his dismissal, or his walking away, depending on whose story you believe. Co-star Rod Taylor was another boozer, but both he and Harris had promised not to touch a drop until the weekends. To get through the week without a drink they developed a secret code between themselves. On Monday morning they'd hold up four fingers to each other, meaning four days left. On Tuesday it was three, Wednesday two and so on. When Friday night arrived it was no-holds barred boozing and whoring until dawn on Monday.

One notable role that Harris was offered at this time was Zed, a futuristic superman in John Boorman's sci-fi movie *Zardoz*. First choice Burt Reynolds had fallen ill and backers 20th Century Fox wanted Harris after the success of *A Man Called Horse*. Boorman wasn't sure Harris had the physique for what was a highly physical role, but went to see him at his London home. Boorman was dazzled by the interior design, all mock medieval and decorated with props from *Camelot*. 'It was chaotic.' With Harris's hung-over mates wandering in and out and their kids running amok, Boorman found it impossible to conduct the meeting. What about next weekend, suggested Harris who was going to be in Dublin for a rugby match. 'OK, why don't you come out to my house for Sunday lunch,' said Boorman who lived not far from the city. It was agreed. But one o'clock came and went and Boorman waited, and waited. At three o'clock lunch went ahead without him. 'There was no sign of Harris,' Boorman later told Hollywood executives. 'If he can't show up for the audition, what will it be like once he's got the job?' Years later their paths crossed again and Harris apologized. He'd had a heavy Saturday night after the rugby match and was hung-over. He noticed it was already past noon when he hailed a cab and told the driver to go hell for leather. Halfway to Boorman's house the driver offered him the day's paper. Harris looked at the date. It was Monday. 'Turn back to Dublin,' he said, 'and stop at the first pub.'

At this time Harris lived in a splendid mansion in Kensington, next door to Michael Winner. 'My mother adored him,' recalls the director. 'He used to come round and borrow sugar. My mother thought he was the most charming man. I was very fond of Richard, too. When he died his children rang me up and asked if I could get them into the house, which was now owned by Jimmy Page of Led Zeppelin, because they wanted to pay a last visit to that part of their childhood. I got them into the house, Jimmy let them in. But Richard was a very similar type to Oliver Reed, he did things when he was drunk and then regretted them, but tried to hide the fact that he regretted them.'

Harris came to live in that house thanks to a curious twist of fate. He claimed that years before he became famous he woke up one morning after a heavy night on the town in the garden of this beautiful house and knew that one day it would be his. Sure enough he eventually bought the place. But he didn't live there alone. Harris claimed the place was haunted by the ghost of an 8-year-old boy who lived in the tower. Harris didn't mind sharing his dream house with a ghost, save for the fact that he could never get enough sleep. The spirit would often wake Harris up at night by slamming doors and running up and down the stairs to the tower. Historical records showed that an 8-year-old boy had been buried there within its walls. Harris tried explaining to the ghost that an actor needs his sleep and that if he didn't stop making all the late night noise he'd have him exorcised. This didn't solve matters so Harris had a nursery made in the tower, filled with games and toys, and that helped settle the spirit down.

One wonders what on earth induced Peter O'Toole to appear in his next film, a musical version of the Don Quixote legend, *Man of La Mancha* (1972), besides the obvious one of acting opposite Sophia Loren, whom he playfully nicknamed 'silicone'. A remarkable woman, Sophia was born in a hospital charity ward and raised in poverty by her single mother, yet managed to turn herself into one of cinema's greatest ever sex symbols. 'The more I was with Sophia, the more edible she looked,' O'Toole claimed.

O'Toole's sparring relationship with Sophia was akin to the one he'd earlier enjoyed with Katharine Hepburn. 'I love that cow!' he said at the end of filming. But when he heard that Sophia was to make a film with Burton next, O'Toole couldn't resist writing a mischievous note to her: 'The news is all over Ireland that I am spitting blood at the moon, aghast because you have abandoned me for a bandy-legged pockmarked little Welshman.'

Man of La Mancha had been a huge Broadway hit, running well over 2,000 performances and for cinema audiences there was now the prospect of witnessing O'Toole singing on screen. Or not, as the case may be. In spite of admitting that he had a singing voice akin to 'a broken bottle going under a door', O'Toole gamely trotted out the numbers. 'But apparently it was horrendous, so they brought in a highly paid opera singer to do the high notes.'

After *Man of La Mancha* O'Toole took a sabbatical from the cinema. He'd grown restless with the film-making process, the spark had gone and it took another three years to return. He was also suffering from ill health, the bane of his life, problems that in just a few years' time would almost put him into an early grave. It wasn't just ill health, though, that perturbed O'Toole. For years he'd also suffered from the most dreadful insomnia. He'd always been a night person anyway and detested having to get up for early morning film calls. 'The man who invented mornings was no Christian. I prefer to go straight into the afternoon.' From time to time he'd tried numerous cures for his insomnia: hypnosis, drugs, the lot, even a special cushion from Japan that you plugged into the mains and which was supposed to vibrate you to sleep. 'All it did was give me a sore ass.' Next he bought a record that consisted of soothing sounds. 'Soothing sounds!' he ranted. 'What a bloody awful record.' In the end O'Toole came to realize that the only thing that was keeping him awake all night was wondering why he couldn't sleep.

To the surprise of many Oliver Reed had become the world's most unlikely country squire, buying a huge mansion in Surrey called Broome Hall, with 52 bedrooms. He came to own the vast sprawl in the first place because of his horse, Dougal, which he'd intended to enter in show jumping trials, only to realize the animal was allergic to coloured poles. Drowning his sorrows in his local pub, numerous pints later he had a brainwave: what Dougal needed was a little bit of land to graze in that could be filled with coloured poles in order for him to get used to them. Reed was off like a shot across the road to the estate agent's. 'I want to buy a field,' he announced. 'What sort of field?' The man asked. The question temporarily threw Reed: 'A field with grass in it.'

Most of the fields in the estate agent's books had either a house or a cottage attached to them, but one property in particular caught Reed's interest – Broome Hall. It definitely had a field, plus a further 65 acres. Back in the pub the landlord heard that Reed was thinking of buying Broome Hall and laughed that of all the people in the world, Ollie was joining the country aristocracy. 'Sod you,' blasted Reed, stormed back into the estate agent's and got his chequebook out there and then.

Reed set about restoring the stately pile to former glories, supervising up to 30 workmen paid full time for years. More often than not the workmen were found in the local pub rather than working; Reed's fault, of course, he'd come down most days to where the men were working and holler, 'Come on, let's go down to the pub. Only for a short time, mind you. You've got fucking walls to build.' Afterwards he'd go into the garden and complain to friends, 'Look, they've dug absolutely nothing today.' 'But you took them down to the pub, Oliver,' his friends would say. 'All day!'

Broome Hall came complete with a wine cellar. 'Predictably that is where I am often to be found.' Reed opened his own bar down there and pride of place was kept for the Thorhill Glass, an old crystal glass that held the equivalent of a bottle of port. Part of the tradition of coming to Reed's private bar was to drink its full contents and then stay in the room for 20 minutes afterwards without being sick.

Broome Hall was the scene of numerous wild parties, notable among them the time Reed invited 30 members of his local rugby club over. The evening started off in the pub when the lot of them stripped naked and sang 'Get 'em down you Zulu warrior,' crammed 15 of their party into a single ladies' lavatory cubicle and then went on a cross-country run to the house in their jockstraps. Once at Broome Hall the real fun began. In all 50 gallons of beer were consumed, 32 bottles of whisky, 17 of gin, four crates of wine and 15 bottles of Newcastle brown ale. Then for an encore they smashed dozens of eggs on the kitchen floor to slide around and play mock ice hockey. 'It could have been worse,' Reed's girlfriend said. 'A lot of them were in training and off the drink.'

Reed loved his rugby, especially the earthy humour and no bullshit of the people who played it. One day he went into Doncaster rugby union club, slapped a £50 note on the bar and said, 'Buy all these working class pigs a drink.' Reed later denied the members were upset by his comments, indeed the word pig was a term of affection in his household, and anyway the club made him a life member.

Reed not only loved showing Broome Hall off to his mates, but also to visiting journalists. A lot of interviews were conducted there; sometimes the invitation came with the caveat of bringing a change of clothing. 'You're going to be pushed in the pond or the swimming pool,' Reed would warn them. Lots of drink was consumed too, with Reed doing the pouring, his eyes fixing on the reporter, daring him not to say stop. One journalist drank so much he was sick in the garden. Ollie followed the poor retching hack advising him, 'No, not on the roses, or the path. That's right, in the bushes.'

When top celebrity photographer David Steen was invited over to photograph Reed in a series of typical lord of the manor poses he was startled by the sheer size of the place, particularly the room they were using which had four French windows and was some 50 feet long and 30 feet wide. After the photographs had been taken Reed announced, 'Right, let's have a drink.' Usually with Ollie that didn't mean a glass or a bottle and so out came a case of red wine. The two men drank well into the evening, and then Reed suddenly disappeared out of the room for an hour, returning riding a white horse. It was a balmy night so the huge French windows were open. Steen watched in utter disbelief as Reed charged out of the window on to the terrace, over the balustrade and off into the countryside.

Of all the terrible films Richard Burton made, and there's a *lot* to choose from, *The Klansman* (1974) must rank as his creative nadir. Burton's co-star was Lee Marvin, who ran Burton a close second in the drinking Olympics. He was a monumental boozer. Filming *The Dirty Dozen* in London Marvin attended a cocktail reception where the equally volatile Sean Connery counted amongst the guests. Rather the worse for wear Marvin spied a quaint old lady sitting on her own in the corner, and, staggering across the room, propositioned her in the most vulgar manner possible. So slurred was his speech that the woman had trouble understanding, so innocently asked him to repeat it. Marvin obliged. It was then that someone whispered to him that the old dear in question was in fact Connery's aunt and that the man himself had heard what was happening and was on his way over. *Dirty Dozen*'s producer Kenneth Hyman saw the danger and desperately leapt into the breach. 'Don't hit him in the face Sean,' he begged. 'He's got close-ups tomorrow.' Just in time Connery saw the funny side of it. 'You fucking producers,' he roared.

John Boorman won't forget his experience of working with Marvin either on *Point Blank*, shot in LA. He and some friends went to dinner with Marvin at a sea front restaurant. When it was time to leave Boorman could see that Marvin was in no fit state to drive home and told him so. 'Fuck you,' said Marvin as he missed with a punch at the director's head. Boorman grabbed the keys to Marvin's own Chrysler station wagon and got in. Like a wild animal Marvin prowled around the vehicle, bashing it occasionally, until finally climbing onto the bonnet and up onto the roof rack. Everyone pleaded for him to come down but he refused. Carefully Boorman drove along the harbour front hoping some of the sea air might sober Marvin up. It didn't, he just snarled and refused to budge. The streets looked pretty deserted so Boorman decided to take a chance and drive down the Pacific Coast Highway towards Malibu. Just minutes later he saw flashing lights in his rear view mirror. He pulled over. The patrolman walked purposefully to the car, looked up, looked at Boorman and said, 'Do you know you have Lee Marvin on your roof?'

To give you some idea of the terror Marvin could inflict on a production, this is what Joshua Logan said about him after directing the star in *Paint Your Wagon* in 1969. 'Not since Attila the Hun swept across Europe leaving 500 years of total blackness has there been a man like Lee Marvin.'

Burton had never worked with the wild American before and they met for the first time on location at Oroville, a small town in California standing in for a bigoted community full of Ku Klux Klan supporters. Before a gathering of pressmen Marvin announced, 'I suppose you know I get top billing in this.' Burton countered, 'Yes, but I'm getting more money.' Liz Taylor, who had arrived to be by Burton's side, a desperate last chance to save their marriage, saw the perfect photo opportunity and sidled up next to the two men and audibly wished Marvin luck. 'Why don't you just fuck off sweetie,' responded Marvin. They never spoke again for the rest of the shoot.

As part of the ongoing publicity Marvin was invited to a nearby hotel to cut a big St Valentine's Day cake. He listened to innumerable speeches from local dignitaries, getting gradually more pissed, until as guest of honour it was time for him to cut the cake. Rising unsteadily to his feet Marvin opened his mouth and then collapsed headfirst into the sponge. Staggering back up, dripping with cream, he walked outside to address a crowd that had gathered. 'Cocksuckers of Oroville,' he shouted. 'United we stand.' The townsfolk were not amused and demanded an apology.

The tension between these two macho hellraisers was so taut that private bets were laid among the crew on which of them would take the first swing at the other. But as the film progressed Burton and Marvin got chummy and often went out to lunch together. Only the courageous or plain stupid ever went with them: lunch might consist of 17 martinis each before going straight back to work. One crewmember later recalled how he saw Burton down an eight-ounce tumbler of vodka in one gulp before breakfast.

Burton had arrived to work on *The Klansman* drunk and stayed drunk throughout filming, consuming three bottles of vodka a day, a routine he'd been following for the past six months. The film's publicist announced to the press, 'If you want to interview a drunk or see a drunk fall in the camellia bushes, come ahead.' His drinking got so bad that midway through the schedule doctors informed the actor that he only had three weeks left to live. 'I'm amused you think I can be killed off that easily,' he answered them. But director Terence Young was so concerned that he seriously wondered if Burton would be able to finish the picture. He was getting progressively more ill and having to force his whole body just to speak a line of dialogue. His complexion was white, sometimes blue, and then yellow. When Young was shooting Burton's death scene in the film he complimented the make-up man, 'You've done a great job.' The make-up guy replied, 'I haven't touched him.'

Young quickly shot the scene and then organized Burton to be raced to hospital in Santa Monica where he received an emergency blood transfusion. He was on the edge for about a week but pulled through. By getting him to hospital when he did Young was convinced he'd saved Burton's life, which he probably did. Burton was hospitalized for six weeks as doctors fought to repair his battered system and wean him off alcohol. During the drying-out process Burton had to be fed through a tube because he was shaking so much. Eventually he recovered, even getting back into some semblance of shape, but he would never be quite the same man again.

By the mid-70s it seemed Richard Harris, like Burton and O'Toole, was finding good films difficult to come by. *99 and 44/100 Per Cent Dead* (1974), a dismal gangster picture that even its director John Frankenheimer called 'probably the worst movie I ever made' was a case in point. Harris himself admitted that he gave a performance on autopilot and that he was only making such films 'to get money for booze'.

The only good thing to come out of the experience was meeting former model Ann Turkel who'd secured her first acting role in the film. As a teen Ann had idolised Harris, *Camelot* was her favourite movie and she'd pin-ups of Harris as King Arthur on her bedroom wall. During filming they fell in love despite the fact that Harris was 25 years her senior and she was closer in age to his son than she was to him. They enjoyed an old-fashioned courtship for months, during which they'd exchange nothing more than kisses. Harris proved a hopeless romantic. Having always said he'd never marry again, and condemning the institution as 'a custom thought up by women where they proceed to live off men, eating them away like poison fungus on a tree', Ann changed Harris's mind and they married in 1974. However, she was blissfully unaware of the psychological and alcoholic dependency of her husband and over the next eight years her life became dominated by his unpredictable mood swings and drinking bouts. 'The stories I could tell would make every other Hollywood exposé look like a Disney movie,' she once explained.

Ann realized what she had let herself in for when she organized a surprise birthday party for her husband. 'Harris got very drunk. He didn't even know who I was. He then broke a mirror and slashed his wrist so his driver and bodyguard took him to hospital. I was terrified. The next day he came to me and said, "This only happens once a year, to release pent up energy," and I believed him! I had no idea what was in store for me.'

A much better film vehicle arrived for Harris courtesy of *Three Musketeers'* director Richard Lester. *Juggernaut* (1974) was one of a rash of disaster movies inflicted upon the public in the early to mid-70s, though this one ranks amongst the best. Harris plays a bomb disposal expert out to stop a mad blackmailer blowing up a cruise liner. The exceptional supporting cast included Omar Sharif, Anthony Hopkins and David Hemmings. Lester found Harris 'always a delight, I thought he was terrific and a wonderful actor'. But his hellraising was never very far from the surface. 'There was only one time I had a problem with him. Richard had had a fairly heavy night and when he was having his hair extension put on for the part fell sound asleep, sort of recovering, and didn't realize quite how tight it was. We started shooting a very tense sequence about trying to defuse a bomb, and suddenly he said, "I've got to stop, the wig's on too tight and it's pulling me to pieces, I'm in terrible agony." And I said, "Look, just cut the bloody thing off, we've got to keep going." We were in the middle of this important sequence and couldn't stop. So between us we came up with the idea that he would suddenly reach into his bag and put on a woolly hat, which he did. It seemed a good idea at the time but when you see the film you think, why the bloody hell does that man – trying to defuse the bomb, and with cutters in his hands – suddenly stop and put on his woolly hat!'

Harris didn't prove very helpful either when it came time to shoot the most hair-raising moment of the film, when a team of bomb disposal experts parachute into the sea and then climb up the ladders of the boat in a force eight gale. 'All the stunt men were flown in by helicopters the night before,' recalls Lester. 'And we'd hired this Russian ship and the vodka was about threepence a shot, so you could have triple vodka for nine pence. So the stunt men arrived and Richard was in the bar and one thing led to another and at one point I thought, this is getting ridiculous because it's three o'clock in the morning. I said, "Lads, you know, we're in a force eight, there's a huge swell out there, and you've got to climb about a hundred feet in frogman suits up these swinging ladders." The leader turned round and said, "Piece of cake, guv. Don't worry about it." And of course they were all being egged on by Richard. Well, by the following morning when we shot the sequence they were dropping off the ladders like flies. Thank God we had four zodiacs swirling round the boat picking them up and dragging them back. Most of it's in the finished film.'

Peter O'Toole also seemed to be bouncing from one nonentity movie to the next, and even then he wasn't first choice, such as the time he was asked to replace Robert Mitchum on *Rosebud* (1975), a kidnap drama about Palestinian terrorists, because the American's drunken antics had so exasperated director Otto Preminger. During one scene Mitchum and some hoods had to survey a map, only this young actor repeatedly got his lines wrong. Pissed off, Mitchum roared, 'I should take out my dick and show him the map.' 'Take out what?' asked Preminger incredulously. 'I should piss on his arm!' Mitchum spluttered. 'Bob, we are rolling!' said Preminger. 'I'd take out *your* dick, if I could find it,' Mitchum continued. 'Bob, please, there are ladies present.'

After more rows with Preminger, Mitchum quit the movie and within days O'Toole was hired. When Mitchum heard the news his response was. 'That's like replacing Ray Charles with Helen Keller.'

Filming in Paris O'Toole was the victim of a bizarre practical joke. He turned up to work one day and found a note in mirror writing in the apartment where they were filming: 'To Peter O'Toole, the so-called Irishman . . . we have planted a bomb in the building.' It was signed by the IRA. Preminger was taking no chances and cleared the building. 'This was the height of the bombings,' O'Toole recalled years later, 'Bloody Friday, Bloody Sunday, my forebears were getting together and blowing things up. You had to take these things seriously.'

Eventually word got back that there had been a party in the apartment the night before and that the note had been written as a gag by critic Kenneth Tynan. Preminger was furious and phoned the critic's Paris home to let him know it. When filming resumed O'Toole went missing. He'd found Tynan's address and arrived there with two beefy members of the crew and proceeded to beat the crap out of him. 'But I thought you'd see through it!' Tynan kept repeating in his defence.

Tynan threatened to sue O'Toole for assault but in the end nothing came of it, although the two never spoke to one another again, an awful result since Tynan had been such a champion of O'Toole, whom he called an 'insomniac Celtic dynamo'. When Tynan's diaries were later published this episode was discreetly cut out. 'I wouldn't tell the story,' O'Toole explained. 'Well, I didn't want to make him look too much of a twat! He claims I kicked him in the balls . . . I may have done. So that was the end.'

Ten years earlier, Tynan had interviewed O'Toole for *Playboy* magazine, and they'd had this wonderful exchange: Tynan: 'Are you afraid of dying?' O'Toole: 'Petrified.' Tynan: 'Why?' O'Toole: 'Because there's no future in it.' Tynan: 'When did you last think you were about to die?' O'Toole: 'About four o'clock this morning.'

Preminger had a fearsome reputation as a director. During the filming of *Saint Joan*, Jean Seberg (playing Joan) was about to be burned at the stake. To the horror of the cast and crew, the pile of wood below her actually caught fire. Despite cries and screams of horror Preminger would not allow the flames to be extinguished until he had finished the scene. O'Toole, however, found him an absolute delight. 'We were in Berlin, filming, and Otto, as you know, fled the Nazis . . . and he was fine for a few days, and then he got more and more and more depressed. He wouldn't even get out of the car when we were filming. All he'd do was wind down the windows and go: "Action! Cut!"'

O'Toole next made a couple of films in Mexico, a country he fell in love with, buying property in Puerto Vallarta, where Burton and Liz Taylor had a house. He also began an affair with a local woman 20 years his junior. Not surprisingly his marriage to Siân began to unravel; it had been under strain for some time. It was not unknown for O'Toole to arrive home drunk as a lord and loaded with friends and expect Siân to cook a meal for everyone. Some of O'Toole's friends were as potty as he was: Donal McCann for instance. He came round for drinks one day, sank two bottles of vodka and collapsed asleep on a sofa. Siân came into the room and saw that McCann's cigarette had set fire to his hair so grabbed a soda siphon and put him out. McCann woke up, surveyed the scene and then held out his glass for a refill.

Another of O'Toole's daft friends was Irish actor Jack MacGowran. The pair had known each other at Stratford when MacGowran owned two goldfish called King Lear and Cordelia. After a pub crawl MacGowran returned home pissed and peckish and had one of the unfortunate fish grilled on toast. On another occasion MacGowran made a bet with O'Toole that he wouldn't drink for a whole month. 'You're on,' said O'Toole. MacGowran's dry month was to begin the next morning. It lasted exactly 17 seconds. O'Toole joyfully timed it.

Since the late 60s it seemed that Oliver Reed and Ken Russell were inseparable. Even when he wasn't starring in Russell's films he still turned up for work, appearing as a railway guard in just one scene in *Mahler* (1974), his payment three bottles of Dom Perignon, and in *Lisztomania* (1975) turning up merely to open a door for Roger Daltrey – this time his reward was four bottles. *Tommy* (1975) was different.

The Who, on whose rock opera the film was based, expressly asked for Ken Russell to direct and Russell in turn insisted on casting Reed for the part of Tommy's uncle Frank, a strange decision considering that the whole film was to be sung and Ollie couldn't carry a tune in his head. When Reed arrived at The Who's recording studio in Battersea for his first *Tommy* rehearsal, a disturbed Pete Townshend was pacing up and down, and swigging neat brandy from a half-pint beer mug. Russell was waiting in the control room. 'OK, Ollie. Grab a mic and start singing.' Accompanied by Townshend on the piano Reed croaked as best he could through one of the songs. Townshend stopped, downed the remainder of his brandy and blasted in Reed's face, 'Are you fucking joking?' Reed was sent home with a tape of the score and ordered to learn his numbers by heart.

During the filming of *Tommy* Reed developed a close friendship with Keith Moon, drummer of The Who. Moon was the undisputed wild man of rock whose antics were already legendary when he hooked up with Reed. This was a man who once gulped down a horse tranquillizer that put him out cold for two days. Their first meeting was auspicious indeed.

Reed was relaxing in the bath at Broome Hall when he heard an almighty roar from outside. It was Moon paying a visit, but being a rock star he was turning up in a helicopter. Reed thought he was being invaded by some lunatic and ran downstairs in his bathrobe brandishing an antique sword that he kept for such emergencies. Reed also kept a double-barrelled shotgun by his bedside and was quite open about his threats to shoot any trespasser. He'd been known to take pot shots at photographers. Moon stepped out of the helicopter and introduced himself. The pair spent a riotous weekend together. Halfway through dinner Moon suggested that they should play a game. 'I was supposed to run round the fields,' remembered Reed, 'while he chased after me with a car to see if he could hit me.' They also had a sword fight with those big double-edged swords up and down the hall. The next night Moon came in and asked Reed to see a dirty home movie he and his girlfriend had made. 'I didn't know what to say. Well, what are you supposed to say about this delightful girl with no clothes on? I just said, yes, that's pretty, Keith; artistic – very artistic. Good night.'

One of their parties resulted in Reed being banned from two Los Angeles hotels, something of a record. It was a huge birthday bash for Reed's brother David at the plush Beverly Wiltshire, and when a naked lady burst out of the cake that seemed to be the signal for mayhem. Moon demolished the place, shattering the huge crystal chandeliers with a chair and then slashing at the expensive wallpaper with a fork. Guests started screaming and running out, while bodyguards began punching the odd person. Sitting on his own in a corner was Ringo Starr, shaking his head as if he'd seen it all before (he probably had). Reed was forced to manhandle his friend into the kitchen. 'He had gone completely berserk.' And was later lumbered with an £8,000 bill for damages and barred. When word got around he was also barred from the Beverly Hills Hotel. Richard Harris had earlier been barred from the same establishment for bringing back hookers to his room and then broadcasting the fact on the *Johnny Carson TV Show*. However, when the Sultan of Brunei bought the hotel in the early 90s he lifted the ban on Harris and Reed.

Kindred spirits Reed and Moon were practically inseparable during the filming of *Tommy*, sharing the same hotel away from the rest of the cast and crew. One night they sat up drinking in Moon's suite, emptying a bottle of brandy. When the drummer tried to order up another, the porter wouldn't answer the phone – so Moon picked up the television and threw it out of the window. It landed outside the main door of the hotel, and the porter came running out. He thought a bomb had exploded. Moon yelled, 'Answer the fucking phone or my bed's coming next!'

Within a few days, as word spread of Moon's wild all-night parties and groupies, the rest of the crew moved in with them. It was like Sodom and Gomorrah. One night Reed was besieged in his bedroom with six bunny girls pressed up against the glass fire escape door, all waving dildos at him, trying to get in.

Even the mighty Reed sometimes found it tough keeping up with the anarchic Moon. Roger Daltrey occupied the bedroom next to Reed and one day Moon discovered he'd left his favourite jacket in there and no one could find the key. No problem, he borrowed an electric drill from the film crew and was in the process of hammer-drilling his way through the adjoining wall when the key was discovered.

On another occasion Reed arrived early one night to find yet another of Moon's parties in full swing and 14 girls drinking champagne in his room. 'Good evening, what can I do for you?' They told him, but Reed was too damn tired and instead ordered them to leave. They refused to budge so Reed went in search of Moon. He found his friend flat on his back, totally starkers, with two Swedish models sitting on his face. 'Excuse me, Moony,' Reed said. 'Umm,' said Moon, or something equally unintelligible. Reed began to explain the difficulties he was having removing several bits of crumpet from his bedroom. 'Just tell 'em to fuck off!' Reed said he'd tried that with no success. 'Oh all right.' Moon stood up. 'Excuse me darlings,' he said to his Swedish playmates and marched down the corridor naked, causing one maid to flee in terror. Barging into the room he picked up a tray of champagne glasses and hurled it at the girls who ran out screaming. 'See you in the morning,' Moon said to Reed as he walked back.

After *Tommy* Moon left with The Who for a US tour and asked Ollie to look after a few things for him while he was gone. Asleep in bed at Broome Hall Reed was awoken suddenly by the sound of a large removal lorry. The foreman handed him a note from Moon which asked Reed to take care of his Great Dane called Bean Bag who'd inherited several of his master's bad habits, such as head butting glass doors, and also a rhinoceros called Hornby. 'What bloody rhino?' Reed demanded. 'This one,' said the foreman, dragging out a full size replica of a charging rhinoceros. Ollie ended up keeping them both for years.

After being told by doctors to rein back on the booze or die Richard Burton entered a period of convalescence. From time to time, when dangerously out of condition, Burton would go on the wagon for months on end; but just as suddenly resume drinking to excess again. It was part of his well-worn image, most people saw him as a great extrovert who lived only for booze, rugby and women and he did very little to dissuade them from this opinion. 'I rather like my reputation, actually,' he said as he approached the big 50. 'That of a spoiled genius from the Welsh gutter, a drunk, a womanizer.'

It was during this period that he finally decided to divorce Liz Taylor. 'We burn each other out,' he said once of their love. Well the flames had gone out at last after ten years of marriage. The divorce settlement was considerably weighted towards Liz, though Burton didn't complain, he just wanted out. The joke around town was that Liz got the diamond mine and he got the shaft.

Burton was asked to play Winston Churchill in a television co-production between NBC and the BBC called *Walk with Destiny* (1974), but when shooting was due to start had gone AWOL and was eventually tracked down by director Herbert Wise to his home in Mexico at Puerto Vallarta. 'We found him there,' recalls Wise, 'in the swimming pool. We chatted and he told us how he was on the wagon and that he had a nurse. But then when the producers were talking to his lawyers on the phone Burton slipped off to the kitchen and I saw him open this huge ice box and take out a bottle of vodka and just drain three-quarters of it, put it back in the fridge and come back out. This was him being on the wagon!'

Burton invited Wise and his two American producers to dinner the next night, a special occasion he promised that also included the presence of the American consul and his wife. 'We arrived the following evening,' recalls Wise, 'and there was Burton sitting on a veranda which had a whole open vista looking out to sea. He sat there, with his nurse in attendance, and we started chatting and he was obviously pissed. Then he insisted on reading bits of the script because he wanted to show us what he was going to do with it and bored the pants off us and he was getting more and more plastered as well. After an hour of this we all looked at each other and began wondering when we were going to eat, because there was no sign of this meal we'd been promised. Then in mid-sentence, as Burton was reading the script, he fell asleep. There was complete silence, the nurse didn't know what to do, she just sat there. Finally the wife of the American consul said, "Well I think we'd better go." And we said, "I think we'd better." So we went. To leave that room you went down some steps, there were several levels to that house, and we went down and I hung back because I found it so dramatic, and I was the last one to go down and as I went I looked back and I saw this idol of millions of people, this film star, totally out for the count with this glorious vista behind him, it was wonderful.'

Wonderful, yes, unnerving, too. Could Burton pull himself together for what was going to be a challenging and arduous film? Wise didn't think so and told his American backers that they were taking a tremendous risk hiring him after what he'd witnessed. 'What's the alternative, then?' they asked. 'What about Peter Ustinov?' Wise said. 'Usti... who?' was the inglorious reply. 'How about Richard Attenborough?' Wise next suggested. 'No, never heard of him.' 'Olivier?' said Wise, feeling confident this time. The American executive picked up his phone and bellowed down it, 'What were the ratings for the last TV show Olivier did?' They came back. 'Not good enough.' All these names bounced around but in the end it was Burton they wanted and Burton they got. It was up to Wise to keep him under control.

Rehearsals for the film had yet to begin when Huw Weldon, then head of BBC television and a fellow Welshman, organized a reception for Burton. 'So at lunchtime in the BBC club there was this huge assembly of everybody connected with the show,' Wise recalls. 'Burton appeared and I was standing near him and behind me was the table with all the drinks. Then Huw Weldon leapt on a table and said how wonderful it was to have Richard Burton here, a great honour etc, and finally he said, "I want you all to raise a glass to this enterprise, you too Richard," and Burton turned round and said, "I'll have a large vodka." He was supposed to be on the wagon but from that moment on the whole show was ruined because he was on the piss again. Now, who needs enemies when you've got friends like that! Obviously Huw Weldon didn't do it deliberately but I mean how fucking stupid can you be when everybody knew what Burton's reputation was. So, that was the start of it.'

Almost from day one Wise had problems with Burton, 'because a lot of the time he was pissed but also all that drinking from years gone by and all the detoxing had had an effect on his brain, so he was not the sharpest and sometimes could not follow my direction. He was a nice enough man, I had no personal grudge against him whatsoever except he posed a tremendous problem because I couldn't rely on him and in performance he was very inconsistent. One morning he arrived at the studio in his Rolls-Royce, still dressed in his tuxedo from the previous night's festivities, absolutely plastered, and I saw him and said, "Richard." He went, "Urghhh." I said, "Richard, turn round." He turned round. "Get back into your car." He said, "What!" I said, "Get back into your car." He did and drove away. I knew he couldn't work that day.'

During the course of the film drink was never very far from Burton's mind. Midway through shooting they tackled one of the film's most emotional moments where Churchill sits alone at night time writing in his diary, with the menacing booms of an air raid going on outside. 'Burton asked me,' says Wise, '"What shall I write?" and I said, "Write whatever you like; I'm not going to do a close up on it." So he wrote something and at the end of the day the production manager said, come and have a look at what he wrote, and it was: *I can't wait for this film to finish because I've got to get back to my drinking.*'

Despite all the troubles Burton did endear himself to Wise, turning up with just a make-up man and the ever-dependable Brook Williams. 'He was quite modest in that sort of way. I would say he was a very nice man if he hadn't been poisoned by alcohol. But it is a disease. Funnily enough a lot of Welsh and Irish, all that Gaelic lot, they do seem to have that propensity for booze, like Harris and O'Toole.'

Amazingly, less than a year after the divorce the Burton/Taylor circus was rolling again. In October 1975 they remarried in Botswana, toasting their vows with champagne amid the distant grunts of hippos. 'The best man was a rhinoceros,' Burton joked. It was indeed an odd place to be married. 'I remember thinking, what am I doing here,' Burton said later. 'It was very curious. An extraordinary adventure, doomed from the start of course.' The omens looked bad when Burton came down with malaria.

Richard Harris was still making shit movies, like the disaster movie *The Cassandra Crossing* (1976), which he only did because it meant playing opposite two sex sirens. 'I'm a Limerick lad,' he explained, 'so it was a wet dream to be acting with Ava Gardner and Sophia Loren in their corsets and bras.'

When he did make a good film, like Richard Lester's wonderful *Robin and Marian* (1976), it was only a cameo appearance; the star role of Robin went to his pal Sean Connery. Harris didn't even get to play the sheriff of Nottingham; that went to Robert Shaw, so he had to make do with King Richard and just two scenes, powerful though they were. 'Practically the whole of that cast were bloody tax exiles,' recalls Lester. 'So we shot in Spain. There were some fair drinkers there too, Shaw, Harris, and Denholm Elliott who left the hotel quite early, found himself a cell in a monastery because there was a tasty red wine made there and we never saw him again, except for the shooting. He stayed there and very piously drank them out of house and home, or rather out of monastery and home.'

Distressed at the low calibre of scripts he was being offered Harris decided to write his own, but no studio was prepared to back these projects, scared of his reputation. Harris knew he had only himself to blame. 'I was a loose cannon. Who would trust me? I was a casualty of 20 years of photos in the paper with some big titted scrubber, with a glass in my fist, telling the world, fuck off! I crucified myself. Then when it came to walking humbly back and saying, gee, could I have ten million dollars to make this . . . doors shut in my face.' The experience did little to endear Hollywood to him, a place Harris had little warmth towards anyway. 'If you go to a whorehouse you expect to get fucked, don't you.'

At least there was the 'supposed' stability of his marriage to Ann Turkel, who was determined to create a happy family home in spite of Harris's penchant to smash it all to pieces. There were periods of time when Harris stayed off the booze but for Ann these were too few and far between. 'Richard didn't drink if we were alone together, but the minute anybody else was with us, he would start drinking into obliteration – a true symptom of an alcoholic.' Harris liked to joke that he'd formed a new group called Alcoholics-Unanimous. 'If you don't feel like a drink, you ring another member and he comes over to persuade you.'

Divorce for Ann, at first, wasn't an option; she was determined to stick to her marriage vows, literally for better or worse. 'It was terrifying,' she said, aware that, if Harris had drunk excessively the night before, just saying the wrong thing could make him explode in anger. Inevitably a degree of violence entered the marriage. According to Ann, she was physically abused by Harris, 'beyond anything you can possibly imagine.' His drinking and erratic mood swings were also, she later claimed, why she chose not to have children with him, despite Harris's desire for a daughter: 'How am I going to handle a baby and handle Richard?' But the bad times were often outweighed by the good and Harris, prone to extravagant gestures, could be incredibly loving. He threw a surprise wedding anniversary party for Ann and flew their families over from the US and Ireland to London. It was this side to Harris's character that made it so difficult for Ann to leave him; later Ann admitted that she should have walked out the first year after it dawned on her what Richard was like.

Peter O'Toole was also suffering marital problems. However, in early 1975 he needed Siân as never before. An abdominal irregularity he'd been carrying for years and persistently ignored (he hated doctors and hospitals) finally erupted and he had to be rushed to hospital. The press believed it was a liver complaint as a result of his drinking, but it was worse – O'Toole believed he was dying. He was incapable of taking solid food, and pure water had to be fed down a pipe directly into his stomach. Tests proved nothing so it was decided to carry out exploratory surgery. Something very wrong was going on inside O'Toole's digestive system and what they found caused such alarm that a major operation was hurriedly performed. Several yards of intestinal tubing were removed, leaving an eight-inch scar. 'I suggested they put in a zip, they were opening me up so often,' he later joked.

For years O'Toole was nervous about disclosing what the surgeons discovered. 'My plumbing is nobody's business but my own.' American tabloids reported that his pancreas was removed, but O'Toole denied this. What was true was that O'Toole came as close to dying as you can do without actually snuffing it. 'It was a photo-finish, the surgeons said.' Stomach problems had been the bane of O'Toole's life since the age of 19. No one really knew what was wrong with him and so he drank sometimes just to ease the pain: 'Madame Bottle, the great anaesthetic.' But no more. There was now so little of his digestive system left that any amount of alcohol would prove fatal to him. Having come so close to death O'Toole was determined to live each day to the full.

Years later in interviews O'Toole stressed the point that he gave up the booze not because of his near-death experience but out of fear that he might one day become addicted and not be able to stop; he'd watched that happen to too many of his friends.

Following his recovery from his illness, though, Siân finally left O'Toole for a young actor, Robin Sachs, 17 years her junior. O'Toole bought her out of the Hampstead house, but she got almost nothing else; even her jewellery was sold at Sotheby's. She left behind her two daughters, even her mother, who continued to live with O'Toole, who affectionately called her 'the old witch'. The star also learnt that he was practically uninsurable in Hollywood. To cap it all his father died, as did his beloved dog. 'The things that happened to me were almost biblical.' But at least he was still alive, though the ravages of alcohol would be clear in that haggard (if still lively) face forever more.

To help him quit the booze O'Toole chewed gum. 'Now at least they make it sugarless so your fucking teeth don't rot out.' The wild boy had gone too, at least the drunken one. 'Only ninnies make booze the excuse for their wild escapades. I can still make whoopee, but now I do it sober. I no longer anaesthetize myself into unconsciousness. That makes the escapade pointless.' So the hellraiser was dead. 'The time has come to stop roaming,' he lamented. 'The pirate ship has berthed.' Or had it?

Oliver Reed consolidated his fame in the mid-70s by appearing in a succession of films. *The Sellout* (1976) was directed by Peter Collinson and co-starred Richard Widmark. One evening Reed asked a few of the crew to come and have a drink with him in his hotel. Widmark wisely refused, but the rest went up to his suite. 'It was about eight o'clock in the evening,' recalled production manager Tom Sachs, 'and Ollie asked for the drinks to be sent up, but when the waiter brought them, he also brought the bill for signing.

Ollie saw how much it was and said, "I'm not paying that!" I thought – this is going to be a short evening. Ollie rang his driver from the bedroom, and 15 minutes later, in came the driver with eight "flunkies" behind him, each of whom carried a box. He had gone out and bought eight boxes of booze. It wasn't just wine; it was spirits – the place was like a pub! When we woke up next morning, still in Ollie's suite, half the boxes were empty and Ollie had drunk as much as the rest of us put together! He hadn't been to sleep. He went straight onto the set and into make-up – stone-cold sober. I don't know how he did it. He was unbelievable.'

When Oliver Reed agreed to appear in the western *The Great Scout and Cathouse Thursday* (1976) he faced the challenge of sharing the screen with a man whose hellraising and boozing matched his own, Lee Marvin. By the mid-70s, however, Marvin was an ailing alcoholic who was at that stage in his illness, according to one of the film's executives, 'when just unscrewing the top of a whiskey bottle and sticking his nose in made him fall over'. When Reed arrived in Mexico the director said, 'You know Lee enjoys a drink. Please don't encourage him.' Reed was happy to comply, only to hear later from Marvin that the director had said exactly the same thing about him.

The stars were also warned about the town they were shooting in; Durango had a reputation for violence. That first evening the cast and crew met up in a local cantina. The instant the director and producer left for their hotel Marvin looked across at Reed, a twinkle in his eye. 'Bourbon, large, on the rocks,' he barked at a waiter. When the man returned with a treble Marvin looked at it incredulously. 'I said large!' Not to be outdone Reed snapped his fingers. 'Bourbon, large, two.' The challenge was on. After a few rounds it looked like Marvin was wavering as he staggered to his feet and joined in with the Mexican cabaret, telling them how to play their instruments before crashing to the floor. Reed tried reviving him by stuffing ice cubes down the back of his shirt, worried the director might return and see they'd reneged on their promise not to booze – on the first night! Shaking his comatose co-star Reed spied an evil looking Mexican take out his revolver and fire three times into the ceiling. Reed ignored it and carried on trying to resuscitate the now snoring Marvin. Another none-too-civilised looking Mexican got up and approached them. 'Hey gringo,' he said. Reed pretended not to hear and dug Marvin violently in the ribs. 'For Christ's sake Lee wake up before we all get a bullet up our arses.' The Mexican tried again. 'Hey gringo,' and followed it up by firing into the ceiling. One of the other actors, Strother Martin, was getting anxious too. 'We've got to get Lee outta here.' And together they somehow managed to carry the hulking Marvin out of the club, much to the amusement of the locals.

The next morning Marvin appeared at breakfast looking as if nothing had happened. 'Know any good bars, Strother,' he asked. Reed hoped the answer would be no, as he'd a bugger of a hangover. But Strother Martin did indeed and they got pissed all over again. Not surprisingly Reed and Marvin became great friends and the American star presented his British colleague with what he called his drinking cloak in recognition of the night he was outdrunk.

Years later the pair met again in Tucson, Arizona. Marvin phoned Reed at his hotel and invited himself round for Saturday night. The hotel switchboard were listening in and the manager hired two private security guards, armed with riot gas, loaded guns and night sticks to be stationed at either end of the bar come Saturday. Marvin never showed, but when he did a few days later Reed told him of the manager's precautions. 'Fuck 'em,' he said. 'We won't drink here.' Reed suggested a restaurant he knew, but warned that it was a bit on the posh side. When they strolled in Marvin was instantly recognized and a gaggle of middle-aged women flustered round him asking for their menus to be signed. 'Later, sweetheart,' he said. Eight bottles later Marvin decided it was time to fulfil his promise and lurched over in the women's general direction. As they held out their menus Marvin collapsed and fell full length across their table. Three of the women screamed, one fainted, and another fled in hysterics while the rest burst out laughing. Trying to rectify the situation Marvin hauled himself back up, but fell heavily again against the table, banging his head, this time spraying the place with blood. The horror show prompted the remaining women to scream uncontrollably and join their friends in running out into the night.

Out in Durango, Reed was quite capable of getting into drunken mischief without any assistance from Marvin. One of the crew had been foolish enough to invite his wife over to the location, the only one to have done so. The couple were having a quiet meal one night in a restaurant when

Reed approached their table. 'Good night Dave,' he said. 'Are you going to bed, Ollie?' the crewman asked. 'No, you are.' The poor man assumed he'd offended the star in some way and began apologizing profusely. Ollie leaned forward. 'Dear boy, nothing of the sort, only I'm going to smash this fucking place up in ten minutes and I wouldn't want your lady to get hurt.' As the couple left and were crossing the courtyard outside they heard the sound of two dining tables being hurled through a window.

A few days later a rather young and pretty production assistant came to collect Ollie from the hotel restaurant. 'Sit down and have a drink.' The already nervous girl obliged, sensing that her charge had been drinking heavily throughout lunch. Suddenly Reed leapt to his feet. 'Well, this isn't much of a party,' he said and balanced a full ice bucket on his head and danced through the crowded restaurant showering fellow diners with ice cubes and freezing water.

Reed's close encounter with another Hollywood legend didn't pass off so smoothly. *Burnt Offerings* (1976) was a substandard horror movie but the real nightmare was the relationship between the two stars. Bette Davis detested Reed, referring to him as 'that man' and only speaking to him when they shared screen dialogue. During filming, Miss Davis used to have a food trolley sent up to her hotel room carrying her evening meal. One day when Ollie, his stand-in Reg Prince and a few friends were returning from an evening out, they saw this food trolley and Ollie turned to Reg with a grin and said, 'I bet I can ride it farther than you.' The bet was on. Taking it in turns the gang would take a run and a leaping dive on to the trolley and go careering down the corridor, the remnants of Miss Davis's evening meal going all over the place. Not surprisingly, after filming Miss Davis declared that Reed 'is possibly one of the most loathsome human beings I have ever had the misfortune of meeting'.

In London Reed got a phone call from old friend Michael Winner offering him a small role in his all-star remake of *The Big Sleep* (1977), jockeying for space on the screen with the likes of Joan Collins, Sarah Miles and James Stewart. Reed also shared a couple of scenes with the film's main star, Robert Mitchum. 'Now there was a wonderful man,' says Winner. 'But he was a pain in the arse when drunk. I wouldn't call him a heavy drinker, but occasionally he'd go over the top. Mitchum wasn't particularly nice when drunk. Reed was jolly and stupid when drunk,

Mitchum became quite antagonistic to people. But he was drunk very seldom.'

Winner hadn't worked with Reed for almost ten years and noticed that his old friend was drinking more than before. He was still never drunk on set but sometimes would have been so drunk the night before that he'd arrive for work a bit wasted. They were filming at a sumptuous London house and Reed, Winner and Mitchum were all sitting in the garden resting between set-ups when Ollie suddenly stood up and said, 'You know, Bob, last night I was playing this game where two people have their legs astride a pole and they're naked and they hit at each other to see which one can knock the other off the pole. It completely did in my bollocks. Would you like to see them?' Mitchum pulled an unpleasant face. 'Not really,' he said. Oliver was having none of that. 'I'd like to show you,' and with that unzipped his trousers to reveal red raw bollocks, not just to Mitchum but a few members of the public who were watching over a low wall. Finally Winner had had enough. 'We really could live without this Oliver. Honestly, we could.'

So Richard Burton was back with Liz, but not for long. On a skiing holiday he spied 27-year-old blonde former model Susan Hunt. 'She could stop a stampede,' he said. At the time Susan was in the process of divorcing her husband, the motor racing champion James Hunt. Instinctively Liz sensed danger, and she was right. Burton asked for a divorce, he wanted to marry Susan. Liz was livid, although her daughter went public blaming the split on Burton's drinking: 'His binges were a problem. There are no half measures. Either he doesn't touch a drop or he drinks until he can't stand up.'

The divorce from Liz when it came was painful. The settlement all but cleaned him out; she took the jewels, their house in Mexico, the yacht and their paintings. Some friends said that the only reason Liz had married Burton a second time was because she had failed to get all the jewels in the first divorce. No wonder Burton blindly accepted the $1 million on offer to star in *Exorcist II* (1977), rightly hailed as a turkey of the first order.

Burton married Susan in August 1976 and he often said that it was Susan who saved his life. She certainly took an active part in it, not just as a wife, but as a nurse and personal assistant. She didn't hide the bottles of gin and vodka that always lay around the house; instead she helped him in his resolve to fight alcoholism, although Burton hated the word alcoholic, preferring 'drunk'. There was a difference in his mind: alcoholics can't give up the booze, Burton knew that he could and often went on the wagon, always falling off though. He had the odd glass now and then, or several, but his recent punishing illness had left his system with a much lower tolerance level than before. People later commented that even a small brandy would turn him from a sober man into an utter wreck.

This new resolve also had a lot to do with his impending return to Broadway, the first time since his appearance as Hamlet brought New York to a virtual standstill 12 years before. The play was *Equus* and Burton was set to take over from Anthony Perkins in the role of a psychiatrist trying to find out why a teenage boy blinded several horses. Rehearsals were tortuous. Officially Burton was on the wagon, but everyone knew that Brook Williams was smuggling in bottles of booze wrapped up in brown paper for him to consume in his dressing room. Onstage he staggered through the role, often stumbling over his lines, covering up the fact with a joke. With just a week to go before Perkins left the production and Burton took over on the Monday performance director John Dexter had to face the fact that his new leading man didn't know the part at all. His plan to save the show was radical; he intended to put Burton on the Saturday matinee when audiences wouldn't be expecting it. 'I won't be ready on Saturday afternoon,' Burton said. 'You'll be ready on Saturday afternoon and you'll go out on stage and you'll do it,' Dexter hit back. 'On Monday night the press will be in and there'll be no excuses. On Saturday, you'll be able to get away with murder.'

Burton wasn't happy but he persevered, only for rehearsals to get worse. He was stumbling over lines again and again. Suddenly Dexter's patience evaporated and he exploded in anger. 'Richard,' he blasted, 'you're disgracing yourself in front of your compatriots. You're a lazy, drunken fool.' Burton stood there in a daze. 'Well, it's very difficult,' was all he could muster. The Saturday matinee came and Burton was a disaster. He was shaking, looking down on the floor for the first half hour of the play, fluffing lines. The rest of the cast helped him through when he dried, saying things like, 'Excuse me doctor, I think I should tell you that . . . to help bring him back to the plot. But most of the time Burton was inclined to say, 'Well that's all I have to say to you,' and leave them flummoxed.

He looked like a man who'd never set foot on a professional stage before. It was heartbreaking stuff.

Burton returned to his hotel in disgrace, staying there for two whole days, but when he emerged again he gave a performance on Monday night that garnered him a standing ovation and rave notices. When he appeared in the film of *Equus* (1977) he was quite rightly handed his 7th Oscar nomination for Best Actor. The bastards still didn't give it to him though.

Burton claimed that appearing in the play *Equus* was the first time in his life he'd been on stage without a drink. 'I've never been so bloody scared. I shook and shivered.' Jim Backus, a friend since they'd made the awful *Ice Palace* together in the 50s, saw Burton in *Equus* and afterwards they dined together. Burton decided to have a double martini to celebrate. 'One drink and he was absolutely blotto,' said Backus. 'I've seen one glass of alcohol turn him into a gibbering wreck. Two drinks and I've had to put him to bed.' Age had certainly hampered Burton's ability to drink. He now suffered bad hangovers and his powers of recovery had lapsed. 'I just can't drink as I used to in the good old days.'

Richard Harris was still having trouble finding decent product. *Orca Killer Whale* (1977) was an OK piece of escapism about a killer whale wreaking revenge on the fishermen who had slain its mate, but hardly up there with *This Sporting Life*. At least it reunited the actor with the director who gave him his first break in movies and his first taste of Hollywood, Michael Anderson. 'By this time Richard had this great reputation for boozing and he said to me before shooting, "I promise ya, when we're working together Mike, I'll not touch a drop." And he didn't. He said, "I'll be as good as gold." And he was, all through the picture and it was a difficult picture to make physically. He was absolutely wonderful. For me he was a joy to work with.'

Having not made a movie with Harris for almost 20 years Anderson detected a change in the man, not surprisingly, especially the way that his boozing reputation preceded him wherever he went. 'His career was on a downward trend when we made *Orca* and this was a major part and he was very conscious of the fact that he had this reputation so he went out of his way to really be at his best on this movie, which he was, in both performance and behaviour.'

It was a reputation that Harris could never truly escape from. The producer of the film *Golden Rendezvous* (1977), told reporters that the movie lagged 44 days behind schedule because Harris was often too drunk to act, allegedly drinking a bottle of vodka a day. The producer even tried to get Harris arrested for breach of contract. Not only did Harris deny the accusation but also believed it to be ruinous to his reputation and sued for £14 million.

Orca was shot in Canada and Malta and Harris stayed in touch with his wife Ann, back in Hollywood, by telephoning her every day, resulting in an astronomical phone bill, over $10,000 a week. Once they were on the phone for four hours straight. After hanging up the operator called to tell Harris, 'I just wanted to let you know that you've beaten Richard Burton and Elizabeth Taylor's record on the phone.'

Despite Ann's benign influence on Harris, the actor was still capable of getting dangerously hammered. One morning he woke up and there was blood all over the pillow. Then Harris realized that he could only see out of one eye. Scrambling out of bed he stared at himself in the mirror, noticing one eye weeping and closed and stitches in his face. Incredibly he had no recollection of how he'd got into such a state. Going downstairs he hoped Ann or his brother Dermot who were breakfasting might be able to illuminate him. 'What happened?' he asked. Both stared back at him. 'What happened! God, there's a restaurant in Santa Monica and you've wrecked it. And you wrecked it laughing – you weren't even angry.'

After his illness Peter O'Toole appeared in one of the best films of his career, *Rogue Male* (1976) about a man out to assassinate Hitler. It was made for BBC television by his old *What's New Pussycat?* collaborator Clive Donner. Ironically it was due to be shown in the same week as the first episode of the drama series *I Claudius* starring Siân. Both shows vied for the prestigious cover slot on the *Radio Times* – O'Toole won. When he visited the *I Claudius* set to see Siân he remembers being 'as popular as a pork sausage in a synagogue'.

O'Toole had kept in sporadic touch with Siân since the split but when they finally divorced at the close of the seventies all ties were severed and they never spoke to one another again. Years later they bumped into each

Whilst publicising *Lawrence of Arabia* in New York, the film made all the wrong sort of headlines when O'Toole was caught up in a drugs bust with controversial comic Lenny Bruce.

Mutual friend Kenneth Griffith warned Sian Phillips off marrying O'Toole, saying 'He is a genius, but he is not normal.'

Filming *Lord Jim* in Cambodia included dysentery and encounters with deadly snakes. O'Toole said how much he hated the place and was banished by the king.

In Paris shooting *What's New Pussycat?*, O'Toole saw two policemen attacking a prostitute and later took revenge by duffing up a totally innocent *gendarme*.

On *How to Steal a Million* O'Toole got his co-star, the incomparably elegant Audrey Hepburn, so drunk that she crashed a car and demolished the set.

During one night's boozing O'Toole was refused service because it was after hours. A problem for lesser men perhaps – O'Toole promptly bought the place.

As a serial killer Nazi in *The Night of the Generals*. O'Toole had a lifelong obsession with Hitler, or as he memorably called him, 'that strange mincing little dude.'

O'Toole could get bladdered off very little booze. Dining with *The Ruling Class* director Peter Medak he swigged so much champagne that he toppled down a flight of stairs.

O'Toole originally refused the role of a faded Hollywood star in *My Favorite Year* because 'People might think this clapped-out drunken old fart was me.'

O'Toole's theatrical disaster *Macbeth* made front page headlines because it was such a total fuck up. 'When I think about it, my nose bleeds'.

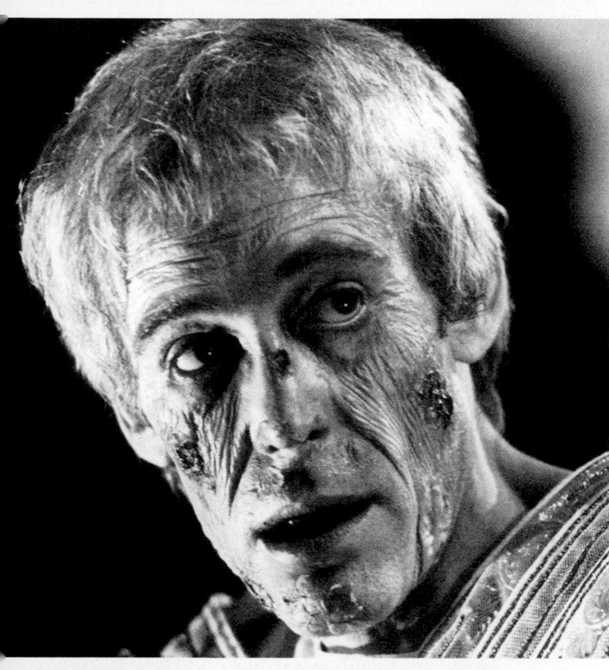

Caligula – notoriously the director, Tinto Brass, inserted hard-core porn scenes. Unimpressed, O'Toole remarked, 'It was about as erotic as bath night on HMS Montclare.'

With journalist and fellow boozer Jeffrey Bernard whose life O'Toole immortalised in the stage play *Jeffrey Bernard is Unwell.*

At the 2002 Oscars, O'Toole was to receive a lifetime achievement award. However, on discovering the bar served no alcohol, he threatened to walk out. Panicked producers had some vodka smuggled in.

other in Piccadilly, 'and she didn't even recognize me. Hadn't the faintest idea who I was. I said, "Hello," and she looked up and said, "oh!"'

O'Toole had no regrets about his marriage failure and was quite philosophical about his own inadequacies that helped consign it to the waste bin. 'Ooh, I was a hopeless husband. Hopeless. I'm a loving man, but not a particularly well-behaved one.'

In the middle of 1976 O'Toole appeared in *Caligula*, a film that wouldn't see daylight until 1980. It was an epic based on the debauched life of the Roman emperor, financed by Bob Guccione, the proprietor of sex magazine *Penthouse*. O'Toole was in prestigious company. In the title role was Malcolm McDowell, a heavy boozer himself who was in such a drunken haze throughout shooting that little if anything of it was retained in his memory. Also there was Helen Mirren and poor John Gielgud who paraded around the set as grandly as he could trying not to notice that the girls flanking him in most scenes had their tits out. 'We both enjoyed ourselves enormously,' said O'Toole. 'We started off looking at all the naked bodies and then after a while compared our operation scars. Half the cast went round wearing four-foot rubber phalluses strapped to them and Malcolm had a nice little gold lamé number. I called him Tinkerbell.'

Tinto Brass, who O'Toole infuriated by calling Tinto Zinc, oversaw the whole sorry mess and on the first day of shooting approached O'Toole and said, 'How you like to be paralyzed in picture?' O'Toole thought about it and replied, 'Anything you like, smiler.' 'So I got myself a naked Sumerian girl to lean on from start to finish. She became known as Betty the Collapsible Crutch.'

According to Guccione O'Toole disliked Tinto Brass on sight, nor did the actor endear himself much to Guccione when he told the producer of his intention of launching a girlie magazine to rival his own *Penthouse*. It was to be called Basement and would include such features as 'Rodent of the Month' and 'Toe Rag of the Year'. 'I don't think I ever saw him sober,' said Guccione about O'Toole years later, getting his own back. 'He doesn't drink any more, or at least he wasn't drinking then, but he was strung out on something. From time to time it took a little longer than usual to get him on the set, and when you've got six or seven hundred people standing around, his little habits can become goddamn expensive.'

Gore Vidal had written the script with good faith and high hopes but was soon asking for his name to be taken off the picture when Guccione inserted some choice slabs of hardcore porn to spice things up; all to no avail. 'As for being erotic,' said O'Toole, 'I'd say it was about as erotic as bath night on HMS *Montclare*.' Malcolm McDowell was appalled, though, and has never forgiven Guccione. 'It was absurd, because the footage didn't even match. There would be a shot of me smiling, looking at what was supposed to be my horse or something, and then suddenly they'd cut to two lesbians making out. It was just awful.' Incredibly the final cost of the film came in at a little over $17.5 million. 'For that kind of money, I could have made over 200 porno films,' lamented Guccione.

With performances such as he gave in *Caligula* O'Toole was fast becoming a parody of himself: a caricature faded film star, though he'd never given two stuffs about fame. Interviewed in a Los Angeles hotel beside a swimming pool he saw only too well the absurdity of it all, of asking a lackey for a drink or indeed anything else he desired. 'I tell them I'm a film star. They don't give a fuck, but somehow I amuse them. I told the pool man who was cleaning here earlier that I was a movie star and he couldn't have cared less. He probably cleans Zsa Zsa Gabor's pool, and I can get stuffed.'

A film that was in a similar vein to Reed's most recent box office hit *The Three Musketeers* was *The Prince and the Pauper* (1977), which reunited him with his *Oliver!* co-star Mark Lester, and was filmed in Budapest where he couldn't resist getting into trouble. In order that Reed couldn't cause too much damage the producers wisely kept him away from everyone else in a separate hotel. 'Budapest is essentially two towns divided by a river,' says Lester. 'We were in the old town and Ollie was across the river in a hotel alone so that he wouldn't upset too many people.' On Reed's days off he and Reg Prince would go boozing in Budapest's roughest nightspots, expeditions that usually ended in brawls. One local came back for revenge the next night only to be knocked out again by Reed. The police intervened and both men spent a night in the cells.

Even on set Reed was hard to handle. One afternoon he was scheduled to meet a journalist but never showed up. The film's publicist sent out a search party but he couldn't be located anywhere. Finally when he did surface Reed wasn't exactly clear about the previous 36 hours; save for the fact that he remembered standing on a bridge over the Danube debating whether he should jump in or not for a bet.

Mark Lester turned 18 on the film, an event he's never forgotten. 'The producer had laid on a huge dinner for me, all the cast and crew were there and Ollie brought me a present from the streets of Budapest, it was a Hungarian hooker. Ollie, who was completely paralytic, dragged in this poor girl and she took one look at everybody, gasped in fright and then legged it. Fortunately for me, because Ollie didn't have the best taste in women, I think he had his beer goggles firmly on at that time. Ollie then joined the party. He got up on the table and decided to do some antics which involved putting a cake in one of the producer's faces and then falling backwards off the table. When he worked Ollie was completely straight and very professional, but there was this other side to him. It was more than just naughty schoolboy type pranks, it was actually things that were so embarrassing you wouldn't expect the local rugby team to behave in such a manner, jokes not appreciated by everybody.'

More antics followed. One evening Mark Lester joined Reed and 20 other people from the film for a slap up meal in a restaurant, only Ollie decided to have the meal in reverse. 'We started off having brandy and a cigar, Ollie was drinking all the time this bull's blood wine, but we were all fairly merry. Then when the chocolate pancakes came one of the camera crew lobbed his pancake across the room and within minutes there was this huge food fight and everyone was just covered in chocolate and the manager came over and just threw us all out. We were literally thrown out into the street.'

Amongst *The Prince and the Pauper*'s galaxy of stars, that included Rex Harrison, Charlton Heston, and George C. Scott, was Raquel Welch. She and Reed had dramatically fallen out on the set of *The Three Musketeers* when Ollie turned her down at a party, preferring instead to dance with her hairdresser, an affront to Raquel's sex symbol status. 'Raquel is someone I can live without,' Reed told a reporter at the time. 'She loathes me and I can't say she's one of my favourite people. We've got some love scenes together and I am dreading them!'

Reed mischievously sent a telegram to Richard Harris boasting of his forthcoming love scenes with Miss Welch and offering him a job as his stand-in, providing his wig didn't fall off in the clinches. 'With his toupee and her falsies they would be perfect for each other.' Reed was always sending telegrams of that sort to Harris and receiving a few back in the same vein. It was a curious relationship, as the two men never socialized. Reed raised the stakes a few notches when during an interview he challenged Harris to a punch up. 'Never mind Richard Harris, or Mr Ireland, or whatever he calls himself. Bollocks to him and his Mayfair punch ups. Next time you see him, tell him that if he wants to meet a real England heavy, he should meet me.' Harris's reaction was to send Reed a recently published book of his poetry. On the flyleaf he wrote: 'To Oliver – Mr England. Since you have not yet attained superstar status and salary and therefore cannot afford to buy this book, here is a copy free.' It was signed 'Richard – Mr Ireland.'

This rivalry and mock backbiting continued with both stars playfully slagging off each other, much to the delight of Fleet Street. 'People say Richard Harris and I have been having a great feud,' Reed jested. 'It's not true. After all, how could we be feuding for years? I'd never heard of him until two weeks ago.' When Reed was in LA and heard that Harris was in town he rang to invite him over for drinks at his hotel. 'I dare you to accept.' 'Don't move,' said Harris. 'I'll be right over.' Reed sat in the hotel bar for two hours steadily getting pissed but Harris was a no-show. As Ollie wearily got up and left through one door, Harris, pissed himself, arrived through another. Feeling stood up Reed challenged Harris to a fight at the Royal Albert Hall.

Harris responded swiftly with another letter: 'It appears Mr Reed, that you are having some difficulty in locating me. My address, should you require it, is Buckingham Palace and the flag is still up with the monarch still reigning. If I decide to abdicate, I will let you know.' With the letter, Harris sent Ollie a 'gift' neatly wrapped in brown paper. Inside was a pair of Victorian crutches, one inscribed with the name Glenda Jackson and on the other the name of Ken Russell. Attached to them Harris had written a note stating, 'In my Royal opinion you should not dispense with these, otherwise you will fall flat on your arse.'

By now the press were having a whale of a time, not bothered if the feud was real or merely an elaborate hoax fixed by the two stars for publicity purposes. Who cared, it was great copy. In interviews they'd ask each of them for their opinion of the other. When questioned directly about Reed,

Harris simply replied, 'I always ignore bores.' And there was a rocket from Reed directed at Harris: 'I'm the only public school actor there is. Harris is very uneducated. He's Irish.'

'Harris!' went the voice on the other end of the phone. 'When I see you I'm going to kick the shit out of you and I'm going to stamp on your face and break both your arms.' Harris guessed it was Reed. 'Where are you?' he demanded. 'El Pedrino's,' replied Reed. 'Don't move.' Harris arrived at the LA bar just minutes later. The big encounter had at last arrived. 'Do I start with you,' Harris asked a muscle-bound minder who'd come to stand next to Reed, 'or do I begin with Oliver?' 'You begin with me,' said Reed, waving away his aide. Onlookers gasped as the two stars squared up and glared at each other. Then all of a sudden Reed asked politely, 'Drink?' 'Don't mind if I do,' replied Harris courteously. Both men shook hands and gave each other a massive bear hug before getting down to some serious drinking. 'Sober he was a great guy,' said Reed of Harris. 'Drunk, he was even better.'

Since his first encounter with Richard Burton way back in 1950 producer Euan Lloyd had carved out a successful career, notably the coup of casting Sean Connery and Brigitte Bardot together in the western *Shalako*, but had always harboured a desire to work with the Welshman. Then in 1976 a book called *The Wild Geese* came into his possession. 'Despite the battering he had taken in the 26 years since we met, here, at last, was my chance. From a single reading I determined that Richard Burton and only Richard Burton would play the leading role. The character was a booze-ridden mercenary leader, past his prime, who is set on rescuing an African president from certain assassination. A man who has been there, seen it all, but is determined to succeed on one final mission. I could see no other actor in that part.'

It was common knowledge that Burton had appeared in some duff movies of late, that a lifetime on the booze had badly dented his image, possibly beyond repair, and that he was in poor health due to a crippling back problem; consequently getting insurance cover for the ageing star was highly doubtful. 'I had cautioned Burton's agent that setting up a potential epic production with Richard in the lead would be a hard slog. I needed a categorical assurance that Richard no longer slept with a bottle at his bedside. I need not have worried, he was now firmly on the wagon.' And drinking Tab by the bucket load. Burton asked if his favourite soft drink could be made available on location. Since it wasn't sold in South Africa Lloyd had to import 2,000 bottles from the US.

Casting the remaining leads became a huge challenge. Burt Lancaster was suggested for the role of second in command Rafer Janders, but then Lloyd got a call from a Hollywood agent. 'When he suggested Richard Harris in place of Lancaster my heart stopped beating. I had heard that Harris had recently made a film, which suffered greatly from his drinking. The completion bond company concerned had vowed never to "cover" Richard again. But Richard's skills as an actor had long impressed me and I considered it worth fighting for him.'

Lloyd was told bluntly that no insurance company would be mad enough to offer the Irishman cover. It had become general practice in the business that once told Harris was in their film directors added a week to the schedule as an insurance against drunken days he couldn't work. For Burton they automatically added three weeks. But so determined was Harris to play the role that he agreed to defer half of his salary as evidence of his determination to behave and not drink. Still, Hollywood thought Lloyd had flipped his lid hiring two of the biggest hellraisers around. 'Why in God's good name would you want to have two famous drunks in one picture?' he was asked.

Lloyd ignored the dissenting voices and bagged a third star for his film, Roger Moore. 'Now Roger enjoys his drink more than most,' says Lloyd. 'But unlike any star I've known he can handle it without the slightest hiccup. I have seen him down six martinis in one evening and remain as articulate as ever. But I did catch him unprepared one morning on *The Wild Geese* when, driving to the location around dawn, I passed Roger's apartment and caught him standing on the front lawn in his underpants, eyes tightly closed, his right hand holding a garden hose over his head! It must have been a late night.'

Filming got underway in northern Transvaal under the supervision of veteran action director Andrew V. Mclaglen. 'He had the awesome responsibility of getting great performances from Burton and Harris when they were both fighting demons within,' says Lloyd. 'Whenever you feel like a drink,' Harris said to Burton one day on location, 'do like I do, jump up and down.' For the rest of the production both men were seen daily in all sorts of unlikely situations hopping like kangaroos. 'Both had been told by their doctors to ease up on the booze,' says John Glen, the film's second unit director. 'In Burton's case it was essential because he was really very ill, his liver was absolutely gone; another drink would've probably killed him. But those were wild days when those guys were young and they had everything at their feet. All that fame, it has a price, doesn't it?'

Lloyd had been expecting trouble during filming. Could Burton and Harris be trusted not to misbehave and go on the ultimate bender? But he was pleasantly surprised when they acted more like angels on set. The reason may have had something to do with the local ganja that was in prodigious supply. Ronald Fraser, cast as one of the fighting mercenaries, recalls a gardener mowing the lawn outside his rented home and then traipsing in with five bags of cuttings. 'What the hell are you doing bringing this stuff into the house? Take it outside,' he yelled. 'It's not for burning,' the gardener told him, 'it's the stuff you roll in paper and light.' Harris, Burton and Fraser happily indulged, rolling deadly joints of Durban poison. 'We were all so happy,' Fraser recalled. 'Convinced we were doing Shakespeare.'

To make everyone feel at home in the African bush the art department converted a large *rondavel* into a typical English pub, christened The Red Ox. Halfway through production, delighted with the film's progress, Lloyd organized a party there. Things went smoothly until midnight approached and he pulled the plug in the interest of filming at dawn the next day. Come morning the third assistant told Lloyd that Burton wanted to see him urgently in his trailer. 'When I knocked at the door a burst of expletives came forth and I entered to find a seething Richard, red in the face, glowering at me. No request to sit, I stood and suffered the worst abuse imaginable. "I have only one thing to say to you. You are a shit. How dare you insult me like that in front of the crew?" Totally baffled, I hadn't the faintest idea what he was talking about. Then it came out. He thought that I had pulled the midnight plug on the party to make sure he would not be drinking.' Lloyd told Burton that he'd misunderstood his actions, but if any offence had been caused he apologized. Still not pacified Burton grunted, turned to his script pages and allowed the producer to make a quiet exit. 'Around six o'clock in the evening Richard knocked at my door, entered smilingly and promptly gave me a huge bear hug. "Forgive me, old chap, for this morning. That was downright stupid of me. I'm afraid the gremlins were at work inside me. It happens sometimes." It was never mentioned again.'

The film company managed to get full insurance on Harris, and the star was told to behave, or else. To make sure he did, a nightly report was sent to the London insurance company confirming that the actor had 'performed to the letter of his contract'. Lloyd had never encountered such a condition being imposed on an actor in a film before. All went well until two-thirds of the way through shooting when the stunt men invited the whole cast to dinner. 'Once again the third assistant knocked at my door soon after shooting had commenced the next day,' says Lloyd. 'The boy looked very upset when he asked if I could see Mr Harris urgently on the set. I drove into the bush at once and found Richard sitting silently on an exposed root of a tree, head in his hands. With great trepidation I approached and stood over him. Slowly he turned his head to gaze at me. "Richard," says I, "are you ill? What's the trouble?" He rose and whispered, "Guv, I was a bad, bad boy last night. I was out with the lads and somehow I fell off the wagon. But I promise you, and this I mean to keep, it won't happen again, EVER." I was convinced he meant it. I said this incident would be a secret between us, and so it was. Thereafter, he went from strength to strength in the role.'

Burton and Harris could often get irritable at the sight of others drinking when they couldn't touch a drop themselves. One night both were at a restaurant with their wives and the crew were boozing it up nearby and being boisterous. 'These men are all drunk,' Burton suddenly announced. 'Drunken men are such bloody bores.' Ann Turkel burst out laughing because only the previous night Harris had said to her, 'I can't bear being with all these drunks. They're so bloody boring.' The wives asked their husbands, 'I don't suppose you thought you were boring when you were drunk?' Both stars looked briefly taken aback. 'Of course not,' they finally replied. The wives looked at each other and then at their husbands: 'You were. You were both bloody bores.' Harris later came to accept the accusation grudgingly. 'But I would never have dreamt I was a boring drunk at the time.'

Both Burton and Harris were delighted with how *The Wild Geese* turned out and with its commercial success in the summer of 1978. 'I'd been plodding through sewage,' said Harris. 'And then at the end of the tunnel, there it was, a romp with the boys, a night on the town. Was *The Wild Geese* a movie? I thought it was a summer holiday.' Those weeks spent in the South African bush also deepened Harris's fondness for and friendship with Burton, whom he idolized till the day he died. 'There was talent!' One day on the set Harris sidled over to Burton and said, 'You know, I've made this picture before, when I was in Limerick as a kid. I would always be daydreaming that I was off in Africa. Or fighting people, or saving my gang.' Burton smiled. 'So was I, a little kid in Wales, always in the trees with a machine gun.'

After the high of *The Wild Geese* Richard Harris finished the decade on a low; films like *Games for Vultures* (1979), about black freedom fighters in Rhodesia, he later admitted not even remembering doing. The industry had changed, too. This was the era of *Taxi Driver* and *Star Wars* and Harris seemed to not have a place in it. 'It was the same for Burton and O'Toole. Their careers had been mighty. And then, where were we all?'

To dull the pain Harris sedated himself in booze (up to two and a half bottles of vodka a day) and then a new predilection for cocaine, which very quickly became a 'social necessity' for him. Then, according to Ann, when coke didn't give him the same rush – he became immune to it – he would take both coke and drink, 'which made him like Dr Jekyll and Mr Hyde'.

He spent a fortune on it and it almost killed him. He was also plagued by bouts of sudden and prolonged fainting fits. Told by doctors that he should stop drinking if he wanted to stop falling into these comas Harris just took more drugs in order to wean himself off the booze. When the problem didn't go away he returned to his doctor. 'What's the fucking trouble here? I'm not drinking and still the comas. What's wrong? I want it sorted out.' Asked if he ever took drugs Harris replied, 'No, never touch the stuff.' The doctor was confused, unable to pinpoint the problem, so asked what Harris took in place of alcohol. 'Oh I use that white stuff, up me nose. I smoke some weed, that kind of thing. But I never take drugs. I wouldn't be caught dead taking sleeping pills or aspirin or any of that muck.'

The comas – and sometimes fits – continued. One in LA was so bad that Ann rushed her husband to hospital. Doctors were so concerned by his condition they informed his family that there was little hope of survival. He was placed on a life support machine and newspapers around the world started compiling his obituary. Even a priest was rushed to his bedside to administer the last rites. When Harris woke to see the man offer him a rosary he said, 'Father, if you are going to hear my confession, prepare to be here for days. By the end of it, I can guarantee you will very much regret your vow of celibacy.' The priest bolted.

Harris pulled through. When he got back home, traumatized and frightened, he flushed $6,000 worth of coke down the toilet. 'The doctors said if my cardiovascular system hadn't been so strong I would have died.'

But the years of boozing were catching up with Harris and one morning in January 1978 he woke up and declared, 'This is it. I'm stopping drinking for life.' Ann laughed; she'd heard it all before. But Harris was serious this time and there was a reason for it. His hangovers were getting worse. 'Sometimes they would last for three days.' But mostly it was because of Burton. On the set of *The Wild Geese* Harris had seen a man full of courage in his battle to stop drinking. 'But there was agony and pain in his abstinence. I thought, well I'm beyond that stage. I was as bad as him in the early 70s, so why carry on and get that way again.' Talking on location, the Welshman had regaled Harris with tales of their three previous meetings; Harris could remember only the one. 'And the stories he tells about the other two meetings are hilarious and totally unprintable. So what's the point of doing things that only other people get a kick out of? That's not leading a life at all. After all, your life is your memories. So what life have I had?' Some of the crew on *Geese* had also worked on *Mutiny on the Bounty* and were saying things like, 'Remember the day you and Brando did so and so?' Or, 'Remember when you and Trevor Howard went to such and such a place?' Trouble was, Harris didn't remember any of it. 'That shocked me. They were hilarious stories and I didn't even have the joy of remembering my own exploits.'

Nervous Harris underwent medical checks and everything inside seemed to be OK. 'I was ahead of the game, so I stopped. The crazy period of my life is over. Maybe things won't be as exciting in the same way, but at least I'll be able to remember them the next day.'

In January 1979 Harris walked into a bar to celebrate a year off the booze. 'And I drank myself stupid.' He'd noticed that the barman had recognized him and was probably wondering if it was true that Richard Harris drank as much as the press made out. So there was sometimes within Harris an element of him trying to live up to his own reputation. 'It taught me a lesson. I couldn't get out of bed for two days after that.'

Like Harris's and Burton's, Peter O'Toole's career was in poor shape come the end of the decade, making films like *Power Play* (1978), a lacklustre drama about a coup d'etat in a mythical country, and *Zulu Dawn* (1979), a star laden sequel of sorts to the classic, and much better, *Zulu*, that no one really wanted to see. With the rise in the 70s of directors like Scorsese and Spielberg and a new breed of American acting personified by the likes of Dustin Hoffman and Robert De Niro, O'Toole's theatrical performance style looked positively prehistoric and was affecting the kind of films he was being asked to appear in. O'Toole never had much truck with 'gibberish spouting' method actors. 'When you're playing Hamlet and you and Horatio are up on the battlements, Horatio says, "But, look, the morn in russet mantle clad/walks o'er the dew of yon high eastward hill." Well, it doesn't! You're looking at Charlie the prop man with a fag in his gob. It's pretend, for God's sake!'

O'Toole was drifting out of fashion with little prospect of ever again attaining the fame he commanded in the 60s. Then suddenly along came the role that brought him back to public prominence: Eli Cross, a maverick director who hires a criminal on the run as a stunt man on his new movie. The man behind the story, director Richard Rush, had been a fan of O'Toole for years and couldn't understand why he was being used so badly in film.

Desperate to land his favourite actor for his pet project, *The Stunt Man*, Rush got himself invited to a party he knew O'Toole was attending. 'I met him there, and we chatted for half of the evening,' remembers Rush. 'I never brought up the screenplay because it seemed like such a tacky thing to do at a party. When he walked out the door I remember saying to myself, "You chicken shit bastard, why the hell didn't you mention it?" Then fate interceded. It so happened that an actor O'Toole had come to the party with was a fan of one of my pictures and on the way out to the car told O'Toole, "You know that guy has done some very interesting films," and he mentioned *Freebie and the Bean*. O'Toole came dashing in and said to me, "Did you direct *Freebie and the Bean*?" I said, "yes," and he said, "I'm crazy about that picture." So I said, "I've got a screenplay for you." A week later he called me after reading it. "I'm a literate and intelligent man, and unless you let me do your film I will kill you." Which I thought was about the best answer one can possibly get.'

By the late 70s though Hollywood executives considered O'Toole commercial death, his movies hadn't taken a dime at the box office for years and Rush faced a major battle convincing his backers that O'Toole was the man for the job. 'There was no chance of yielding on my part. Once O'Toole said yes the picture had to go with him as far as I was concerned.' Rush was also warned about the star's reputation for being difficult on set. 'But Peter had a deified position in my mind that placed him above all of those trivialities. As it turned out he was an absolute dream to work with. You couldn't ask for a more perfect working companion. It was like having a Stradivarius to play that was quite willing to be played.' This was a view shared by the cast and crew. Barbara Hershey, his co-star, put it best: 'When you meet Peter O'Toole, he does not disappoint.'

Much has been written about O'Toole basing the character of the rather crackpot and tyrannical movie director Eli Cross on his old *Lawrence* collaborator David Lean. O'Toole was certainly instrumental in refining the role of Cross, though it didn't change overly much from Rush's own original conception. O'Toole was also careful to select the right costume. Every morning he'd go to Rush with a new set of clothes and the director would offer suggestions. 'One day Peter came to me and said, "How's this?" and I said, "That's it, that's exactly the look I've been after, the Americanization of Peter O'Toole." And I didn't realize that he was dressed exactly as I was and it wasn't until noon that day that I finally figured that out. The rest of the crew were aware of it and it caused some amusement.'

In the words of O'Toole, *The Stunt Man* was not released, 'It escaped.' No one in the States would touch the film at first. 'It didn't fit into the wrapper that the distributors had prepared that they send their hamburgers out in,' says Rush. 'They would always say when they saw the film, what is it, is it a comedy, is it a drama, is it an action adventure? Is it a satire? And of course I would say, yes! It's all those things.'

Shot during 1978, *The Stunt Man* finally saw daylight in 1980 and the critics raved. Single-handedly it resurrected O'Toole's movie career and remains a cult favourite. It also earned him another Oscar nomination. 'He was staying at my house at the time of the academy awards,' recalls Rush. 'And he came out of his room that morning and said, "I am a movie star!" He was getting in the mood for the ceremony.'

Today Rush recalls fondly his time with O'Toole. 'He was great fun to work with because he's such a bright man and such an eagerly enthusiastic man about everything in life. He had a great sense of humour.' The poster art for *The Stunt Man* was a devil figure sitting on a director's chair looking through a camera. Originally it was drawn as a dwarf-like devil but then changed into a graceful Peter O'Toole devil. Rush thought it best to show this image to O'Toole first in order to get his approval. 'So I sent him a copy and he called me back and said that he took one look at the picture of this devil with that massive tail thrusting forward between his legs and said, "How did you know?"'

Since *Tommy* Oliver Reed and Keith Moon had continued their rabble-rousing friendship. Once in Los Angeles they kidnapped David Puttnam as a prank. The British film producer was leaving the Beverly Wilshire Hotel when he was grabbed from behind and bundled into a waiting car, which then sped off onto the public highway. 'It was mad,' Puttnam later recalled. 'They were laughing and it was stupid and edgy. I knew I could handle Keith, but the two of them together I certainly couldn't handle.'

It wasn't just the playful side of Moon that appealed to Reed; he also must have identified with the violent streak that ran through the drummer like fat through bacon. Sitting in a pub one afternoon Moon whispered gently into Reed's ear, 'I'm going to chuck that table through the window.' Ollie watched as the musician hoisted the table on his shoulders and demolished the entire window frame. Reed's own violent nature was much in evidence at this time. One of his favourite haunts of the late 70s was Stringfellows nightclub where he enjoyed a game that he christened 'head butting'. Each player was required to smash his head against his opponent until one collapsed or surrendered. A regular victim was The Who's bass player John Entwistle, who, after being knocked out three times, pleaded with the nightclub's owner Peter Stringfellow to either ban the game or bar Ollie.

Reed could also behave just as outrageously in public as Moon. At London's Grovesnor House Hotel he turned a soda siphon on himself and other celebrities attending a charity boxing match. He then climbed into the ring and entertained everyone with his own version of 'The Stripper'. Another time he was in a posh restaurant in France with a friend and there was no sign of the waiter. Growing irritable Reed wanted to leave but was persuaded to hang on. Half an hour later they'd still not been served. 'Right,' said Ollie. 'I'll show you how to get some service.' He picked up a chair and hurled it through a window and into the street. Within seconds an irate manager and five waiters had surrounded the table. 'Ah yes,' said Ollie. 'I'll have some fish soup please.'

By 1978 Keith Moon was well past his devilish peak and had grown increasingly dependent on booze. Ironically the prescription drugs he'd been given to wean him off alcohol ended up killing him. On September 6th he attended a party thrown by Paul McCartney. It would be his final fling. The following day Moon died in a London flat. The post mortem found 32 pills in his system, 26 of which were undissolved. Reed was devastated when he heard the news of his friend's passing, but can't have been very surprised.

Reed had much more to worry about anyway, like the fact the films he was making, turkeys like *A Touch of the Sun* (1979), by remaining unreleased weren't even getting the chance to flop. This hopeless thriller was shot in Zambia and about the only good thing to come out of it was the decision by Reed to go off on a safari holiday to nearby South Africa. In one town he befriended a white farmer who invited him back to his farm. The whisky came out and the two men got steadily pissed. Reed mentioned the fact that he was on safari and the farmer explained that he'd once been a white hunter. 'Oh really,' replied Reed fascinated. 'I used to be in the army and I was a sniper.' Reed's porky pies impressed the farmer so much that he produced a rifle and pointed to a clothesline with some pegs on it 40 yards away. 'Do you think you could hit one of those?' Still bullshitting Reed said, 'Which one would you like me to hit?' 'The second one from the right,' said the farmer. Reed picked up the rifle, took aim and fired through the window. To his – and everybody else's – utter amazement he scored a bullseye. 'Wow man that was fantastic. I've never seen shooting like that,' the farmer hollered, getting to his feet. 'Do you think you could shoot this cigarette out of my hand?' Reed figured that since he could hit a clothes peg from 40 yards, a fag a few feet away would be a doddle. Reed aimed and fired and hit the man straight through the hand. The farmer just stood there, blood pumping from the wound. Reed was about to leg it when the farmer announced, 'That was fantastic, man. You were only an inch out.'

Things picked up slightly with an appearance in a moderately good horror film called *The Brood* (1979), directed by cult favourite David Cronenberg. Filming on location in Toronto, Ollie enjoyed a four-hour lunch on one of his days off, during which he personally drank five bottles of wine. He decided to walk back to his hotel sans trousers, just a shirt, tie and shoes. When stopped by a pair of bemused police officers Ollie asked, 'You mean you can't walk the streets of Toronto with your trousers off at Christmas?' Both policemen shook their heads, to which Reed confirmed that he didn't give a brass monkey what they thought. He was escorted to his hotel room.

A few weeks later Reed was guilty of wrecking a pub. He'd challenged the bar's regular drinkers to an arm wrestling competition that descended into a fistfight. Arrested, he spent a night in jail, putting his shoes outside the door of the cell to be cleaned, and later apologized to the court for his behaviour. He even sent flowers to the police; a gentleman to the last.

The Blotto Eighties

Richard Burton took a massive gamble at the start of the new decade by returning as King Arthur in a new theatrical production of *Camelot* that was set for a year-long tour round America. The show was a hit with both public and critics alike and played to standing ovations every night. Highly gratified Burton wondered why audiences were responding in such frenzy. 'Is it that the audience know so much about me from my highly publicized and infamous past?' he mused in his diary.

Off the booze Burton's mind was rarely off the subject. He wrote this in his diary: 'Ah! How I'd love the panacea of a drink now, a double vodka martini straight down and the warm flood of painkiller hitting the stomach and then the brain and an hour of sweetly melancholy euphoria. I shall have a Tab instead – disgusting.'

Occasionally he did drink, only moderately, but sometimes that was enough. He only drank wine, steering clear of spirits, depending on his will power. One evening, with *Camelot* scheduled to open in just two days' time, he dined with its creator Alan Jay Lerner. The waiter was taking their order and Burton said, 'I think I'll have a vodka and martini.' Then he looked over at Lerner. 'Richard, don't you look at me. You can have anything you want; because I know you won't let this play down.' That gave Burton pause and he called back the waiter: 'Well never mind, perhaps I'll have some Perrier.'

Sadly everyone was watching and waiting to see if Burton would succumb to the demon drink. A week after *Camelot* had opened in New York the curtain came down halfway through the first act. Burton was slurring his speech and staggering about the stage incapable. 'Give him another drink,' someone cried out from the stalls. The understudy took over but hundreds walked out demanding their money back. Scenting blood photographers camped on Burton's hotel doorstep while the papers debated whether he was back on the piss for good. The excuse when it came was flimsy: he'd taken a mixture of drugs that had made him ill. In truth, Burton had indulged in a couple of glasses of red wine with Richard Harris over lunch that afternoon, so by the evening was totally zonked. He called the producer the next day saying it would never happen again.

The next night he was back on stage, terrified about the reception he would get from an audience who all would have read the papers. The moment he set foot on the stage there was a massive roar that turned into a three and a half minute ovation. 'I just stood there, and I could feel the audience supporting me and the affection and the warmth,' Burton said afterwards. 'It was one of the most extraordinary experiences I have ever had in the theatre.'

Curiously it wasn't the booze that destroyed Richard Harris's marriage to Ann Turkel, just a gradual parting of the ways. God knows she'd felt like walking out years before. Life became an exhausting round of picking up the pieces after him: flying to a film set in Montreal where he'd walked off because he didn't like the script; breaking up a fight at their home in the Bahamas. Such incidents might have drawn them closer, instead they spent less and less time together and Ann finally decided to leave. 'My health couldn't take it any more.' Inevitably in 1981 the couple divorced, but they never severed their relationship, often meeting up in New York or London and chatting on the phone most days. 'It was like we were still married,' Ann said.

Harris blamed divorce number two on nobody but himself; he knew it was his behaviour that had driven away the women he most loved in his life. Harris was never going to be the type of husband who did the washing up, played with the kids, put his feet up and watched the telly on the couch. Ann and before her Elizabeth knew this; their mistake was to think they could ever change him. 'I have made 70 movies in my life,' Harris once confessed, 'and been miscast twice – as a husband.'

Harris also knew he'd failed pretty miserably over the years as a father, too. Only much later did he come to realize how hard it must have been for his sons to read of his exploits in the newspapers while still at school. Many a time they'd ring up home and say, 'Mum, what's dad doing? He's in the papers again. He was in jail last night and who was that woman he was with?' Although he later developed a close friendship with his children Harris felt guilty for the remainder of his life at being an absent father.

Arguably Harris's nadir as a film performer was his execrable turn in the infamous Bo Derek Tarzan movie. Bo first encountered Harris on the set of *Orca Killer Whale* and never forgot him. 'We'd go out for dinner or to a bar, and you wouldn't want to go to sleep at night, you'd just want to sit and listen to his stories. On the set, he'd tell stories right up to "Action!" then give some incredible performance and then go back to his story.' She also saw the darker side of the Irishman. 'Richard would often end up punching one of his drinking buddies. I'd find out because they'd come in the next day with a black eye, but they'd be buddies again and go drinking the next night.' This didn't deter Bo from casting Harris in *Tarzan the Ape Man* (1981), as Jane's father, lost in deepest Africa and tracked down by his daughter.

He was still hitting the bottle, and the production was held up several times when Harris overdid it and collapsed. He also behaved rather eccentrically on location in Sri Lanka, where the heat was unbearable. Not giving a stuff for convention Harris would turn up minus trousers and sans underpants at the lunch buffet with his undercarriage swinging about, saying, 'Excuse my balls, it's just such a lovely day.' His larking around concealed a growing malaise about making movies; the whole process now annoyed and, worse, bored him. *Tarzan* was a 44-day shoot and on his first night Harris opened his diary and wrote: '43 days left.' He was seriously considering jacking acting in altogether.

While Harris endured his film nadir Peter O'Toole was about to embark upon the most controversial and embarrassing episode of his entire career, and also one of the all-time great theatrical disasters. Not for nothing do actors say that productions of *Macbeth* are cursed. At a preview of Laurence Olivier's 1937 stage version his sword broke during a fight routine and a fragment flew off into the audience, striking a spectator who promptly died of a heart attack. When Alec Guinness took on the role in the 1940s he fared little better when the entire set caught fire. O'Toole's efforts, characteristically, were to eclipse everything before it.

Returning to the stage after a 17-year absence O'Toole was aware that the role of Macbeth was a killer for any actor and required great physical stamina. Having only recently undergone major surgery and describing his current career as 'tepid', O'Toole was out to prove himself again. He also believed totally in the theatrical superstition that Macbeth brought bad luck to companies who staged it and refused to refer to the play by any name other than 'Harry Lauder'. He'd rush around touching wood whenever someone mentioned Macbeth and at one point curled himself into a moaning foetal ball on the stage imploring, 'Say Harry Lauder, please or we'll all die.'

The play was put on at the Old Vic in London, run by actor Timothy West. But O'Toole was to have total artistic control over the production. It soon emerged that the two men were poles apart both in temperament and in their approach to theatre. It didn't help that O'Toole always addressed West as Eddie Waring, the famous rugby commentator. Their relationship was akin to a warring husband and wife living under the same roof but ripe for divorce. It didn't bode well for a happy working arrangement.

An already nervous Bryan Forbes, hired by O'Toole as director, was beginning to harbour grave misgivings too, particularly over his star's obsession with making this the bloodiest *Macbeth* on record. 'Do you know how many times the word "blood" appears in the text, old darling?' O'Toole said to Forbes one day, volunteering the information that, 'If you stab a living man, blood spurts seventeen feet.' He also proudly proclaimed that he was having a double-handed sword made of the finest Toledo steel for his duel with McDuff and when this fearsome weapon finally arrived at the theatre the actor playing McDuff visibly paled. Oddly HRH Princess Margaret paid a visit to one rehearsal and during a break the subject of blood came up yet again in conversation. 'What you need is some Kensington gore,' the princess told O'Toole, meaning the stuff deployed in the old Hammer horror films. 'We use it all the time in St John ambulance demonstrations. It's very realistic.' Forbes saw O'Toole's eyes light up.

As the opening night loomed relations between West and O'Toole went nuclear. They spoke only through intermediaries. O'Toole hated the posters and tore them all down, and when West complained that the production was going over budget O'Toole had him barred from final rehearsals. Poor

Forbes was caught in the middle. West defied O'Toole and secretly watched the last dress rehearsal and was appalled by what he witnessed. He pleaded with Forbes that radical changes had to be made to avert a full-scale disaster but the director felt that to confront O'Toole 'would provoke an explosion that could destroy us all'.

Worse was about to happen. On the opening night as the audience took their seats Forbes went into O'Toole's dressing room and was stunned to find him stark naked except for a Gauloise in his mouth. 'Peter, old son, aren't you leaving it a bit late to get into costume?' he said, trying to remain calm. 'Can't wear them, darling,' replied O'Toole. 'They're hopeless.' 'Ah!' Forbes exclaimed, panic taking over him. 'We don't have much alternative, do we? But let me see what I can do.'

Outside Forbes grabbed fellow cast member Brian Blessed, a close friend of O'Toole's; he was Forbes's only hope. After hearing the sorry tale Blessed said, 'Do you think his bottle's gone?' The thought was too hideous to contemplate for Forbes. 'God help us if it has.' Blessed shook his head: 'Leave him to me. Can't promise what he'll look like, but I'll get him on.'

By some miracle Blessed dragged him onto the stage that night, haphazardly dressed though O'Toole was, including for some bizarre reason jogging trousers and gym shoes. 'There was madness in the theatre that night on both sides of the curtain,' Forbes later said. Several journalists tried to get Forbes to admit that O'Toole was drunk, but Forbes knew that since surgery the actor had not touched a drop.

There was also O'Toole's much promised bloodbath. One of the stagehands had been sent on a shopping errand to purchase several gallons of fake gore and O'Toole was slapping it on with wild abandon. Traditionally for the scene in which Macbeth returns after the off-stage killing of the King the actor soaks his hands in 'blood', not O'Toole, he immersed himself in a crimson-filled zinc bath. The effect produced a mixture of horror and hysteria throughout the audience. Forbes wrote later, 'From that moment onwards the play was doomed.' During the same scene on another night, as O'Toole came down the stairs, dripping with blood, an ambulance howled all the way up Waterloo Road. 'I got the giggles,' O'Toole later confessed. 'The audience got the giggles. It was bloody marvellous.'

The first intimation that a full-blown public disaster was on the cards was when a reporter turned up in Bryan Forbes's kitchen the next morning and a TV news crew parked itself outside the door wanting reaction to the news that West, and by implication the Old Vic, had publicly disowned the production. Perhaps for the first time ever a play took over the front pages of the national press, while the critics lambasted the production, principally O'Toole's performance, in a way few in the business could ever remember. 'The performance is not so much downright bad as heroically ludicrous. The voice is pure Bette Davis in her Baby Jane mood, the manner is Vincent Price hamming up a Hammer horror,' said the *Daily Mail*, while *The Sunday Times* critic called it, 'A milestone in the history of coarse acting. Mr O'Toole's performance was deranged.'

O'Toole took the abuse unbowed, despite his Hampstead home being besieged next morning by reporters. His housekeeper had told him the bad news that the reviews were stinkers and that there were a couple of journalists outside the front door. 'When I opened it, there were about 100. What could I do? My shaver is electric so I could not cut my throat.' That evening O'Toole fought his way into the theatre through crowds besieging the box office for tickets that had already sold out. The production had transcended awfulness and, like a car crash, everybody wanted to see it. 'It's all wonderful,' he said, by way of greeting his bewildered cast. 'This is what the theatre is all about.' Katharine Hepburn agreed, phoning O'Toole with the advice, 'If you're going to have a disaster, have a big one.'

When Burton heard that O'Toole had taken a pasting he called him up from America while still touring *Camelot*. 'I hear you've had a bit of stick from the critics.' 'Yes,' O'Toole replied. 'How are the houses?' Burton asked. 'Packed,' said O'Toole. 'Then remember, my boy, you are the most original actor to come out of Britain since the war and fuck the critics.' 'Thank you,' said O'Toole. Burton went on, 'Think of every four letter obscenity, six, eight, ten and twelve letter expletives and ram them right up their envious arses in which I'm sure there is ample room.' 'Thank you,' said O'Toole, no doubt touched. 'Good night, Peter. Don't give in and I love you,' declared Burton. 'I won't,' said O'Toole. 'And it's mutual.' 'Good night again,' Burton finished. 'Good night Richard and thank you.' It was like the bloody Waltons.

Things went from bad to worse on the third night when a bomb scare halted the performance temporarily. After a quick search it was deemed a hoax and the audience was let back in. Then as the curtain was about to be raised a second bomb threat was received. 'You didn't take me seriously, did you,' said an ominous phone voice. 'It'll go off in the interval.' The performance was cancelled. This merely added to the play's notoriety and tickets started to change hands at incredible prices; the West End had seen nothing like it. *Macbeth* went on to sell out its entire London run and played to capacity crowds during its subsequent six-month tour round the provinces.

Months later, as the scandal died down, O'Toole was able to look back more philosophically on the event and recognize it for what it was – a total fuck up. 'The opening night was a fiasco. When I think of it, my nose bleeds.' O'Toole admitted that banging into scenery, forgetting his lines, and wearing trainers was perhaps not the best way to approach Shakespeare.

Oliver Reed could only dream of the sort of headlines O'Toole was getting. His career was in the mire, with appearances in movies nobody wanted to see like *Venom* (1981), actually quite a suspenseful little thriller about an escaped snake inside a house where a hostage situation is being played out. Directed by Piers Haggard, taking over at short notice from Tobe Hooper (he of *Texas Chainsaw Massacre* notoriety) who left the production under mysterious circumstances, the film was chock full of larger than life personalities (polite terminology for eccentrics or drunks), including Sarah Miles and Nicol Williamson. And there was Ollie, of course. 'Oliver was one of the finest film actors that we had,' recalls Haggard. 'He had enormous power. But he was a handful. And he would test you all the time. When I met Oliver for the first time in the canteen at Elstree studios he played a trick on me, pretending that he was going to walk out and leave the film because I'd insulted him by saying something completely spurious. But it was just a hoax. He was just testing me.'

Reed's co-star was the equally outrageous and near psychotic Klaus Kinski. The two actors, according to Haggard, detested each other on sight, 'which was a bit difficult because they had most of their scenes together.' By the close of shooting Haggard thought the black mamba was the nicest person on the set. 'Oliver used to amuse himself by going to Klaus Kinski's trailer and shaking it. Don't forget Oliver was as strong as an ox. So he'd shake Kinski's trailer and shout, "You fucking Nazi bastard!" And then

Kinski would come out trembling with rage and swearing back as best he could.' Actually Kinski was born in Poland and was an immigrant to Germany, 'But he passed for a Nazi in Oliver's eyes,' says Haggard.

The film was funded by the Guinness family and one day some of its more auspicious members arranged to visit the set. This of course coincided with a major slanging match between Reed and Kinski that was taking place on the top of the set. 'I was on the studio floor,' Haggard remembers, all too vividly. 'And you could hear – "You fucking Nazi bastard" and "You fucking English cunt." They were effing and blinding. Oliver was clearly goading Klaus, who unfortunately had no sense of humour. Oliver, on the other hand, had a fabulous sense of humour, very wicked, but he definitely liked a laugh, and he definitely liked a laugh at Klaus Kinski's expense. Anyway, just at the point where the Guinness family, led by our producer Martin Bregman, walked in the door, Oliver and Klaus came hurtling down the stairs; you thought bloody murder was going to be done. And Martin turned round and said to the family, their nanny, the children, Lord this and Lady blah blah, "I think we'll go and have a look in the other studio," and led them all out as quick as he could.'

Next Reed was stuck in Iraq making the forgettable *The Great Question* (1983) in what was essentially a war zone; at the time Iraq and Iran were at loggerheads and occasionally sending missiles over the border, but that didn't stop Ollie having a good time, especially since he'd only recently discovered that in his forties his capacity for booze was going up, not down.

One night Reed joined the crew for numerous drinks in the hotel bar and, looking in the nearby restaurant, saw a Texas oil billionaire whom he knew. Jumping up, obviously drunk as a skunk, he rushed upstairs to his room. 'When he came back down he was wearing a western shirt and cowboy boots and walked John Wayne style into the restaurant to see his buddy,' recalls stunt man Vic Armstrong. 'Inside he gave this guy a Texas handshake as he called it, which basically means lifting your leg up and smashing your cowboy boot down on the table. So Ollie walked up to this guy's table, surrounded by women and other dignitaries, and smash, all the cutlery and glass went flying in the air. Suddenly Ollie looked at the guy and it wasn't his mate at all, it was some Arab with his harem, deeply offended that this westerner had come stamping on his table and upset everything. The police were called and Ollie was arrested. He didn't go to jail thank God.'

Back home Broome Hall continued to be a huge burden on Reed's finances, but he adored the place. A regular guest was snooker ace Alex 'Hurricane' Higgins. Reed had taken up the sport and turned the chapel into a snooker room. Higgins came over to play a match there one day and was mightily impressed by the fine décor, especially an installed lemon tree that allowed him to pick his own fruit to freshen up his drinks. After the match, where Reed was annihilated, Higgins was invited to the private bar, on whose walls no framed picture was intact, for a drinking challenge. Higgins drank like he played, fast, and soon got very drunk and rather nasty and was thrown out. But Reed remained impressed by his snooker skills. 'Hurricane smashed out of his mind could beat me stone cold sober.'

The pair remained friendly for years. During another drinking session Reed put some Chanel No. 5 perfume in a glass and told Higgins it was a gorgeous malt whisky. 'Wow Alex, it's wonderful. Try that.' Higgins replied he couldn't drink whisky. 'Fucking chicken,' taunted Reed. Higgins grabbed the glass and downed it in one. His face screwed up in pain and he spat out what he could. Higgins was ill for two days. He had his revenge though by treating Reed to a Fairy Liquid crème de menthe. 'Ollie was burping bubbles for weeks.'

Famous for his own terrifying behaviour, Higgins has admitted that Reed often frightened the shit out of him. After a particularly hectic afternoon in the pub Higgins passed out in an armchair back at Ollie's home. He was rudely awoken by a real sword jabbed into his ribs. 'Get up,' growled Ollie. 'How dare you fall asleep in my company. For that insult, sir, I require satisfaction.' Higgins was thrown another sword. 'Now, sir, prepare to die.' Reed attacked with a series of mighty blows and Higgins did all he could to defend himself. 'I was genuinely scared for a moment that he had at last flipped,' said the snooker star, 'and was going to kill me.'

Higgins made the mistake of falling asleep again in Ollie's presence and this time was hunted down with an axe. He ran into his room and bolted the door but that didn't deter Reed who started chopping at the solid oak like Jack Nicholson in *The Shining*. It took him just a few minutes to weaken the wood and Higgins saw the tip of the axe peek through the door. 'I was terrified. I honestly thought I might be about to breathe my last if he got through.'

When he wasn't boozing with pals at home Ollie was at his local pub restaurant. During one lunchtime drinking binge Reed left a group of friends at their table and without them knowing climbed up a massive stone fireplace, stretched out on the chimney ledge and fell asleep. Unable to locate him Ollie's friends left and the landlord locked up for the afternoon. Six hours later Ollie woke up to the smell of food wafting into his nostrils and climbed down. Dirty and dishevelled he bowed as regally as he could to the dumbstruck diners before planting a sooty kiss on the barmaid and walking out.

Reed was just as much a menace in the grounds of his own home. Returning with his gardener from a drinking session, driving his open top Rolls-Royce, he approached the gates of Broome Hall. A mischievous grin took over. 'Let's see how fast we can get this up the drive.' He speeded up and smashed into the masonry of an old bridge. The car was a complete write-off. He got out and slammed the door. 'Never fucking liked it anyway.'

Rip-roaring weekend parties were still a regular occurrence at Broome Hall and most evening get-togethers with friends would begin with Ollie drinking a full bottle of wine from his fabled Thorhill glass. 'If anyone refuses to follow, I tend to sulk.' He loved to shock first time houseguests too by shouting at his girlfriend Jacquie when the meal arrived, 'This food is filth,' and hurling it against the wall. When she entered one evening with a big pot of gravy Reed put his shoe in it and made gravy marks all over the walls. Unable to reach the ceiling Ollie got a broom, dipped his shoe back in the gravy, popped it on the handle and covered the ceiling in dirty foot prints. After the dining room was redecorated such frivolity had to stop. One is amazed how poor Jacquie managed to survive it all, although to the press at least she confessed how she loved living with the madman because she couldn't predict anything: 'There are never two days alike.'

But as the years went by Jacquie found life at Broome Hall increasingly difficult to cope with. It all came to an end on New Year's Eve when Reed couldn't wait for it to become midnight, so he put the hands of the clock on the kitchen wall to twelve o'clock and bellowed, 'Now it's midnight, now it's New Year,' and, getting out his shot gun, blasted the time piece off the wall, bits of it ricocheting round the kitchen causing more damage and mess. It was the final straw. 'That's it,' said Jacquie, and left. Reed sold Broome Hall within a month of her departure.

Richard Burton continued to tread the boards in his American tour of *Camelot* but was growing increasingly weak and ill and the pain became intolerable. Witnesses told of how the sheer will power Burton employed to combat the pain, not to mention the eight performances a week to packed houses, would have killed a lesser being. But the man was in a terrible state; even the pills he took to deaden the pain caused nausea. Sometimes in between scenes he'd dart off stage to be sick. He also suffered from a pinched nerve in his right arm, which often meant he couldn't even lift Excalibur. Still he battled on. When the tour hit LA, however, Burton survived only six performances. When the end came it was sudden. 'I was sitting in my dressing room. I had my cape on and my crown on my head and I was staring blankly into the mirror. I was paralyzed.' At the hospital it was agreed that a back operation was the only course of action, but Burton was so underweight and exhausted he was sent to rest in order to build himself up.

It was almost a month later that a team of top surgeons opened Burton up and discovered that his entire spinal column was coated with crystallized alcohol, which had to be scraped off before they could rebuild the vertebrae in his neck. It was a dangerous operation that carried with it the risk of permanent paralysis. Susan was by his side, as she'd been throughout the *Camelot* tour. Elizabeth Taylor sent flowers. The world waited. The news was good, Burton was out of danger and two weeks later was released from hospital, though still taking a considerable amount of medication to kill the pain. Months later he collapsed again, this time undergoing an emergency operation for a perforated ulcer. Released from hospital, because of the ulcer Burton was unable to take the painkillers for his back, so had to cope with even greater discomfort.

It was obvious to everyone that the star's touring days were over, but *Camelot* was booked up for months in advance. A replacement was needed, but who the hell could replace Richard Burton?

Richard Harris was in New York when he received a frantic phone call. The *Camelot* producers had come to the conclusion that the movie King

Arthur was their only salvation. Problem was, Harris had decided to take a break from acting. 'But Burton himself has requested you to take over from him,' said the producers. 'If it's true,' Harris answered, 'let him call and ask me personally.' Later that day Harris's phone rang. It was Burton. 'Dickie, you'd be doing us all a favour.' How could Harris refuse?

Harris hadn't set foot on a stage for nearly 20 years, but he needn't have been nervous about his return; the tour was a huge success, fractured only by Harris's own illness. In Detroit he collapsed in the middle of the first act. When a call for a doctor in the house came up on the loud speaker 28 people queued up outside his dressing room to examine him and ask for autographs. In hospital the diagnosis was not good. 'I think if it goes on like this you have about 18 months to live,' a doctor said. Harris asked what he had to do to survive. 'Stop the piss.'

Harris's intake was as prodigious as ever, two bottles of vodka a day or 25 pints of beer in a single session. Harris knew he was drinking himself into oblivion. Once he collapsed suddenly in the street; a few days later he lost consciousness during a dinner with friends. They urged him to check into a specialist New York clinic for blood tests and it was here, finally, that the life-threatening hypoglycaemia, the root of years of suffering, was revealed. A chronic condition, hypoglycaemia involves a lack of sugar production in the body. 'I'd fucked up my pancreas when I was drinking too much.' The organ was releasing too much insulin. His blackouts weren't the after effects of booze sessions, but insulin comas. 'And one day,' his doctor warned, 'you won't come out of it.'

The medical verdict was that booze had to go; otherwise he was staring death in the face. One summer evening in 1981 he walked into Washington's Jockey Club for one last drink. On the wine list there were two bottles of Chateau Margaux 1957 at £600 each. He ordered them and slowly and methodically drank the lot. 'I treated them like you'd treat making love to the most gorgeous woman in the world. If you knew you only had one orgasm left, you'd say, "I'm holding it up, babe, because I don't want this to end."'

Harris was true to his word this time and friends were astonished when he kept the pledge for 10 years. 'The liquor industry went into a panic when they heard I wasn't drinking any more,' Harris joked. 'Have you noticed how much the shares have dropped?' In the early 90s he did return to the booze, but only moderately, having a glass of Guinness which remained his daily companion till the day he died. Friends said that he became a different man once the demon drink was conquered, more mature and reflective. The only problem was that much of his past was unknown to him. Whole days, even months, over the last 20 years had been erased from his memory banks because of booze. He kept running into people who'd say, 'Remember me?' and Harris would answer, 'I've never seen you before in my life.' They then would have to explain things like, 'But Richard, you spent four weeks at my house.' One man even told Harris that he'd proposed marriage to him. 'He should have accepted,' the actor joked. 'I pay very good alimony.' One of the reasons Harris gave for turning down a £1m advance to write his autobiography was, 'Because I was far too drunk to ever really recall what happened.'

Back on the *Camelot* tour Harris found it punishing but satisfying. He was nearly killed during one rehearsal but for a diving stagehand who bundled him clear of a rapidly descending one-ton piece of scenery. His life long love affair with booze had also caught up with him. One critic in his review of the show said, 'Let me describe Richard Harris to you. For those who may not have seen his movies, from his neck down he's built like an Adonis, but from the neck up he looks like a dried-out prune.'

Spurred on by his success in *Camelot* Harris negotiated to buy the touring rights. The deal was the canniest and most rewarding of his life. Over the next six years *Camelot* earned $92m, of which Harris personally grossed almost $8m. It put him in the wonderful position of making movies only if he wanted to. 'What *Camelot* has given me is fuck off money,' he said, with a hint of hard-earned pride.

After the very public humiliation of *Macbeth* Peter O'Toole's next film project went a long way to rejuvenating his reputation. *My Favorite Year* (1982) was produced by Mel Brooks's film company and based on his own experiences when, as a young comedy writer on a TV show in the 50s, he was drafted in to keep Errol Flynn sober and out of trouble until he'd made his guest star appearance. Flynn was a notorious rabble-rouser and drunk and was frequently banned from drinking on film sets. Necessity being the mother of invention, the savvy star soon developed a solution which was to inject oranges with vodka and eat them during his breaks. Indeed, Flynn's drinking at Warner Brothers, where he was under contract, got so bad that he directly influenced the studio's policy on serving alcohol during studio hours. On the set of 70s disaster movie *The Swarm* Michael Caine, Henry Fonda and Ben Johnson were enjoying lunch at the Warner Brothers commissary when they were joined by Olivia de Havilland. There were complaints that no booze was being served. 'That's because of Errol Flynn,' said de Havilland. 'He used to get so drunk he couldn't work so Mister Warner said no more booze.'

The script of *My Favorite Year* also drew heavily upon another Hollywood acting legend, that of John Barrymore, who once said, 'You can't drown yourself in drink. I've tried; you float.' Barrymore was the movie's earliest hellraiser, a distinguished actor who boozed and whored like a good 'un and who sired a family of thesps that still permeates Hollywood; Drew Barrymore is his granddaughter. Barrymore was a legend and hero-worshipped by many, not least Errol Flynn. When Flynn retreated to a house up in the Hollywood Hills it became a refuge of sorts for Barrymore and every night the old guy stood by the bedroom window and urinated out of it in the hope of spraying the Warner Brothers studios in the valley below.

The best Barrymore story goes like this: after a few drinks too many at a popular Los Angeles bar the great man stumbled by mistake into the ladies' room. Slashing away merrily in a conveniently located pot plant he was disturbed by a female visitor. 'How dare you! This is for ladies.' Turning around, his penis still exposed, Barrymore responded, 'So, madam, is this. But every now and again, I'm compelled to run a little water through it.'

To many O'Toole seemed perfect casting for the role of a sozzled and faded Hollywood film star. At first he refused the offer, 'Because of the possible danger that someone might think that this washed-up, clapped-out drunken old fart was actually me.' In fact so allergic to drink had O'Toole become that even a drop of it passing his lips could prove dangerous. One scene in *My Favorite Year* had his character waking up in bed with a stewardess and immediately downing one of those mini airline-size bottles of scotch. A whole case of little bottles had been prepared, each one emptied of liquor, washed and re-filled with coloured water, but somehow a real bottle slipped through and when O'Toole drank from it during a take it made him so ill he had to leave the set for several hours.

In the end he enjoyed the filming immensely, but for one strange incident that occurred during a scene in which a crowd of extras playing crazed fans mobbed his fictional film star. 'I don't think I've witnessed anything quite so bizarre in my career. God only knows what was on their minds. These extras – these animals, as it turned out – were supposed to simply mill around me, very passively I might emphasize. Instead of that they jumped all over me like rabid dogs. One cheeky prick took hold of me by the ear and wouldn't let go. I mean, he would not let go! I finally had to bash him in order to get free. They went absolutely bonkers. I think they'd been in Hollywood so long, they'd lost their grip on reality.'

Playing a faded star must have given O'Toole pause to ponder his own rapidly approaching old age. 'One of the lovely things about being an actor is that you can go on forever, although I have no intention of uttering my last words on the stage in fucking Macclesfield or something. No thank you. Room service and a couple of depraved young women will do me quite nicely for an exit.' *My Favorite Year* earned for O'Toole yet another Oscar nomination.

Sadly Oliver Reed had never truly conquered Hollywood; though the chance had at one time presented itself to him on a silver platter, only for it to be totally spurned. 'He was offered the Robert Shaw role in *Jaws* and turned it down,' reveals Michael Winner. 'Had Oliver done *Jaws* he'd have been a big star, a serious star, not sort of wobbling about starring in British films. But he was nervous about going to Hollywood, he was nervous of being where he didn't feel secure. Drinking of course is often about insecurity. He was very shy and he needed the drink to give him confidence.'

Reed occasionally made American films, but generally inferior ones, such as the spy comedy *Condorman* (1981) starring his old *Jokers* comrade Michael Crawford. Reed was playing a Russian nasty and as time went by grew ever deeper into his character and began speaking with a heavy Russian accent. One night, on location in Switzerland, Crawford sat by himself in a local bar and saw a grim-looking Ollie barge in. 'Come here and haffff a dreeenk!' shouted Reed when he caught sight of Crawford. 'It's OK, Ollie, I'm meeting someone.' Again, he growled, 'Come here and haff a dreeenk!' 'No, Ollie, really . . .' Reed rose majestically from his seat and pressed his not inconsiderable chest against the increasingly nervous Crawford. 'Cummmmm here into Russian Embassy and haff a dreeenk, you little feathered fart!'

Crawford had no choice but to comply. 'Of course, from that moment on and throughout the rest of the film production, I was known as "Condorman, the Feathered Fart". Thank God it didn't make the billboards.' According to director Charles Jarrott, 'I think Michael was a little afraid of Oliver.'

Reed's other co-star, the glamorous Barbara Carrera, fared even worse. Reed didn't quite feel that Barbara was giving her all in the movie. For instance, they shared a scene together in a helicopter where she was supposed to be terrorized by him, but in take after take, she was entirely unable to project enough fear for Ollie's taste. 'So,' Crawford recalled, 'while they were in flight for a final shot, Ollie actually opened the 'copter door and threatened to throw her out. She had no doubt that he meant every word, and the glance of fear that crossed her face at that moment was very real.'

Jarrott, who'd worked with Burton in the 60s, was initially going to cast Klaus Kinski in the villain's role. 'Thank God I didn't! I rather looked forward to working with Reed. He was such a character and worked like a real professional. Only after the day was over, did he lift the elbow. Strange: at work he was fairly quiet; at night, he was always boozed up and boisterous. One tended to steer away from him then. He spent a day and a night on a British cruiser visiting Nice. I hear the rum flowed like water!'

The first occasion Jarrott worked with Reed was a night shoot in the Casino at Monte Carlo. Reed was immaculately dressed in a white tuxedo and his scenes went like clockwork. He was cool, stone sober. 'We finished at about 2am and I went back to my hotel. After changing and enjoying a drink, I sauntered out on to my balcony, overlooking the Mediterranean. It was a beautiful moonlit night. I glanced down at the calm sea, and noticed a white tuxedo floating away on the waves. Looking back up at the hotel I saw Ollie, stark naked, climbing from balcony to balcony. An English King Kong was abroad!'

Ollie decided to spend the Christmas of 1981 in Los Angeles. He found for a drinking companion an ex-British Army squaddie and, fuelled by whisky and beer, the pair set off for the city's Latin Quarter to search for a tattooist willing to emblazon Reed's cock with the image of two eagle's claws. A visit to several of the more orthodox establishments met with flat refusals. The cab driver ferrying them around came to the rescue. 'I know who'll do it,' he said. 'Then take me there, my good fellow,' said Reed. They travelled down side streets and alleys to a less salubrious district and stopped outside a rundown shop. Inside Reed made his request. The tattooist shook his head, unprepared to work on so vulnerable an area of the human body. At that moment the man's wife appeared. 'I'll do it,' she said. 'Make bigger, please.' Ollie had rather a nice time engineering his cock to a suitable size for the woman to work on. Two hours later he returned to his hotel room, his manhood wrapped in bloodied cotton wool.

Not long after, Reed had an eagle's head tattooed on his shoulder so when people asked why he had an eagle's head on his shoulder he could reply, 'Would you like to see where it's perched?' On holiday in the Caribbean once Ollie got carried away and, as was his usual way, flashed his prick at fellow hotel guests. Alas, the eagle's claw tattoo on his cock was interpreted as a voodoo image and he was chased out of the bar.

Ollie's forays across the Atlantic were never dull. Director Peter Medak recalls standing outside the Beverly Wilshire Hotel when a limousine pulled up, the door opened and somebody on all fours backed out onto the pavement. 'And it was Oliver. He'd arrived at the airport at four o'clock that afternoon, he'd stopped at every bar, and now he was checking into the hotel. We fell into each other's arms and he said, "Come on let's go to the bar, they'll take the luggage upstairs." We go into the bar and within two seconds he had the bartender by his neck; they threw him out of the hotel before he could even check in. Oliver was the darkest of those hell-raisers. Oliver for no reason would start a fight. If he didn't like someone's face or someone said the wrong thing, boom.'

Ollie's dark side manifested itself even when he was in playful mood. Being interviewed in a restaurant he suddenly stood up in front of the journalist, unzipped his trousers and pissed into a half-empty champagne bottle. Finished, he zipped himself up again, placed the bottle back in the ice bucket and grinned puckishly: 'That'll give someone a shock when they pour out a glass.'

In spite of such incidents Reed claimed not to be as nasty or fierce as the press often made out. He did though admit that many of his outrageous pranks were deliberately stage-managed. It wasn't that he wanted to shock people so much as his love of cocking a snoop at the establishment and po-faced conventionality. Perhaps more than as an actor, Reed saw his role in life as that of a showman. People had come to expect him to be outrageous and he didn't like to disappoint them. Give the public what they want was his motto. Once, dining quietly with a friend in a restaurant, Reed realized that the manager was arranging for newspaper photographers to come and take photos, so Ollie obliged. 'Watch this,' he whispered to his colleague. He got up and, passing an empty table, 'accidentally' knocked into it sending the chairs and place settings flying. Next day one tabloid headline ran: 'Drunken Ollie wrecks restaurant.'

Such behaviour also derived from the fact that Reed was easily bored, like a child. While he was sitting in a pub, a woman entered collecting for charity. Ollie took off his jeans and gave them to the startled woman. He also once bet someone that he could pronounce and spell the word 'masseuse' correctly; he couldn't and for his forfeit shaved his head. And who else would own a racehorse called 'Gorn Myson'? It only raced once under that name and afterwards the relevant authorities ordered a change of name as it was unfair to hear the racing commentators apparently call out, as the horses went down the final straight, 'GO ON MY SON!' Reed even took part in the inaugural lawnmower racing championships. Unfortunately he lost control of his machine and demolished the VIP toilet tent, without injury to driver or occupant. 'Luckily, dear boy,' he said, 'because we were both seated at the time.'

By the end of 1982 Richard Burton had separated from Susan. She put most of the blame on his drinking. The final straw was a car accident that resulted in Burton being shut up in a local loony bin. Burton had enjoyed a couple of drinks in a bar near his Swiss home and driving back in his new Mercedes-Benz, up a hill, accidentally jammed the gear stick into reverse. The car went into a spin and four other vehicles smashed into it. Burton himself was thrown through the windshield. Having scrambled home Burton asked Susan to call his doctor. Instead an ambulance arrived that under her orders took him to a mental institution where he claimed he was kept for nine days. 'I thought I might actually go mad in there.' During his enforced stay a tall blonde woman accosted him in the wards. 'Follow me,' she said, and thinking it to be Susan Burton obliged. She drew him down onto a bed and they made love. 'Then I realized it wasn't Susan at all, but another patient – a nymphomaniac. They couldn't get her off me.'

When he got out, Susan announced that she was leaving him, she could no longer deal with his drinking and the burden of his ill health. Burton was now a virtual cripple, his body broken. At one stage he literally couldn't lift cutlery and had to be spoon-fed for weeks. People implored him to rest. Instead he took on the biggest and most punishing film role of his entire career, that of composer Wagner in an epic TV mini-series. The seven months of filming all over Europe, with Burton appearing in virtually every scene, was a killer, but he was determined to do it. The director was Tony Palmer. 'We filmed with Burton for 157 days and lost four days because of . . . let's call it emotional tiredness. He had a physiotherapist with him pretty well the whole time, because he knew this was going to be a long haul, which was one of the reasons he wanted to do it, he was testing himself. I think he saw the Wagner film as an opportunity to prove both to himself and to the world that he was still capable of delivering the works; a big performance.'

Another incentive was the calibre of the supporting cast, especially the chance to act opposite the theatrical knights Laurence Olivier and John Gielgud. All of them were good friends and delighted to be at last working together. 'Richard frequently said during filming, I've never had so much fun,' says Palmer.

According to Palmer, Burton knew he was an alcoholic and the director had taken advice about how to deal with alcoholics, and that it was the level of alcohol in the blood that mattered. 'I had supper with him three nights a week, every week, for seven months and he would have on the table in front of him two glasses, one filled with wine, the other filled with water. I remember one memorable dinner we shared with Olivier, and Richard was telling funny stories and Olivier was being wildly indiscreet about practically everybody you could think of, and Richard just got carried away and his hand went to the red wine. I was sitting right opposite him, watching, and I almost stopped him, but I thought, I can't, it's not my place. Within five minutes, maybe ten, but certainly no more, it was Jekyll and Hyde. So, from having first been he and Larry talking about the old times, ten minutes later Olivier was a cunt who destroyed the British theatre and destroyed his career. It was just a tirade. Olivier was extraordinary; he just sat there and watched it all. Afterwards Richard said to me, "I blew it, didn't I." I said, "Well I think you owe him an apology." And so he went to see Olivier and apologized; they kissed and made up.'

The *Wagner* crew were filming in the mountains of Austria in freezing conditions when news broke about Burton's split with Susan Hunt. He was expecting it to leak out eventually so was quite sanguine about it, but did ask Palmer if he could do his best to keep the press away. The director managed to keep a few hacks at bay but didn't count on the resourcefulness of Royal Correspondent James Whittaker, who'd just taken pictures of the pregnant Princess Diana on holiday in the Bahamas and was now heading with his photographer directly to Austria. 'I kept making diversionary tactics,' recalls Palmer, 'but they hired a bloody helicopter and they went up the mountain to where we were filming and landed and Richard said, "Don't worry I'll deal with it," and out got these two guys in their Bahamian shirts and shorts, you've never seen anything so funny. Richard agreed to pose for a photograph provided they went away. Only the photographer got his finger stuck on the camera; he couldn't take the picture because the whole thing had frozen solid and his hand had actually frozen to the camera. So they asked us if we could get the hospital helicopter to come, and we did and they, humiliated, went away.'

News about Burton's impending divorce went round the world and was music to the ears of Elizabeth Taylor who began repeatedly calling Burton's hotel room at all hours. Unable to get any sleep, Burton asked Palmer if he would mind swapping rooms with him. 'I agreed to this and nothing happened for two or three nights but then, sure enough, three o'clock in the morning the phone rang. "Oh darling, darling, I miss you so much." I let this go on for a bit and then said, "Elizabeth this is Tony Palmer, not Richard." She was desperate to get to the location, to be with Richard, she was crazy about him, always crazy about him. She was also the serious drinker; she could drink anything and anyone under the table;

including Burton. So I said to Richard, "What do I do? Do you want her here?" And he said, "If she comes, I go." So we cooked up a story. The next night she phoned again. "Elizabeth," I said. "There's one tiny little part for you in the film. It doesn't involve lines I'm afraid, but it's perfect for you." She said, "When do I start?" I said, "I'm afraid it's quite soon." She said, "That's no trouble. Can you give me a brief outline of the part?" And I said, "Well Elizabeth, it's to play the role of an Eskimo." There was a pause of a milli-second and she said, "I've always wanted to play the part of an Eskimo." Whether she knew then that it was a joke I don't know, but she never called back and I saw her about a month later and she didn't refer to it so I think she got the point that she was being sent up. Richard thought this had been brilliantly done.'

On the set of *Wagner* Burton was to meet and fall in love with the woman who would become the last person to share his life. Sally Hay was Tony Palmer's secretary and the director saw the burgeoning romance first hand. 'About a month after the story broke on Suzy Hunt, Richard sidled up to me one day and said, "I've got some letters which I need typing out, could I possibly borrow Sally one evening." I said, "Richard she's over there, go and ask her." He said, "I think I'd prefer if you could ask." So I went to Sally and explained things and she looked at me, she was a woman of the world, let's say, and said, "All right but will you promise to come and knock on my door an hour after to make sure I'm OK?" I saw her the following morning and asked what happened. "Nothing," she said. "I turned up, I wasn't even offered a cup of tea, I did the letters, went away, typed them out, brought them back, he thanked me very much and that was it." A week or so later Richard came to me again. "I've got a couple more letters." "Richard, for God's sake ask her yourself." "No, no." Well, he was courting her. He was absolutely courting her. It wasn't until the fourth or fifth occasion this had happened that I said to Sally, "What happened?" And she said, "Well, one thing led to another." I thought that was very revealing about Richard, that he was absolutely formal and proper in his intentions.'

As Burton and Sally drew up plans to marry, Liz Taylor gatecrashed once again, persuading Burton to team up for a Broadway revival of Noel Coward's *Private Lives*. Amazingly both stars were given £42,000 a week, the highest salary ever paid out on Broadway. Worth it, though, the theatre was sold out every night. The critics had a field day, however, trashing a production that was more of a circus than a show. Burton remained sober throughout, but Taylor invariably turned up late and instigated the majority of backstage squabbles and fights. The strains of her squawking, 'This is the last time I'm working with you, you cunt,' would fill the corridors. For Burton it was the last straw: 'This has proved it. I can never get together with that woman again.'

It was during that Broadway run that Burton and Sally married. 'It was the only one of my weddings at which I have been sober.' Suddenly Burton was revitalized, managing to get back into reasonably good shape and displaying a renewed intention to give up the booze for good. 'No doubt the distillers and the tobacco barons will be weeping over the loss of such a good customer.' Life was looking good, with numerous projects in the pipeline, and he gave one of his most chilling performances too as the torturer O'Brien in the screen version of Orwell's classic book *1984* (1984).

Originally Paul Scofield had been cast in the role of O'Brien, but proved unavailable and Burton's name was mentioned. The producer rang Tony Palmer to check if Burton was reliable. 'The last thing they wanted, being on a tight budget, was a raving drunk turning up they couldn't control. I told them that not only was he absolutely under control, 99% of the time, but also it was a stroke of genius that casting and I was sure he'd deliver the goods, because he's one of the few really great screen actors who understands that less is always more. It was a great performance.' Few knew at the time that it would prove to be his last film.

At 58 he looked old and physically frail. He was in pain and weak, unable even to put on his jacket without assistance. One crew hand on *1984* remarked, 'He's like a wild beast whose spirit has gone.' One day on the set an aide brought Burton a ready-opened can of Diet Pepsi and many wondered if he was having them laced with vodka. Word got back to Burton and the next day he offered everyone a swig to prove it was OK.

Mostly true to his vow of giving up drink, Burton could go on the wagon for weeks, sometimes months, and then indulge in massive binges. On the set of the TV mini-series *Ellis Island*, for which he provided a short cameo, he drank heavily. 'He just hated life without drinking,' said one crewmember. A visiting journalist to Burton's home asked one houseguest what it was like up there. 'Wall to wall empty bottles,' was the grim reply.

Work was still coming in though. Euan Lloyd, the producer of *The Wild Geese,* was determined to land Burton for the much-anticipated sequel. 'Get Reggie Rose to do the script and I would certainly be interested,' went Burton. The plot this time had the mercenary gang out to rescue Rudolf Hess from Spandau prison in Berlin. In three months a script was ready and a director was in place, Peter Hunt, who'd made one of the best of the Bonds, *On Her Majesty's Secret Service.* The icing on the cake was the casting of Laurence Olivier as Hess. Burton and Lloyd met up in Geneva to tie up the final details. Burton told of his delight at working with Olivier again and agreed to report for work during the second week of filming.

Sadly it was never to be. On Sunday August 5th Burton complained to Sally of a headache and decided to retire to bed early. In the morning Sally noticed he was breathing very heavily and that he couldn't be woken. Something was wrong. She called an ambulance and at the hospital it was discovered that Burton had suffered a cerebral haemorrhage. He was rushed to a medical facility in Geneva for an emergency operation. It was likely to take hours, Sally was told, she'd be better off at home instead of pacing up and down corridors, but once back there she just sat and waited by the phone, dreading its ring. When it did it was a doctor pleading with her to return fast. She was too late. Burton was dead. There was some consolation in the fact that even had the operation been successful Burton would have ended up confined to a wheelchair, unable to speak. According to one report Sally found her husband's last words in a note on his night-stand; Burton had jotted down a line from Shakespeare's *The Tempest*: 'Our revels now are ended.'

Euan Lloyd had been shooting in Berlin for ten days on *Wild Geese 2* when he got an early morning call from Brook Williams. 'Brook was in Switzerland at Richard's home. He gave me the devastating news. My responsibility to the cast and crew took second place to the magnitude of his passing. I slipped into depression.' The film's backers, EMI, gave Lloyd just seven days to replace Burton, or else. With the film collapsing before his eyes Lloyd suddenly heard Burton's voice inside his head. It was an echo of a conversation they'd had years before in which he told Lloyd how impressed he'd been by Edward Fox's performance in *The Day of the Jackal*. Bingo, Lloyd had found his replacement. 'But alas, *Wild Geese 2* turned out to be a distant cousin of the first,' confesses Lloyd. 'And still, the tragic loss of Richard hurts to this day.'

Tony Palmer too was shocked when he learnt of Burton's passing, as the last time he saw the actor he'd been fit and well, 'although Richard did have quite a serious collapse after we finished filming *Wagner*, just from absolute exhaustion. I visited Richard and Sally fairly frequently in Switzerland, really to support Sally who was going through quite a tricky time. She was keeping him off the drink, but he did become very depressed and rather morbid and thought he'd never work again. Then after he recovered I saw them again and he was absolutely full of beans. He was shooting *1984* and he and Sally came round several times to have supper and he was absolutely in fighting form, he wasn't physically on the decline at all. So it was a real shock when he died.'

As in life Burton caused chaos in death. The family wanted him laid to rest next to his parents in Wales, but Sally insisted he be buried in the tiny Swiss town of Celigny that he had made his home. Still, Burton went into the ground a Welshman, adorned head to foot in red with a copy of the complete works of Dylan Thomas. His coffin was covered with a large wreath decorated with the Welsh flag and as it was lowered into the plot his family suddenly burst into song with a bawdy Welsh rugby anthem. There was only one person conspicuous by her absence: Elizabeth Taylor, reportedly too struck with grief to attend; perhaps she didn't make an appearance out of deference to Sally. Elizabeth made her pilgrimage to Burton's grave a week later, bringing with her, predictably, the world's media. Even in death, Burton couldn't escape the prying camera lens.

Harris was asked to take part in a Hollywood memorial tribute to his old friend and thought how apt it would be to start his eulogy with a quotation from *Richard II*: 'Let us sit upon the ground . . .' But as the words came out he found he couldn't go on; instead he broke down and left the podium. Out of sight of the audience Richard Harris wept uncontrollably. Back on stage he forced himself to continue the line, '. . . and tell sad stories of the death of kings.' Later in his speech Harris admitted to the audience, 'If Richard could have seen me a moment ago he would have been howling with laughter.'

Burton's death predictably made front-page headlines around the world. Critics hailed him, others mourned the fact that he wasted his gifts, that had he not sold his soul to Hollywood and stayed in Britain and been true to the craft of theatre he would have equalled if not surpassed the pinnacle achieved by Olivier. 'I had an enormous amount of respect for Richard,' claims Waris Hussein, director of *Divorce His* and *Divorce Hers*. 'I thought he was a wonderful person. But his literally was a Faustian pact: he sold his soul and he never really got over it. He had the talent of the greats. He was a great stage actor, a wonderful voice; he looked incredible in his early years. You don't often get that combination of looks and talent. I remember seeing him as Hamlet at the Old Vic and he was just charismatic. I was walking around in a daze for about a fortnight afterwards, I just thought I'd seen a deity come down; he was just amazing. Years later when I was working with him I told him that I'd seen his Hamlet and thought he was wonderful and he literally started to get tears in his eyes and said, "Do you remember that?" I said, "Yes," and he said, "Not many people do." It was very sad.'

Maybe the Hollywood fame was simply to mask a deep-seated insecurity. 'I think Burton was a fragile man his whole life,' says Tony Palmer. 'I think he was desperately insecure and I think the vulgarity came as compensation because he thought, if I can be brash they won't notice that I need two whiskies to get on stage, which is something John Gielgud told me. He said, all great actors are nervous of going on stage, but Burton more than most. So the bravura, and all the money and yachts, were all somehow to compensate for this insecurity.'

More than anything Tony Palmer was struck by Burton's sheer magnetism; even at the end of his life, with Burton a shadow of the man he had once been, power oozed off his frame. 'He was immensely cultured and knowledgeable. He once told me he could recite every single one of Shakespeare's sonnets, all 151 of them. I never challenged him, but I bet he could, that would not have surprised me. Brook Williams always swore that he could. This was a miner's son; he'd got to his position by his own power. In the end it's the power of his personality which was overwhelming. You were aware of a presence, and it wasn't simply because he was legendary. Of course that adds a bit of gloss, but there are undoubtedly certain people for who, when they come in the room, you stand up, and Richard never came into the room and I didn't want to stand up; even when I'd had supper with him the previous night and knew the colour of his underpants, as it were, you always wanted to stand up, he had that effect on you.'

Rather apt was this observation from a commentator saying that Burton was Dylan Thomas as played by Casanova, directed by Mel Brooks. 'Wealth was not enough,' wrote another. 'It had to be opulence. Fame was not enough. It had to be notoriety.'

Not long before his death Burton was asked to look back over his life and sum it up if he could. 'Much of it has been a circus,' he admitted, 'played out in full view of the public. And, to be honest, I've loved every terrible minute of it.'

God bless you Richard Burton.

Not long after Burton's death Harris and O'Toole met up in a London pub and talked into the night about their recently departed friend. 'Richard once told me,' Harris said, 'that we spent a third of our lives drunk, a third with a hangover and a third sleeping.' There they sat quietly in a corner, two of the biggest hellraisers of all, sipping their tonic water. 'Ooh, what I wouldn't give for one glass of red wine,' pined Harris, 'just one.' A friend was sharing the evening with them and O'Toole picked up the man's glass of muscadet, held it to his nostrils and took in the heavy bouquet before replacing it untouched on the table. 'Aaah,' he said, in fond remembrance of drinks past. Then a minute's silence was called, not just for Burton, but for all thespian chums who had recently taken their final bows and moved on to that great saloon bar in the sky: 'Richard, Finchy, Larry Harvey, Bob Shaw, all my mates,' said O'Toole, shaking his head. 'They did drop like flies; everybody, all young.'

Harris was not enjoying sobriety very much. It was a bore: 'There must be other things in life besides drinking, though I haven't discovered what they are yet.' At least he was waking up in the morning and actually able to remember what he did the night before: 'Trouble was it wasn't worth remembering.' Minus the booze, though, he was still able to enjoy the craic. 'Richard Harris may no longer be a wildcat,' wrote one journalist, 'but he is certainly not a pussy cat. Perhaps the description "amiable tiger" will do.'

He still loved to go back to the pubs in Ireland where some of the best story tellers in the world congregate. 'First rate liars all of them. I love listening to the beautiful words coming through the Guinness froth.' But Harris knew that he couldn't have gone on the way he was drinking and that going back would lead to calamity. 'I can resist the first drink,' he told the press, 'but I cannot guarantee that I could resist the second one. I used to enjoy hangovers. I used to love to wake up the next morning with a roaring head because curing it was the perfect excuse to start all over again. But then it was taking me days to recover and I was getting genuinely sick.'

Peter O'Toole's own battle with booze had for a long time been won. 'I drank because I enjoyed it, not to solve a problem or because I needed a crutch. It was easy to give up.' He missed, though, the simple pleasure of boozing and still frequented pubs, careful to order nothing stronger than lemonade. 'I like being around men with jars in their hands. Sober people, they're not for me.' Such abstinence reminded him of the example he would have loved to have followed himself, that of the old comedian Max Miller who was told by his doctor to cut all his activities by half. Miller duly sat on his yacht for six months doing nothing. Then he returned to six months of working the clubs, eating and drinking heavily and bonking like mad. 'What a perfect division,' thought O'Toole.

Smoking was now the only act of defiance left to the actor. His preference was for Gauloise cigarettes that he chain-smoked in a long, black holder, equipped with a filter as a concession to health. 'I give up smoking from time to time,' he said, 'but, as a kid, I always had what Dylan Thomas called a "conscious woodbine" hanging out of my gob.' Such was his devotion to the habit that a friend once complained, 'Peter, you smell like a French train.'

Even without drink O'Toole was determined to give free rein to his eccentricities. 'I can still cause mayhem,' he gleefully said. Too true: in October 1984 he insulted a celebrity audience at a gala night in Dublin and half the audience walked out while the rest booed. The TV station carrying the show hastily ran a commercial during O'Toole's outburst. 'I'll always love to frolic, but now I can remember what I've done.' Like most drinkers O'Toole had suffered memory loss. 'That's the great snag of booze, oblivion. So sobriety's a real turn-on for me; you can see what you're doing.'

Now in his fifties, those decades on the piss had taken their toll on him. O'Toole cut an almost cadaverous figure, his great mop of straw-coloured hair long faded to grey, and his heavily lined face a testament to the excesses of his past. Despite his Grim Reaper appearance O'Toole had recently been cast as a teacher who has an affair with a young student, played by Jodie Foster, in *Svengali* (1983). The American TV movie was shot in one of the more dangerous areas of New York where transvestite prostitutes plied their trade nearby and a pyromaniac set fire to cars in a parking lot used by the film crew.

The director was Anthony Harvey, who after *The Lion in Winter* had met O'Toole quite often, going for long walks over Richmond Park, but he never truly got to know the actor; few people did. The two men hadn't met for years prior to *Svengali* and Harvey relished the opportunity to work with him again. 'Peter had enormous intelligence, a great sense of humour and huge energy, like a machine. He also had what all great actors must have, and that's an enormous sense of danger; you wouldn't like to mess with him.'

Most notably though, *Svengali* marked the first time Jodie Foster had stepped back into the limelight after she was the unwitting motive in an assassination attempt on the then incumbent US President, Ronald Reagan. When John Hinckley gunned down Reagan it was to prove his warped love for the actress, after becoming infatuated with her ever since she'd played a prostitute in *Taxi Driver*. It was O'Toole who helped Jodie face the movie camera again, his wealth of experience proving invaluable; after all he was a star before she was even born. 'It is all so unfair,' he told reporters, 'that this tremendously nice and talented girl should have become the target for every nutter in the land.' The pair struck up a touching friendship on set, with O'Toole mischievously calling her 'Midget'.

Although most of his recent work had been in America, O'Toole still made a habit of visiting Ireland. On one trip he was accompanied by a journalist who noted O'Toole's behaviour and observations on the cabin crew with some amusement. Sitting on the plane, and unaware of a priest close by, O'Toole broke into a broad smile as the stewardess, a quite robust little blonde in a tight fitting tweed uniform, walked by. 'Oh, look at that arse!' he roared, his face aglow. 'That ass is covered with tweed made in Connemara, where I was born. Nicest asses in the world, Ireland. Irish women are still carrying water on their heads and carrying their husbands home from pubs, and such things are the greatest posture builders in the world.'

As for Ireland itself, O'Toole, just like his father, had no intention of ever going back there for good. 'God, you can love it! But you can't live in it. Oh, the Irish know despair, by God they do. They are Dostoyevskian about it. Forgive me, Father, I have fucked Mrs Rafferty. Ten Hail Marys son. But Father, I didn't enjoy fucking Mrs Rafferty. Good, son, good.'

In 1985 Oliver Reed married for the second time, his bride named Josephine Burge. They'd met when she was just a 17-year-old schoolgirl in a Sussex pub from which, predictably, he was later banned for boisterous behaviour. He'd seen her there a few times with her gang of mates, even saying to the barman, 'See the skinny one. I'm going to marry her.' One day he plucked up the courage to introduce himself. Taking the ring-pull tab off the top of a can of beer Reed went over and put it on her finger. She wore it for the whole of her summer holidays, although when she came back to the pub Reed had trouble remembering her name. The press made much play of the fact that Josephine was 25 years his junior, three years younger than Reed's own son, Mark. Even his friends and family were shocked by it all.

Reed not so much planned the wedding as he planned the stag night and the reception. He wanted to hire a coach to take his mates and himself roaring round the countryside showing porn films and football matches. 'That way we can't be thrown out of any pub.' In the end Reed and his gang took over a boozer in Surrey and drank for three days solid: beer, cider, half pint mugs of gin and vodka and gunk. Reed, naked but for a kilt, presided over the booze orgy and friends arrived in shifts to replace revellers who had fallen by the wayside. Local villagers kept their fingers crossed that sleep deprivation might render Reed harmless. 'He's in there with a real rough lot,' said one quaking neighbour. 'They could take the village apart.' But come the third day the boozers were still going strong, pausing only for a cuppa: two teabags in a litre of scotch heated in a kettle, of which everyone had to partake. Periodically food in the form of sandwiches was sent in from a nearby hotel. The manager placed the tray outside the door. 'I dare not enter because Ollie sees me as representing authority. If he got half a chance he would grab me and I'd never be seen again.'

As the press watched from the relative safe distance of the car park small groups of Reed's handpicked boozing chums who could no longer stand the pace staggered out into the harsh daylight. 'I can't keep up with the man,' said one. 'I don't know where he's putting it.' By the end of it all there was but one drinker left in the pub, Reed himself.

By comparison the wedding itself was a relatively calm affair. 'I have talked to the police,' the registrar in charge told the press, 'and assured them that it will be a quiet and quick ceremony.'

After downing a reported 104 pints during the two-day reception Reed announced to Josephine and the world his plan to be a new man; his hell-raising days were over, he vowed. Alas, just two weeks later he was embroiled in a bar room brawl. 'Once a pirate,' he excused, 'always a pirate.' Besides he'd only recently come off a wager to stay off booze: 'My life against twelve and a half pence was the stake.' It was an experience he didn't particularly care for. 'I like the effect drink has on me. What's the point of staying sober?'

Not long after their marriage Reed and Josephine moved to Guernsey. Many pondered that the reason was because Ollie had been banned from every pub where he lived, most notably the Bull's Head where he climbed the chimney naked, shouting 'Ho! Ho! Ho! I'm Santa Claus!' One regular drinker at his old local did lament his departure. 'We just hope that for the sake and sensibilities of the good people of Guernsey that Mr Reed refrains from a regrettable habit of his insisting on showing complete strangers his tattoo.'

That was the least of the islanders' concerns. Over the years Reed had visited Guernsey often and havoc, as usual, hadn't been far behind. One hotel even took the precaution of installing bars on the windows of his first floor room. Why? The room overlooked the outdoor swimming pool and one evening Reed charged across his bedroom and dived headfirst through the open window, sailing over the terrace patio and into the water. To prove his feat was no mere fluke, he did it again.

Then there was the occasion he was challenged to a drinking contest by a bunch of sailors and just couldn't refuse. 'But we were having quadruple measures of chugalug, one after another, and I am afraid they sank me.' Reeling from the effects of too much rum Reed put his fist through a hotel window and was arrested in his underpants, covered with dirt and blood, after squaring up to the police. 'Come on,' he bellowed. 'Come on, have a go if you dare.' Finally he collapsed and was arrested and dragged comatose to the police station. In court he later admitted the charge of damage and 'acting in a disorderly manner while drunk'. He was fined £100. Released, Reed apologized on bended knees to Josephine and promised reporters to give rum a very wide berth indeed from now on. Josephine, on the other hand, seemed remarkably relaxed about things. 'He's much more fun when he's drunk. He can be rather boring when he's sober.' Josephine recounted the occasion when she woke up at home one evening to find Reed sitting on the bed, wearing a policeman's helmet and swapping jokes with a strange man. 'I just went back to sleep.'

True he was invariably fun, but a drunk Reed on a film set could be an accident waiting to happen. One time, wardrobe had come to collect Reed who was lunching at his hotel and on his sixth bottle of Dom Perignon. Somehow recognizing them, Reed immediately demanded that they sit and drink with him. His call time was 11 o'clock. Before the wardrobe assistants could coax him off his barstool, Reed downed one more bottle of champagne (in 15 minutes) and declared that he was ready to act. He was unable to stand, so the assistants dragged him by the arms out of the bar, Reed ranting and raving all the while, and deposited him in a car to speed him to the location.

Gently laying him down on the grass, wardrobe proceeded to take off Reed's trousers and boots. On seeing his co-star Reed suddenly whipped out his cock and started pretending that it was a gun. 'Bang, bang,' he hollered. 'How do you like my chopper?' The actor tried not to take any notice. 'It looks better when it's at attention.' Fortunately, Ollie didn't feel the need to prove that.

Reed was then handed a prop pistol for his scene. He was on a hill surrounded by enemy troops and two helicopters hovered overhead. Realizing he was defeated, Reed had to dramatically toss his gun aside.

The cameras rolled, everything proceeded smoothly, until a scowling Reed hurled his pistol at an extra, pulled out his cock and screamed, 'Bang, bang, bang.' The director could scarcely believe it. 'CUT!' Reed just stood there laughing, then stumbled up to another actor and said, 'I know that I'm supposed to just drop the gun, but I think that my only way to survive is to pretend I'm crazy so they won't shoot me!' He laughed more, choked, and then threw up. The eventual shot in the film had to be accomplished using his stunt double.

Reed also still had a habit of dropping his trousers in public to reveal his 'mighty mallet'. One day in the pub with friend Stephen Ford, Ollie brought up the subject of his cock. 'You talking about that silly little thing again,' Ford said in exasperation. 'I bet you right now that I've got a bigger cock than you,' Ollie said. Not having that, Ford said, 'Oh all right, fine. What are you going to do about it?' Reed stood up. 'Right, come through.' Reed pressganged Ford into a small back room which had a large mirror on a wall. 'Right, trousers down,' ordered Reed, who realized he had lost immediately. Still pulling up his trousers Reed went back into the bar. 'Silence everybody, stop. Stop!' A hush fell over the whole establishment. 'I wish to announce that Stephen Ford has got a bigger cock than I have.'

Out of all Richard Harris's brothers Dermot – his business manager – was the one he felt closest to. Dermot had a huge capacity for drinking day and night. It was the booze that wrecked his marriage to actress Cassandra Harris, who would later marry Pierce Brosnan. People who knew the two brothers and saw them together could see that they were nothing but a bad influence on each other.

Touring *Camelot* in Chicago, Harris was waiting in the wings for his opening cue when Dermot said, 'Dick, I don't feel too good. I think I'll go and lie down.' As he walked onto the stage Harris heard himself saying, 'Look after yourself.' When he came off again after the curtain call Dermot was dead. He was only 48. Coming so soon after the loss of Burton, Dermot's death profoundly affected Harris. Some say it changed him. Others were more of the opinion that once a rogue, always a rogue, but at least one that bordered on the loveable. A female journalist told of the time she interviewed Harris at his hotel suite and the star kept telling her, 'You haven't seen the whole suite until you've seen the bedroom.'

Harris was capable of the most obscene behaviour, but a lot of it was tinged with humour and playfulness. 'I've always said the reason I don't feel my age is because I've preserved the child in myself. The child has never grown up.' Harris was the Peter Pan of hellraising. At home in the Bahamas neighbours took to dropping by uninvited. To deter them Harris conceived an impish plot. One afternoon a family living close by turned up. Walking inside they found Harris with two mates sitting naked watching porno movies and masturbating. 'Oh, hello there,' said Harris. 'Come on in.' The poor family fled in terror. It was all an act, of course. Harris had deliberately bought the worst hardcore movie he could find in New York and when he saw anyone coming up his drive shouted to his mates, 'Action station boys,' and they all stripped off. The incident went round the island like all good gossip does and afterwards Harris was left pretty much in peace; the way he wanted it.

In the 80s Harris had moved lock, stock and barrel to the Bahamas but his career was down the pan. By the close of the decade he was reduced to making TV movies, bad ones to boot. His poor choice of material was epitomised by his insistence on playing the detective Maigret (a role Burton had been considering prior to his death) in a TV series in 1988. It was crap indeed and the critics weren't kind. The *Daily Mirror* poured scorn on Harris's Irish brogue. After destroying Maigret, they said, why not go the whole distance: 'How about Sherlock O'Holmes, Paddy Mason, Hercule Guinness?'

The years of boozing, the enemies and grudges left in his hellraising wake had all come back to haunt Harris. The casting opportunities had dried up. Unlike his contemporaries, Caine and Connery, Harris had fundamentally failed to make the critical metamorphosis into late middle-age film roles. By 1989 he was fast approaching his sixties, and Christ did he look it. 'A critic once described my face as five miles of bad Irish country road,' Harris said, almost with pride. 'Every wrinkle tells a tale.' For the rest of his life Harris enjoyed shambling around looking like an unmade bed, sleeping in his clothes and then not changing them the next day. Indeed he'd wear the same outfit for days on end; he didn't give a shit, proudly boasting of the fact that he'd never owned a hairbrush in his life.

At least he wasn't drinking, and for the first time in his life he was rather glad of the fact. 'I've woken up with women whose names I don't remember. I've punched coppers. It all used to be so smashing. The wonderful sensation of a fist going into somebody's face. But now my body just hurts. If one of my three sons so much as grips my arm I say, "Ouch". I live in constant agony, drinking Perrier water while the guys are knocking back the vodkas. But if I touch the stuff my day isn't worth living. Oh yes, it's been a great 30 years, but we've all paid the price in our different ways.'

Peter O'Toole had done many things in his life; child snatching certainly wasn't one of them. But that's exactly what he was accused of doing in 1984. When O'Toole met Karen Somerville, an American model, in 1981 she was 15 years his junior. It was his first meaningful relationship since his divorce from Siân and in 1983 at the age of 50 he became a father again, of a long wished for son, aptly named Lorcan, Gaelic for Lawrence. But when Lorcan was just ten months old the couple split and a bitter tug of love over the child ensued. Karen was awarded custody and moved back to the States with Lorcan; O'Toole was given visiting rights only. On one of these trips over to see his son O'Toole, who had vowed never to let Lorcan go, bolted with the child, turning up in Bermuda of all places, en route to London. During the eight hour stopover Karen phoned friends to organize a lawyer to prevent O'Toole taking the child off the island. Police and officials arrived at O'Toole's hotel just as he was preparing to leave for the airport and he was forced to hand Lorcan over to the authorities.

O'Toole always denied that he was attempting to snatch his son and take him back to England. All Karen said on the subject and of her former partner was, 'Let's just say that he is not a predictable man.' With that in mind, perhaps, Karen employed security guards to watch over her son should there be another 'kidnap' attempt. Back in England O'Toole was heartbroken; the son he had always craved was thousands of miles away, more out of reach than ever. Now living a solitary existence in his cottage in Connemara and in his London home, O'Toole told reporters that any woman contemplating marrying him ought to be led gently to a place of safety. But he fully intended to carry on fighting for custody of his son; and the big show down was yet to come.

As for Harris, the mid- to late-80s was a barren period for O'Toole, with cameo appearances in stupefyingly awful blockbusters like *Supergirl* (1984) or sterile comedies nobody wanted to see such as *Club Paradise* (1986) and *High Spirits* (1988). There was one notable exception, *The Last Emperor* (1987), a magisterial film about Pu Yi, China's final ruler. O'Toole's role, as the young man's English tutor, was relatively small but made a huge impact. The film itself was history making, being the first feature granted permission by the Chinese government to shoot inside the fabled Forbidden City. Security was so tight that when O'Toole forgot his pass one day he was denied entrance to the set.

But the real drama for O'Toole was happening in real life. For almost four years he and Karen Somerville had been locked in an increasingly hostile legal battle over the custody of Lorcan. After the Bermuda incident O'Toole must have thought he'd blown any chance of ever being granted custody but in 1985 he was once again allowed access to his child and the boy was routinely shuttled back and forth across the Atlantic. But the utter desperation O'Toole felt to keep hold of the son he had always yearned for clouded his judgement once again and he refused to release Lorcan after bringing him to London for a holiday. Karen immediately proclaimed that Lorcan had been stolen from her and got the courts to order O'Toole to return the boy. He refused. Tough New York lawyers threatened O'Toole with a daily fine of $1,000 from his earnings on *The Last Emperor* if he failed to hand over Lorcan to his mother. Karen then upped the stakes, getting her lawyers to ask a US federal judge to issue an arrest warrant and a ruling that O'Toole was in contempt of court, which meant he could be arrested the moment he entered the United States.

In May 1988 O'Toole and Karen faced each other in London's High Court; the two former lovers were unable even to look each other in the eye. It was an appearance before the world's press that O'Toole could well have lived without, he looked frail and nervous, a man on the brink of being torn in half. The judgement, when it came, hit O'Toole in the pit of his stomach like poison; the son he adored had to return with his mother to America. Visibly shaken and in tears O'Toole's all or nothing gamble in refusing to hand over Lorcan after the allotted 16-day custody period had failed. He returned with the boy to his Hampstead home and together they packed Lorcan's small suitcase and for a while played in the garden, father and son together perhaps for the last time.

Facing the possibility of never seeing his son again O'Toole appealed the decision to return him to his mother. In August in an American court O'Toole dramatically won back joint custody of Lorcan. The judge ordered that the boy stay with his father and carry out his schooling in London and live with his mother during the holidays. O'Toole had won his greatest battle. For this most private of men, who only consented to interviews out of necessity and had always shunned the glitzy media spotlight, to have to live out this personal trauma in the glare of publicity was an agonizing ordeal. But the reward was sweet and the years of Lorcan's childhood that O'Toole was now able to share brought out the very best in him.

Oliver Reed had been settling in very nicely thank you in Guernsey. As a moving in gift he'd bought Josephine a beautiful antique gold necklace but one boozy evening she'd tied it round their pet dog's neck as a joke. Incensed, Reed took the necklace and buried it in the garden to teach her a lesson. Trouble was that when after a few days he came back to retrieve it he couldn't for the life of him remember exactly which bit of the garden he'd buried it in. The gardener was ordered to dig up most of the lawn and flowerbeds and metal detectors were employed in the hunt. But it was never found.

At his new home Reed converted the large loft into a replica pub. Friends would join him there and they'd drink often till three or four in the morning. Ollie would then sometimes stagger into his study to write poetry, phoning his poor put upon brother Simon to regale him with his latest offering down the phone line. When these recitals became too much for any human being to bear Simon took to leaving his answer phone switched on all night. Asked later for his verdict on brother Ollie's poetry Simon said, 'It was like someone who had taken LSD every night of their lives.'

Reed very quickly established his drinking credentials in the many pubs on the island. 'He is usually OK until about 2 o'clock,' said one landlady, 'but then things tend to get out of hand. His drinking reputation is legendary on this island.' He also enjoyed welcoming visiting journalists to his new world, taking them on tours of the island, usually starting and finishing in a pub. On one occasion Reed was driving a reporter along the coastal road when he suddenly stopped the car and asked his passenger to step out and just smell the beautiful clean fresh air. The journalist did so and in mid-sniff heard the door slam behind him, the car engine rev up. Reed sped off. The poor man was in the middle of nowhere, no house and no person within four miles. When the weary reporter got back to his hotel hours later Reed was waiting for him in the lobby, drink in hand.

After years of nothing parts and being famous only for periodically appearing in the tabloids in various stages of being pissed, Oliver Reed returned to the big time again with *Castaway* (1986), a film based on the real-life story of a business man who places an ad in a paper for a girl to come and live with him on a tropical island. True to form, though, at the glitzy opening night of the film a sozzled Reed shouted out in dismay during the performance when he realized that some of his favourite scenes had been cut out of the movie.

Cast as the girl, and spending the majority of the movie completely starkers, was Amanda Donohoe. In her first real movie role, she was to some extent thrown in at the deep end, having to handle Ollie. 'I don't think that anybody understood the state that Oliver was in when he came to do *Castaway*. Although everybody understood that he drank, nobody knew quite how much. There was this dichotomy; there was this incredibly sweet, charming, sensitive man . . . and the next minute he'd be calling you a bitch. You really didn't know where you were with him. This was at a point in his career where he had been unemployable. I think he really tried to be very good . . . he tried and tried and tried . . . but I just don't think he could resist somehow.'

To promote *Castaway* Reed did more press than he'd managed in years. A reporter was invited to meet him one morning at a genteel hotel in Dorking. Waiting in reception the journalist saw Reed arrive, recovering from a massive bender the night before. 'That's why I'm drinking champagne,' he announced. 'It's a good pick me up. But I think now,' consulting his watch which read 10.45 am, 'I'll switch to gin and tonic.' The interview began with the reporter wondering why Dorking, not exactly the kind of place frequented by film stars or hellraisers. 'I *am* Dorking,' Reed explained, pounding the table with his fists, rattling the coffee cups. 'And Dorking is *me*.'

By far Reed's most notorious public appearance at this time, perhaps of his career, occurred when he agreed to do Michael Aspel's TV chat show. Aspel knew Reed was always a good booking, but on this particular occasion he'd had word from the researcher travelling with him: 'We've stopped again!' and that the star was drinking large quantities of booze. Still, nothing quite prepared Aspel for the apparition that lurched onto the set. He came on looking like the uncle from hell at a boozy Christmas party with his shirt half hanging off and clutching a jug of what one hoped was just orange juice. He then proceeded to forget the plot of the film he was meant to be promoting and hijacked the band to play the 60s hit 'Wild One', belting out the lyrics like a Neanderthal Elvis. It was a performance that few who watched it would ever forget. 'I was delighted,' Aspel later confessed. 'People said "Aspel was furious" – I was thrilled! You don't expect Reed to come on and behave like a bank manager; if he did it would be disappointing. But we knew he was sloshed because he'd taken 15 stops . . . and a couple of pints of gin and tonic. So when he lurched on I thought "This is great!"'

Was Reed out of his head or was it another case of giving the punters what they wanted? 'I don't think it will take that long to rebuild the studio,' said Aspel. It certainly left an impression on fellow guest, writer Clive James – 'It was one of the most exciting evenings since World War II, when I was much further from the front line' – and on the viewers, 600 of whom jammed the station's switchboard to complain, *The Sun* newspaper called them all spoilsports. 'In our view,' they said, 'Ollie Reed drunk is better than Wogan sober any day.' That didn't stop TV bosses announcing their intention to ban Reed, who'd left for home after the Aspel show perfectly delighted with his performance, from ever appearing on their chat shows again. 'On television Oliver was a menace,' says Michael Winner. 'They once said to me, "We're going to do Oliver Reed's *This is Your Life* live." I said, "Obviously you have a better job to go to and wish to leave Granada television in a hail of ignominy." They said, "No, no, all his family say that Michael, you are the only person he respects, so we're going to tell him that he's coming as a guest on your *This is Your Life*." Sadly this never worked out because there was an electricians' strike and the thing was cancelled. On television Oliver was quite difficult. They often called me to sit next to him, because they thought if I was there he would be sober and well behaved, which was only marginally true.'

After other public misdemeanours – on the Des O'Connor chat show

Ollie was only just restrained from producing his cock live on camera – his brother and two sons wrote jointly to inform him how unacceptable and embarrassing his behaviour had become. Reed never replied. To him he was merely giving the public what they wanted. 'Sometimes I go over the top,' he said, stating the obvious, 'but I don't punch people any more. I'm too old for that now.'

But deep inside Reed must have known that he was cutting his own throat with such antics, however glorious they were. After *Castaway*, a critical and financial success, in which he'd given his best performance for years, producers should have been banging on his door with scripts, but his antics scared them all off; people were just afraid to employ him and what should have been a revival ended up another barren wasteland.

In 1987 doctors warned Reed to give up the booze or he'd be dead within two years. His alcoholic intake and rich food diet were leading to possible kidney damage, coronary disease and ultimately heart failure. But did he care? – not really, announcing that he'd rather die than stop boozing. 'Richard Burton was hitting the bottle with John Hurt the night before his death. He knew it was going to kill him, but he did not stop.' Reed didn't like what giving up booze had done to his other surviving acting chums. 'Now Richard Harris and Peter O'Toole have stopped drinking they don't look nearly as robust as they used to. I certainly prefer them in their stamping days.'

Reed hated the thought of a long, lingering death, of vital organs slowly popping off. Thoughts of suicide came into his mind. Drinking himself to death was the preferable option, though it would take far too long. There had to be a quicker solution. In the end Reed made his son Mark swear to perform 'his sacred duty and put a shot gun in my mouth and pull the trigger'.

Who knows just how seriously Ollie contemplated suicide; in any case he had no intention of heeding the health warnings and carried on boozing. By now a life on the piss had taken its toll on his appearance: he was pot-bellied, grey-haired, lined and stooping like an old man; at times he looked like Father Christmas leaving an Alcoholics Anonymous meeting. It was a long way away from the brooding sex symbol of the early 70s. His face was now 'a sad reflection of a dissolute life', as one journalist put it. 'A Hogarthian example of debauchery's perils.' When in 1989 he played Athos once again, in *The Return of the Musketeers*, Reed looked positively prehistoric compared with his co-stars from the original movie. But the hellraiser was still there. Filming in Aylesbury, Reed went to a local pub and after numerous pints boasted to the locals of the tattoo on his cock. He was finally persuaded to place his manhood on a barstool for public examination.

For Reed, however, the onset of old age presented no great fears. 'I'm looking forward actually to getting old and playing the sage. I want to be wheeled around in a wheelchair, carrying a whip, pushed around by a Negro in a white uniform, whipping people if they get in my way.'

That same year Reed was thrown out of a celebrity bash for attacking fellow hard man Patrick Mower. Trouble flared when Ollie stood up and yelled interruptions during some of the speeches. When Mower intervened to calm him down Reed tried to head butt the TV star. Reed later denied head butting Mower, insisting he had 'leant across the table to give him a kiss'. Seated close by watching all this were ex-boxer and stunt man Nosher Powell and wrestler Jackie Pallo who got up and forced Reed back into his chair. Things were quiet for a while until Reed began goading Mower about his young blonde companion. Again Nosher Powell was on hand. Grabbed from behind Reed was manhandled to the door and thrown out into the street. As one guest told the papers, 'Oliver was smashed out of his brains tonight.'

The Pickled Nineties

Richard Harris was pretty much washed up as the 90s began, totally non-existent as a film force having done nothing of note for over ten years. Critics were now placing Harris in the same bracket as Burton, as a man who had wasted his talents on Hollywood pap after his blistering breakthrough in *This Sporting Life*. 'Balls to that,' was his not altogether surprising response. 'I've lived the life I wanted to live. Why should I live up to some critic's expectations?'

Indicative of the lack of opportunities coming his way was Jim Sheridan's offer for Harris to play just a cameo role as a village priest in *The Field* (1990). Years before he'd have been up for the lead, but that vacancy was filled by Ray McAnally, whom Sheridan was eager to work with again after their joint success with *My Left Foot*. Harris told the producers he could do it better than McAnally, but they just laughed at him.

Unexpectedly McAnally, at 63, died from a heart attack and the project was thrown into disarray. Harris seized the opportunity and pitched his name forward, only for the producers to inform him that the backers wanted someone with 'marquee' value, a Brando or a Connery, certainly not Harris. Brando's agent actually rang Harris to ask who these Irish people were that wanted to hire his client. Harris told them they were a bunch of layabouts and couldn't be trusted. 'I was galvanized. I did everything in my power to stop them getting someone else.' Finally after eight weeks of discussion Harris was cast as a farmer who will stop at nothing in order to keep a rented field which his family has tilled for generations and which an American wants to buy. The role rejuvenated him as never before. *The Field* would be his King Lear.

It proved a tough shoot, however. The assistant director called it 'pure hell'. For many on the film Harris's larger than life reputation was well founded and Sheridan struggled to keep the peace. At one point co-star Tom Berenger walked away in disgust when Harris blew his top on the set. The problem was that Harris identified so strongly with the tough, single-minded farmer that he was literally living the role; the character was obnoxious, therefore so was he. His perfectionism became overbearing. 'But any kind of perfection needs ruthlessness; you just won't take second best. So, if that means I'm a pain in the arse, then I'm a great pain in the arse.' Upon completion one of the actors summed up Harris as 'a circus of a man'. Still, Harris footed the £1,000 bill for the crew's boozy wrap party. He himself sat quietly sipping tea.

After *The Field* Harris confessed to being knackered. What he wanted now was to find himself an heiress with an island in the Pacific where he could write poetry all day and shag the servants at night. But all those exertions turned out to be worth it when Harris received an Oscar nomination for his performance. 'About fucking time,' he ranted, though he'd no desire to attend the ceremony. 'Why the fuck would I want to participate in any of this Hollywood bollocks. It's 14 fucking hours there, 14 fucking hours back, two hours of fucking stupidity and kissing people's fucking cheeks. Fuck that.'

It was hardly the kind of attitude to endear oneself to Academy members, and not surprisingly Harris lost out on the Oscar. Still, after describing himself as 'a dinosaur' only a year before he was suddenly in demand again, even 'hot'. Alas the British Academy failed to recognize his work in *The Field* with even a nomination, a decision that deeply pissed Harris off. A few months later, when BAFTA asked him to deliver the opening address during a royal visit to America, he wrote back claiming he had a previous engagement with his television set and suggested they ask the five actors they'd seen fit to nominate for Best Actor instead of him. The rebel was still there. Dragged along to the LA launch of Planet Hollywood, Harris was talking to Ann Turkel when he was cut up by Bruce Willis, who totally ignored him. Tapping the star on the shoulder Harris said, 'Excuse me, your face seems so familiar, but I can't put a name to it. I was actually talking to my ex-wife when you moved into my space. So would you please fuck off!'

Current stars like Willis didn't cut any ice with Harris; to him most of them were ciphers, irrelevant when matched up with his generation.

Someone asked him once what the difference was between the stars of today like Tom Cruise and when he was a major star. 'I said there is a great difference, look at a photograph of me from the old days and I'm going to one of my film premieres with a bottle of vodka in my hand. Tom Cruise has a bottle of Evian water. That's the difference.'

Ever the hellraiser, Harris loved to behave badly, this time not spurred on by the booze. 'Just because I don't drink any more people think I'm not hellraising.' It was showing off really, minus the violence that so characterized his behaviour in his 60s heyday. He'd launch into an impromptu Irish jig in the middle of a crowded restaurant for example or tour the tables kissing the hand of every woman present. During an interview in his hotel suite the phone rang. Harris didn't bother to ask who it was but just shouted down the line, 'Come straight up and take your knickers off.' It was the Royal Shakespeare Company. With another journalist in a restaurant, Harris's interest was piqued by a group of elegant, middle-aged women in pearls taking tea at the next table. He suddenly spouted, 'Would you like to ride the arse off her?' so loud that the women couldn't fail to hear, eliciting shocked embarrassment. Harris roared with laughter. 'Jesus, it's only fun, isn't it. It's what they expect of me. It makes their day.'

Peter O'Toole had begun the new decade on a massive high, back in the West End with a certifiable hit show. *Jeffrey Bernard is Unwell* was based on the real life columnist of *The Spectator*, whose weekly accounts of successive disasters caused by booze, women and horse racing became cult reading. In Keith Waterhouse's brilliant play Bernard wakes up under a table to find that he's been locked in his favourite pub, the Coach and Horses in Soho, after closing time and spends the night reflecting on a life of dissolution. O'Toole was inspired casting and had known Bernard personally for 30 years. The two could almost have been brothers.

Jeffrey Bernard was a real London character and a chaotic drinker; his stomping ground was the pubs and drinking dens of Soho, his tattered frame a permanent feature, sometimes obscured by clouds of smoke from the ever permanent fag in his gob. One great story has him on the town with TV and radio star Tony Hancock in the late 50s. Hancock is so absolutely soused that it takes some time before they can find a taxi which will take him home – the cabbies' reluctance due in no small part to the fact that Hancock has quite obviously pissed his pants. Finally they stop a cab and Hancock immediately collapses onto its floor. Bernard, leaning against the door, is surprised to see Hancock offer him his card and say, 'If you ever need my help, just call me.' Looking at the urine-soaked clown with incredulity Bernard replies, 'Why on earth should I want help from you?' Hancock smiles benignly, 'Because I think you might have a drinking problem.'

At the time of Waterhouse's theatrical homage to Bernard the boozy writer had a column in the *Daily Mirror*. One day he informed his readers that the play about his life was packing them in, punters were literally hanging from the rafters. Later that day Bernard called Keith Waterhouse to say how wonderful it was that they were filling one of London's biggest theatres, to which the playwright replied, 'But Jeffrey, we haven't opened yet. We open in six weeks.' Pissed out of his head the previous night, Bernard had gone to bed, dreamt the whole thing had been a huge success and woken up to write his column.

Unlike Bernard, O'Toole hadn't touched a drop of alcohol since 1975. That all changed in the new decade after a trip to Moscow. He found the Russian capital truly ghastly, a real eye opener. 'There were all these people queuing for cardboard shoes and everyone with forms and clipboards. I found a tea bar where they served sly vodkas. What else could I do?'

Hardly back on the booze big time, O'Toole drank only in moderation, when he felt like it. But his eccentricity hadn't deserted him. Meeting O'Toole you never quite knew what to expect. One journalist was assigned to interview him at the close of the day on the set of a film. As the shooting wrapped she loaded her cassette recorder in anticipation and asked if he was prepared to do the interview. 'No, I'm going to fuck off,' he said, firmly. 'That's what I'm going to do. I'm a tired old fart and I'm cold.' And off he went.

His friends, too, had come to accept his strange behaviour. When Sarah Standing, the daughter of Bryan Forbes and a dear friend of O'Toole's, was pregnant, she sent a note saying she was going into hospital. The birth was about to be induced, with Sarah hooked up to machines, when suddenly the doors burst open and O'Toole, a Gauloise in his mouth, came in shouting, 'The stork has arrived. The stork has arrived.' He sat at the bottom of the bed and had his lunch with Sarah's husband and her gynaecologist. Afterwards the gynaecologist turned to O'Toole and said, 'I think Mrs Standing is about to give birth now, if you'd like to leave.' O'Toole looked puzzled. 'No, I'm perfectly all right where I am thank you,' and continued smoking with the windows wide open.

In 1991 an unusually dense Channel 4 producer decided that it would be a great idea to invite Oliver Reed onto a live late night discussion programme entitled 'Do Men Need to Be Violent?' The second mistake was to supply a well-stocked drinks cabinet that Reed made predictable full use of. Drinking wine from a pint glass he swore at fellow guests and sat next to feminist writer Kate Millett, who he insisted on calling, 'Big tits'. After a lecture on fighting dogs Reed asked the host, 'Is it after midnight yet? It is, good. Well, a woman's role in society depends on whether or not she wants to get shafted.' This didn't go down very well with the feminist writer, nor did Reed's assertion that, 'I've had more punch ups in pubs than you've had hot dinners darling.'

Reed's behaviour got increasingly worse, much to the delight of the watching audience, until Channel 4 were forced to pull the plug for half an hour. During the enforced break the show's host and its producers tried to persuade Reed that he really ought to behave himself. When the show finally returned to the airwaves viewers saw Reed staggering back to his seat uttering the immortal words, 'I've had a slash.' Trying to get back onto the discussion subject, he announced that he'd tried to volunteer for the Gulf War but was so drunk he only got as far as the telephone operator before passing out. Then, after tumbling over a sofa to give the feminist writer a snog, he was reproached by the programme host. Reed took his chastisement like a guilty schoolboy. 'Do you want me to leave?' he asked. 'Yes, yes,' was the chorus from everyone else. Reed slouched off. It's a classic piece of television and one wonders whether Reed deliberately behaved in such a manner in order to send up the gathering of pretentious intellectuals – or was he just pissed out of his box.

For some years Reed had established near legendary status for behaving badly on chat shows. When he appeared on the Gay Byrne programme, one of the most popular shows on Irish television, he stunned the audience by taking off his shirt and making a grab for fellow guest Susan

George (you can't blame him), ending up on the floor with her. Within minutes callers had jammed the switchboard of the TV station. 'Oliver was just doing what he normally does,' said Susan afterwards. The next day reporters besieged Reed's hotel but he refused to talk about the incident. All press enquires were answered with the comment, 'Mr Reed will only speak to you if you promise to put him on page 3 beside a nice lady.'

Other memorable TV appearances followed. On the David Letterman show, America's number one chat show, Reed adopted an American accent for much of the interview, pointed at the camera and shouted, 'I'm after you, Stallone,' replied to some of Letterman's questions in German, spoke nonsense such as claiming he was a fisherman who wore boots in his ears, took the piss out of Letterman's nose by pressing his own down in imitation, and stared Letterman down, forcing the host to plead to his band leader, Paul Schaffer, to help him out.

In 1992 Reed appeared on a bizarre Channel 4 show where celebrity guests were interviewed while having their hair cut by a French barber. Reed was in a very grim mood and so the interview did not exactly go swimmingly. 'So, I hear you were once in the British Army?' 'Yeah. Got a problem with that, frog?'

Reed was fully aware of the fact that such behaviour classed him as a bad boy, but he was secretly proud of the fact that he was truly the last of his kind. 'I've always liked being called a hellraiser. The sad thing is that I'm the last of them. There was O'Toole, Harris and I was the baby. Now I'm the only one carrying the baton.'

While many critics looked down on his infantile rabble rousing, one scribe from the *Mail on Sunday* surely expressed what the majority of the nation thought: 'The world needs Oliver Reed. He's the last great bad boy, a lone, shining beacon in the long dark night of political correctness. Richard Burton is dead and Richard Harris has had to reform to stay alive. No, only Ollie still raises hell day in, day out.'

He was also blissfully unaware of the current climate of political correctness, still espousing male chauvinistic views that made feminists' blood boil. 'I believe that my woman shouldn't work outside the home. When I come home and I'm tired from filming all day, I expect her to be there and make sure everything is cool for me. You know, like drawing my bath and helping me into bed. That's the kind of job she has and in return for it, she can bear my children and if any man talks bad to her, I'll hit him.'

Then something happened to sour Reed's image and call into question his boisterous antics. In 1993 his former stunt double and drinking pal, Reg Prince, sued him over an injury that had almost cost him his life. The incident dated back to the mid-80s and the filming of *Castaway* when the two men were enjoying a boozy night at their hotel. Reed was performing handstands in the restaurant and showing diners the tattoo on his cock. When they moved outside to the balcony Prince claimed that Reed deliberately tipped him over the side where he fell 12 feet onto the beach. Prince suffered a double spine fracture and told the court he hadn't been able to work since. Reed claimed the incident was self-defence, that Prince attacked him with a table knife. But Prince told of how this wasn't the first time Reed had injured him. At a New Year's Eve party in Mexico, so Prince claimed, he'd gone up to Reed to wish him a happy New Year. 'And he head butted me and broke my nose.'

In the end Prince lost the case, but a few years later turned up at Ollie's house with a very large knife. Prince was a man not to be messed with, he was big. He got into the house and crept up behind Ollie, planting the knife across his neck. 'You know I've come here to kill you,' he said. 'I would much rather you had a drink, Reggie,' said Reed, turning to offer Prince a tumbler of gin. The two men talked awkwardly for hours and then Prince left.

Rejuvenated by his role in *The Field* Richard Harris fell in love with making movies again, jumping into work with an abandon he'd never shown before, making in the next ten years some 22 pictures. He also retrieved his theatrical reputation by playing the title role in Pirandello's *Henry IV* in the West End. James Hogg was box office assistant at Wyndham's at the time and recalls that period all too clearly. 'I must say he was excellent in the role and the show was a triumph. However, one thing that we hadn't bargained for at the theatre was Mr Harris's flatulence. Apparently he was famous for it, although I'd never heard anything. We started to get the odd complaint during the previews. Some old ladies in the front row had heard what they thought was someone blowing a raspberry on stage. Naturally we thought nothing of it. Then, as the run progressed, we started to get complaints every other night. To investigate, we gave ourselves seats in the front row, and sure enough, just after Harris made his entrance we heard one. A bit of a corker too. The thing was, Harris really didn't seem to care. Either that or he didn't even know it was happening. The morning after one performance I was sitting in the box office with the manager, having a cup of tea and reading the *Daily Mail*, and there it was, something along the lines of "Star's wind spoils theatre trip." A disgruntled customer had decided to go to the papers and they'd obviously snapped it up. Another part of my job was getting the odd programme signed for special guests and I used to dread going to Harris's dressing room. He had a record player next to his bed and seemed to just play "MacArthur Park" on a loop. I honestly never heard anything else! On top of that he would swear at you for bothering him, throw the programmes back after signing them and, if I was lucky, send me off with one of his specials!'

He was also in rude health, having recently had a medical check which came up trumps. 'I've survived,' he proclaimed, 'but to be honest, I'm surprised that both O'Toole and I are still alive. The last time we met we spent all evening talking about the miracle of still being alive.' For a while, during their boozing heyday, the two men had decided not to see each other, 'because if we did, we'd kill us both,' said Harris. 'We always brought out the worst in each other.'

The two men now regularly saw each other, usually at rugby matches. During one sporting afternoon O'Toole suddenly said, 'Ah, Jesus, I miss waking up in fucking places that you never knew you had been to.' Harris smiled. 'I know. I used to love going to the shop to buy a packet of cigarettes and not coming back for a month.' Both men burst out laughing. As O'Toole recalled, 'We were two old codgers trying to watch a rugby match and stay sober!'

Amongst the best of Harris's new spate of films was *Unforgiven* (1992), Clint Eastwood's revenge Western. Casting the picture, Eastwood called Harris in the Bahamas. 'Who's this?' said the Irishman. 'Richard, this is Clint. I got this picture that I'd really like for you to play a part in. Can I send you a script?' Harris was ecstatic. 'You got to be kidding? Do you know what I'm watching right now? *High Plains Drifter*, it's my favourite Western! You don't have to send me a script for your new movie. I'd love to do it.'

Though they'd never met, Eastwood admired Harris greatly: 'He was a slightly mad Irishman and a truly gifted performer.' The feeling was mutual. 'Clint's one of the few Hollywood heads worth the money.'

Although he was back making 'Hollywood' pictures again, Harris's dislike of the movie capital remained. 'The only good thing about Hollywood is that you know where all the thieves in the film business live.'

Harris had always preferred home-grown talents to the puffed up twits in Hollywood. He admired the likes of Olivier and also Gielgud, an actor Harris admired from afar as socially their paths had scarcely if ever crossed. On the thespian's 90th birthday Harris decided to telephone the great man. 'Happy birthday, Sir John,' he hollered down the line. 'This is Richard Harris phoning from the Bahamas just to wish you happy birthday and thank you for everything you have done for British theatre. We are hugely in your debt.' There was a pause. 'Harris you say,' replied Sir John. 'I don't know a Harris. Of course there is that very loud, vulgar chap from Ireland. Did the *Camelot* thing. Very bad reputation with drink and women, I believe. Very bad indeed. Anyway, I thank you so very much for phoning from Bermuda; so sweet.' 'Bahamas, Sir John, Bahamas.' 'Yes, yes, yes. The sun shines there as well, I believe.'

Alas, Harris had little time for his old 60s chum Michael Caine, whose career, after years in the wilderness, had rejuvenated to such a point that he was being revered as the Queen Mum of British film. Harris could stand it no longer and wrote a letter to the newspapers claiming Caine had got too big for his boots. Incensed, Caine burst into Harris's London hotel suite one day demanding an apology. Harris obliged. Not long afterwards Harris read an interview with Caine in *The Sunday Times* in which the star referred to Burton, O'Toole and himself as 'drunks'. Harris fired back with a letter printed in the following week's *Sunday Times* that referred to Caine as 'a fat, flatulent 62-year-old windbag. If only he had indulged in a few trips to his local boozer instead of breezing past the common man in his Rolls-Royces he might have achieved a modicum of immortality, instead of being part-owner of dreary restaurants.' During an interview when Harris was asked what he thought of Caine he let rip an almighty fart. 'Do you hear that?' Harris asked the journalist. 'That was an automatic fart after hearing his name.' Harris went further: 'I don't care what he says. But don't characterize Burton, O'Toole and me as drunks as if that's all we've achieved in our life, because he could live 20 fucking lives and he couldn't achieve as much as we three have achieved.'

Peter O'Toole found the Harris/Caine spat all rather amusing. 'When Caine made those comments Harris got on the phone to me straight away, saying, "This asshole, Jesus, fuck!" I hadn't read the piece, and I still haven't, though I read what Harris said about him and croaked with laughter.' When pressed, O'Toole refused to take sides, believing both actors could handle themselves perfectly well without him. 'Though,' he told one journalist, with a hint of menace, 'I think a caution to "watch your big mouth" is in order.'

He was a hit back on the London stage with *Jeffrey Bernard*, but alas O'Toole's film career was nowhere near matching his stage success. He was making pictures that went unreleased, unwatched, like *The Rainbow Thief* (1990), which at least reunited him with his old *Lawrence of Arabia* co-star Omar Sharif. Filming one dangerous stunt, Sharif almost drowned on a flooded sewer set. O'Toole naturally saw the funny side of it. 'Come on,' he said. 'There's nothing funnier than an angry, wet Egyptian.' The two men had stayed in touch and were close friends, meeting now and again in a bid to relive their golden heyday. 'The last time Omar and I were together was in Cairo a few months back, and we misbehaved ourselves all over again. Even though we're venerable gentlemen, we can still misbehave ourselves appallingly, and we did what young men do, only perhaps marginally more slowly.'

Another O'Toole movie misfire was *King Ralph* (1991) about a brash American who becomes King of England when the entire Royal Family are killed in a freak accident. O'Toole knew he was making a piece of crap. 'It was meant to be a light-hearted, quick little frolic that suddenly turned into this dull, plodding nightmare.' At least he found solace in the supporting cast of fruity British thespians. 'The only thing that got us through was that John Hurt and James Villiers were on it, so at least we had a decent poker school.'

The star was John Goodman, who didn't hide his complete awe of O'Toole. During a break in filming, Goodman asked to borrow an ashtray. O'Toole, with characteristic flair, flicked his ash on the floor and declared: 'Make the world your ashtray, my boy.'

* * *

Since the late 1980s Oliver Reed had been pretty much unemployable, appearing for the most part in appalling TV movies. 'If you look at Oliver's career as the career of an artist,' says Michael Winner, 'it went into the toilet. It basically vanished.' He made one film alongside O. J. Simpson, but the money ran out and it was shut down. Director John Hough heard one story that Ollie and Simpson were drinking in a bar and got into an argument over whether American football or English rugby was the tougher game. 'Suddenly O. J. charged across the room and crashed into Oliver, sending him flying, and said, "That's what it's like in American football." Up came Oliver and charged back and knocked Simpson all across the room and said, "Well that's what it's like in English rugby." They kept doing it and quickly it got out of hand, they were like two bulls charging against each other. Then this little Welshman, who was sitting drinking his pint of beer in the corner, suddenly stood up and said, "You're spoiling my drink," and with one blow knocked out O. J. Simpson and with the other blow knocked out Oliver Reed. The film's stunt man, who was supposed to be looking after the two stars, jumped in to try and restrain this Welsh guy and he felt his muscles and they were like solid steel. He told me, "There you've got a real tough guy."'

Reed's friend Ken Russell cast him in his own TV film, *Prisoner of Honour* (1991). The two hadn't worked together for years and Russell saw in his old sparring partner that the spark he once loved had burned out. 'There was always an animal lurking under the surface and the animal had either been tamed or driven out of him. It wasn't the same Oliver. He was a different man.'

It didn't take much, though, to raise the sleeping loon within Reed. One night at home in his kitchen he'd been drinking steadily. The lights were on too bright and when he tried to work the dimmer switch he was foiled. Angry, he declared, 'I know how to turn the fucking things off,' and jumped onto the table and punched out each bulb in turn. He cut his hand so badly that he needed hospital treatment.

Reed also made a short appearance in the forgotten British comedy *Funny Bones* (1995), about an American comedian in Britain. It was shot in Blackpool, and regulars of a local pub complained that Reed drank its entire stock of imported lager while working in the city. At least he was fit again after suffering from a bout of health scares. Delighted to be given the all-clear after a medical check up, Reed phoned a friend in London and invited himself over. This mate lived on the fourth floor of an apartment block, which at the time was covered in scaffolding. Reed didn't care. Armed with an eight-pack of beer Ollie climbed up the scaffolding, meeting workers and distributing cans on the way, got on the roof and banged on the skylight of his friend's flat. For the next few days Ollie insisted on using this route to get in, once even stopping off to lay a course of 60 bricks.

When Ollie did manage to land what could have led to a renaissance in his career, such as a role in the blockbuster movie *Cutthroat Island* (1995), he blew it, big time. At the pre-production party he went around showing everyone his cock or his 'mighty mallet' as he still fondly referred to it. Star Geena Davis was not amused and Reed was promptly sent home. 'Thank you very much,' said the producer. 'We've seen your cock, now get on the next plane; we'll have someone else do the part.' For his friends and supporters it was all too common a tale. 'Oliver lost a lot of work through that kind of behaviour, no question,' says Michael Winner.

After a long absence Richard Harris was now back on the booze, but only Guinness or maybe the odd glass of wine, not spirits, 'because they were my undoing'. It was a move precipitated by attending the funeral of one of his brothers. Having lost his father, two sisters and two brothers to hereditary heart disease, it was fear of death that had prompted Harris years before to abstain from booze. Now, he thought, wouldn't his relatives all like to get out of the grave just for five minutes to enjoy a pint of Guinness? Harris searched out the nearest pub and sampled his first pint of stout for 13 years. It tasted better than ever. 'It was delicious. Better than making love to Marilyn Monroe.' Those 13 years of abstinence he claimed were the most boring years of his life. 'Nothing is worse than a group of people having a drink and you're sipping Perrier water and they're getting funnier and you're getting more and more bored.'

From now until his death Harris enjoyed a daily tipple. 'You need to stay lubricated, just to remind yourself you are still living and breathing.' The drink also came in handy on one occasion when in a New York bar a man came up to Harris and for no apparent reason hit him and then fled – but not fast enough. With deadly accuracy and a fair degree of venom Harris hurled his empty pint pot at the fleeing stranger, striking him on the head causing a vicious wound. 'A cracking shot,' exclaimed a triumphant Harris.

Even at this late stage Harris was still never very far away from violence erupting, especially in pubs. Around this time it emerged that Harris had crossed swords with fellow Limerickman Frank McCourt, the author of the best-selling *Angela's Ashes*, which the actor believed was derogatory about his birthplace. They'd first met in an Irish pub in New York, and Harris even then despised the writer's bitter feelings about Limerick. As their discussion grew more heated McCourt suddenly belted Harris on the nose. 'Then, like a hare running from a hound, he raced towards the exit door and ran out of the pub,' Harris claimed. 'I have never yet been confronted by a Limerickman who ran away from a fight. We don't do that in Limerick, we stand our ground and we fight. To run from a fight is not part of the Limerick character at all.'

Director Peter Medak, who'd been a close friend in the 60s, met Harris again in 1997 when he directed him in a TV movie of *The Hunchback of Notre Dame* and discovered that the man had hardly changed at all. 'He was the same. He had that same kind of wonderful madness in him. He just lived every second of his life. I don't think he ever mellowed; Richard was the same person all the way. When I was doing post-production with him in London's Soho he said, "Fuck it, that's it, let's go and have lunch," and it didn't matter where you were in the world with him, whether it was in Prague or in London, or wherever, there was an Irish pub just round the corner. "That's where we're going," he'd say. He used to buy drinks for everybody. He was incredibly personable. But all the great actors were like that; they had no pretence about themselves. They were great stars back in the 60s, not like stars today who are so isolated from the real world, from the public. Back then they were in the street. Burton would go back to Wales into the local pubs, everybody knew him and could talk to him; nowadays they have 18 bodyguards. It's because Burton and Harris and the others came from working class roots and that never really left them. They were real people.'

Medak didn't know that Harris had taken up booze again when they met to discuss the film at the Savoy hotel. 'I called him and said, "Where are you?" and he said, "I'm in the bar." By the time I arrived there were empty champagne bottles and I said, "Richard, you're not supposed to drink." He said, "Fuck it, that's not drink, this is milk." He was knocking it back. I don't know how many we had. It just didn't matter to him. Drinking Guinness or champagne for him was really milk.'

But still the regrets were there; the fact that often he couldn't remember incidents from his own past. 'I often sit back and think, I wish I'd done that, and find out later that I already have.' A story that is pure Harris occurred in 1997 when he was looking through a stack of old photographs and noticed one of himself standing next to a Rolls-Royce, except that he didn't remember ever owning such a car. He called both his ex-wives and they didn't know, so he called his LA accountant who said, 'Yes, it's been in a garage in New York since 1974 at a cost of $400 a month.' Over time the bill had mounted up to $92,000. Immediately Harris had the car shipped to England, restored and put up for sale because he couldn't bear the thought of driving round in a posh car like Michael Caine.

Peter O'Toole continued to appear in absolutely nothing of any worth whatsoever. It seemed that Hollywood producers were choosing to ignore him for major movies. But the O'Toole name still carried with it the aura of legend and he made arguably one of the greatest entrances in television history in 1995 when he appeared on the David Letterman chat show. The host introduced him to the roar of the audience but nobody emerged from behind the curtain. A couple of seconds went by, still no sign of O'Toole. More seconds passed, still no sign of him. Then to the surprise of everyone a camel strode out from behind the curtain with none other than a beaming O'Toole perched atop it. The camel turned fully around in a tight circle at centre stage, O'Toole skilfully manoeuvring the animal with a combination of gentle taps from the end of a long switch. The audience roared their approval as O'Toole commanded the camel to assume a full kneeling position, one that allowed the actor to dismount. Before the audience had a chance to catch its breath O'Toole pulled out a can of beer from his jacket, popped the top and toasted the crowd and Letterman before gulping down a healthy swig.

The crowd was in hysterics by now, but O'Toole had one further surprise up his sleeve. Turning to the camel, which though kneeling still carried its head a good two feet above his own, O'Toole offered the beast the can of beer. Without hesitation the camel's rubbery lips reached out and wrapped themselves around the can, tugging it out of O'Toole's hand and guzzling down the entire contents. Finished, it tossed the empty can across the stage floor, licking its lips in complete satisfaction. Milking the moment, as if he were back on the boards of the Old Vic, O'Toole bowed to the audience and his animal partner before taking his seat next to Letterman. It took quite a while for the applause to finally subside; when it did O'Toole said, 'I think that's called a stupid pet trick!'

In 1995 Oliver Reed moved from Guernsey and relocated to County Cork in Ireland, a long cherished dream of his. He settled in easily and the locals all accepted him and weren't fazed at all by a notorious hellraiser and film star moving in amongst them. Soon after arriving he was invited on Irish comic Patrick Kielty's TV chat show. Reed turned up in Belfast at one o'clock in the afternoon pie-eyed and proceeded to stand in the Green Room with an equally drunk mate shouting Shakespeare at each other. 'My good man, I'm the finest actor,' declared Reed. 'I think you'll find Ollie that I am the finest actor.' And so on. By the time the show went out live in the evening Reed could barely string a sentence together. The production team was running around panic stricken in a bid to rustle up a last minute replacement, but there was no one, it had to be Reed or there was no show. So out he walked to the strains of 'Wild Thing', playing it up to the hilt.

Reed sat down and Kielty opened with the first question. 'Well Oliver, how long have you been in Ireland?' The question barely seemed to register on Reed's befuddled face. Then he answered. 'Young man . . . how long . . . is your dick?' The audience roared with laughter. 'You haven't been here that long then,' the comic hit back. 'It was just a nightmare,' Kielty later recalled. 'We ended up drinking till three in the morning. And . . . oh, just bizarre.'

The career, however, was still a concern; Reed hadn't made a major movie for ten years. It was his old friend Michael Winner who brought him back into the limelight with a role in *Parting Shots* (1999), a black comedy about a man (played by rock star Chris Rea) who learns he only has six weeks left to live so decides to take revenge on the people in his life who've deeply pissed him off. Reed promised Winner he'd behave and not drink and was pretty true to his word. The problems started after filming when Winner was plagued by a series of phone calls from a sozzled Reed, often late at night. The conversation would inevitably begin with 'I love you, Michael,' before sliding into a series of slurred messages. 'That's very nice, Oliver,' Winner would say. 'Is Josephine there?' The phone would be handed over and Winner would chat with Josephine while Ollie shouted thoughts and opinions in the background. Suddenly Winner would hear over the line the dull thud of Ollie hitting the floor. 'I've got to go,' Josephine would then say. 'Oliver needs me.'

During post-production on *Parting Shots* Winner requested Reed's services back in London to dub one particular scene due to an awful sound recording on location. Phoning the Hampstead hotel Reed was staying at, Winner was told by the receptionist that Ollie had gone out the previous evening, got blind drunk and been arrested outside the tube station. Winner dialled Hampstead police station. A desk sergeant answered the phone. 'I understand my friend Mr Reed spent the night with you,' said Winner. 'We've just released him,' replied the officer. 'He was arrested at ten o'clock for being drunk and disorderly, but we haven't charged him because he was so charming.' Just minutes later a taxi drew up outside Winner's house and Reed clambered out. He was in no fit state to dub his voice and the recording session proved useless. As he left, Reed turned to Winner and said, 'You know I mustn't travel without Josephine. She looks after me.' Reed once even rang his wife from California to ask her how the video recorder in his hotel room worked. 'He was very humble and ashamed that he'd spent the night in the cells,' recalls Winner. 'And then he went off, and that was the last time I ever saw Oliver Reed.'

About halfway through production of *Parting Shots* Reed had sauntered over to Michael Winner and said, 'I can't believe it, Ridley Scott wants me to go and read for him. But I'm a star.' Winner said, 'Oliver, don't fuck with me. You're not a fucking star. You're out of work and you're not old enough to retire, you haven't got enough money to retire, so you need a third act to your career. Obviously they think if you're working with me you can't be as drunk as people think you are. So go to Ridley and read. End of story, Oliver. And if he wants you to read twice, read twice.' Reed took Winner's advice. The role was for *Gladiator* (2000).

Once Scott had cast Reed in the role of a world-weary slave merchant and ex-gladiator, the film's insurers, concerned about his reputation, reportedly wrote asking how much he still drank. Ollie returned the form saying, 'Only at parties.' The insurers are said to have written again, asking nervously, 'How many parties do you go to?'

The insurers were right to be worried. Reed was still getting into trouble, recently going on Sky News live where he was asked what his future plans were and he replied, to make love to the channel's female presenter. In January 1999 he was arrested at Heathrow airport for throwing beer over customers in a restaurant. He was given a caution and released. It was to be his last reported misdemeanour.

On the set of *Gladiator* the old Reed mischief was never far away. In a scene opposite stand up comic Omid Djalili, playing a slave trader, Reed squeezed Djalili's testicles throughout the take. Just before the camera rolled Reed had enquired of him, 'Are you a method actor?' and then stuck his big, fat mitts on his balls. 'Not many people can say Ollie Reed has fondled their nuts,' said the comic.

Reed undertook the role in *Gladiator* with little inkling of what its impact would be, or that it would ultimately be his cinematic curtain call. He'd always had a peculiar take on death, particularly the whole rigmarole of what would happen to his body. He had no desire to be laid out for days in his Sunday best: 'And have people gawking at me to see what a dead hellraiser looks like.' Nor did he want to be cremated: the very thought of his body frying in its own fat made him quite queasy. Burial wasn't an option, either. He didn't want maggots crawling up his nose and out of his mouth. Burial at sea was out, too. 'Who wants to be gobbled up by a big fish and become excrement that gets eaten by a sardine whose excrement is swallowed by a prawn?' Reed didn't much relish the thought of being part of a prawn cocktail eaten by some pretty girl in a fancy restaurant, which, when passed through her body, is flushed into the sewer and then into the sea again: 'I don't want to be a permanent shit.' Reed eventually came to the perfect solution. He'd become fertiliser that's spread under a sunflower and made eventually into sunflower seed oil, 'So instead of nibbling me in her prawn cocktail the pretty girl will rub me on her Bristols as she suns herself on a beach in the Caribbean.'

In the end Reed's death was messy, nonsensical and avoidable. Much of

Gladiator was shot in Malta and Reed quickly found the most English bar on the island, a pub called – imaginatively – The Pub. On May 2nd 1999 Ollie had drunk there with Josephine and was about to leave when a gang of sailors burst in. Reed saw them and there was only ever going to be one outcome: 'Let's have a drink,' he roared, pulling them towards him. 'Black rums all round.' Reed downed 12 double measures of rum and then retreated to his more accustomed double whiskies. He also challenged the sailors to an arm wrestling contest, beating a number of challengers.

When the sailors got up to leave Reed happily signed autographs and then slumped back into his chair to rest, snoring audibly. Then the snoring stopped. Josephine noticed his lips were darkening. Something was very wrong. Laid out on a bench, Reed was given mouth to mouth resuscitation while someone called for an ambulance. Quick to arrive, it sped off with Reed to hospital but the paramedics couldn't feel a pulse. Inside casualty doctors struggled to revive Reed but it was too late. The great man had passed over. 'It was very sad because I spoke to him two days before he died,' says Winner. 'A *Daily Mail* reporter was going over to see him and I said, "Do me a favour dear, don't throw her in the pool, don't take her knickers down and hurl her round the room. Please just be very nice to her." He said, "Michael, I promise you, I've only got a couple more shots in the movie and they've offered me *Uncle Silas* on television." So he was very pleased that he thought he was washed up and now he was back. Then I got the call, Oliver Reed's dead, and I just burst into tears. Terrible.'

There was almost an inevitability about Oliver Reed's death, but it still came as an enormous shock to friends and colleagues. 'I was really sad when Ollie died,' says Mark Lester. 'The Americans were terrified of Ollie because of his reputation, but after *Gladiator* I think he would have got a lot more work and a lot more substantial roles in Hollywood. Because he was a very, very good actor, a very powerful actor. But the trouble with Ollie was that he was his own worst enemy, as many of those hellraisers were, and he wasn't as powerful as Burton so that he could get away with doing a lot of the things he did. The trouble was, Ollie was a binge drinker so he could go for days and weeks without having anything, but when he did drink he used to drink huge amounts and in the end I don't think his body could take it.'

'His death was a total nonsense,' is Ken Russell's take. 'It shouldn't have happened. It was very sad. He'd just done *Gladiator* and shown that he was a bloody good actor and was all set for a comeback, and then he resorted to arm wrestling with 18-year-old sailors. It was a terrible waste.'

At least one could take solace in the fact that, just like Bing Crosby croaking it on a golf course, can you think of a better place for Ollie to die than in a pub? 'I am very sorry he has gone,' Reed's old co-star Glenda Jackson told the press, 'but I think he probably went the way he would have wished.' Winner holds similar thoughts. 'There's no question that he missed his resurrection with *Gladiator*. But at least he went quickly. He didn't suffer, not like my dear friend Burt Lancaster who had a stroke and was a zombie for seven years. So from Ollie's point of view it wasn't a bad exit.'

Even better was the funeral. Thousands of ordinary people turned up to show their respect, and when Reed's coffin came out of the wagon spontaneous applause started, and a few raised voices cried, 'Go to it Ollie,' while a single lone piper started to play as the congregation walked into the church. 'I was the only person from showbusiness who went to Oliver's funeral,' is Winner's personal recollection. 'All the people who said he was wonderful, none of them turned up, they couldn't be bothered to go as far as Cork. I didn't cry at my mother's funeral. I didn't cry at my father's funeral. I wept at Oliver's funeral. The coffin was down there in the church, I walked down, touched the coffin, I was in floods of tears.'

Newspapers everywhere carried the news of Reed's passing. As with Burton before him, commentators spoke of a life of waste, a career that had such promise in the 70s thrown away in pubs, chat show embarrassments and gutters of puke. 'When Oliver died a lot of the papers said he had a wasted life,' says Winner. 'It wasn't a wasted life at all, he had a wonderful life. He enjoyed himself. He did a lot of movies, he had a long career considering, he didn't end up broke, he lived in a lovely house in Ireland which he loved, and he had a lovely wife and lovely children. How can that be a wasted life?'

Perhaps the tragedy of Reed is that he created a persona for himself that he felt obliged constantly to live up to. 'If I went around kissing babies and doing good, the public wouldn't be interested,' he once said. 'That's not what the public expects from Oliver Reed. They want him to fall off the edge of a dustbin, get into fights and get drunk and do all the things you read in the papers.' There was nobody better in the world at playing the public clown than Ollie Reed, and thank God he took up the mantle. The only problem was that in the end it obscured the talents of a truly great actor.

Oliver Reed's passing left a gaping hole in so many people's lives. 'He was a great man who did things his own way,' says top chef Marco Pierre White. 'He used to come into my restaurant in Wandsworth and sit on the floor to have a drink before going to the table. On one occasion, he started praising everything – the décor, the service, the food. I said, "Ollie, you've been here dozens of times and I know you like the place. You don't have to say all these nice things." And he said, "Yes, but this is the only time I've been here sober."'

Such antics and blissful ignorance of normal life were priceless; no wonder those who shared his friendship mourned him so heavily. 'Ollie would phone me sometimes late at night, pissed out of his mind,' says Michael Winner, 'but 99% of the time I was with him he was the quietest, gentlest, most considerate and kind human being you could ever meet.'

When Richard Harris heard that his 'old slugging partner' Reed had died he was shocked and unsettled, particularly by the manner of his passing. For Harris, Reed's end would not be his own. 'I intend to die in bed aged 110, writing poetry, sipping Guinness and serenading a woman.'

Ironically, Harris had just finished making his one and only film with Reed, though they never shared any scenes together. He was cast as Emperor Marcus Aurelius, and most of his scenes in *Gladiator* were with young guns Russell Crowe and Joaquin Phoenix. After their first scene together Harris came over to Crowe and said, 'I am going to make one assumption about you, Crowe – I bet you love rugby.' From that instant they were boozing buddies and, although they only worked on the film together for three weeks, developed a close friendship, with the elder statesman tipping the Antipodean star to carry on his bad boy behaviour. 'Russell's a top bloke, a brilliant actor and a much loved new friend. He will carry the baton on. He irritates the hell out of the Hollywood bigwigs, but he's much too good for them to ignore.'

Both, however, couldn't quite fathom out Phoenix. The young actor was incredibly nervous on the set and would ask Crowe to rough him up before their big scenes together so he could psyche himself up into his villainous character. Crowe was at a loss as to what to do and so went over to Harris to ask his advice. 'Mate, what are we gonna do with this kid, he's asking me to abuse him before takes.' Harris thought for a while and then replied, 'Let's get him pissed.' Over the course of several hours and several pints of Guinness, Harris and Crowe managed to relax their young co-star.

Approaching his 70th year, Harris took up residency at London's prestigious Savoy hotel. Such self-imposed isolation worried him not a jot. 'I find myself the best company in the world.' And he loved the fact that if he wanted a sandwich at 4am, he could get one; that the hotel's staff was at his beck and call. For this he considered £6,000 a week cheap at the price: 'If you're paying the mortgage on a home you can't ask the bank manager to fetch you a pint.' He could press a bell and dinner would arrive, press another and the valet came to take his clothes away. 'And as for female company?' asked one inquisitive journalist. 'Oh, you bring those in yourself.'

Harris prided himself that he was still attractive to women and enjoyed a relatively active sex life for a pensioner, though the famous libido was now somewhat limited. 'All of a sudden you can't do it any more, as well or as often. Sometimes it's a struggle.' So he once resorted to using Viagra, but never again. 'It worked too well. I was taking this woman out to dinner afterwards and couldn't zip up my trousers. I couldn't get it down.'

By 2000 Harris was passing into legend. The *Daily Telegraph* saw him as someone with 'the forehead of an Old Testament prophet'. His face indeed looked magnificently battered: 'My life's stamped on it.' At a European film ceremony he received a lifetime achievement award. 'I consider myself in God's departure lounge,' he told the audience, 'waiting for that final plane, but luckily some of my scheduled flights have been cancelled – mostly because I've said I'm not going to die yet.' He'd even taken to helping out fellow hellraisers during their own private turmoils, such as mentoring fallen star Mickey Rourke, holing him up in an LA hotel while he sorted out his fractured career and life.

For a change it was Harris's son making all the tabloid headlines, not him. Jamie had inherited many of his father's hellraising genes and been a regular and hard drinker since the age of 14. At boarding school he'd been fined £1,000 for stealing a cement mixer and driving it two miles back to school after a drunken night out. Harris proudly framed and displayed his son's drunk and disorderly fine in the rear porch at his home in the Bahamas.

Before the curtain finally closed on Harris there was to be one last flourish. When the offer arrived in 2001 to play Professor Albus Dumbledore in the first *Harry Potter* movie Harris did what Sean Connery had done just weeks before, he turned it down. The actor didn't want the hassle any more of early morning calls, or the thought of being saddled to a long running series. 'I hate commitment of any kind – that's why I've got two ex-wives. It scares me.' It was Harris's 11-year-old granddaughter who begged him to reconsider, threatening never to talk to him again if he refused the role. 'What could I do?' moaned Harris. 'I wasn't going to let her down.' The film was a box office phenomenon and Harris became something of a hero to the young cast and a whole new generation of cinema goers.

So it was with great satisfaction that he turned up for work on the sequel the following year, but on the set people noted his weariness and how thin he suddenly looked, not fully aware that he was very ill indeed. But the old lion was still there, not hesitating to call for a re-take or question the lighting. However, when his colleagues deigned to do the same he'd rant, 'Look, there's a war in the Middle East and bombs being thrown all over the world. There's real life going on out there. This is all just make-believe crap.' One evening he teamed up with Alan Rickman and Kenneth Branagh on a pub assault and the trio was still drinking come 4 o'clock the next morning. 'Richard was regaling us with stories about his life,' recalled Rickman. 'We just sat there with our mouths wide open.' The old magic was still there, but for how long?

Finishing his *Harry Potter* duties in the summer of 2002, Harris retreated to his Savoy suite and all but disappeared. Friends grew worried that he was barely eating, and even his bedtime Guinness was proving too painful to digest. Then there was silence: nothing, no phone calls, no visits, and no letters. It got so bad that Elizabeth and his sons went to the Savoy and literally banged the door down. Inside Harris's condition had deteriorated. He was emaciated and weak and they insisted on calling an ambulance. 'When they took him away to hospital,' recalls director Peter Medak, 'the lobby just completely stopped, and Richard sat up on the stretcher and turned back to the whole foyer and shouted, "It was the food! Don't touch the food!" That was typical Richard.'

The diagnosis was Hodgkin's disease, an insidious lymphatic cancer. Reluctantly Harris started a course of chemotherapy that lasted several weeks, with his sons and Elizabeth in constant attendance. He strove to put on a brave face for the world, telling *Harry Potter* director and producer Chris Columbus that if he recast Dumbledore in the third instalment, 'I'll kill you.'

Despite heavy treatment it was soon clear that Harris was fighting a battle he simply couldn't win. At peace with himself, Harris had a life to look back on that was the envy of most of us. That he'd boozed a lot of it away didn't bother him a bit. 'I had the happiest days of my life as a drinker. If I had my life again I'd make all the same mistakes. I would still sleep with as many women, and drink as much vodka. Any regrets would make me seem ungrateful.'

Fearing the worst, Richard's son Jared phoned Ann Turkel in Hollywood, advising her to fly to London immediately. On the flight over the actress didn't believe her former husband was going to die. 'I was willing him to survive. I felt that by being there, there might be some glimmer of hope.' That glimmer flickered out as soon as she arrived at the hospital on October 25th and saw Harris attached to a life support machine. Beside him was Elizabeth, looking concerned, and his three sons. Ann held his hand, spoke into his ear and told him she loved him. 'I'm here, Annie's here, I won't leave. You're not going to go – you've got too much left to do.' Harris slowly closed his eyes. 'I need to sleep now,' he said. A few minutes later the life support machine was switched off; Harris was gone.

As Richard Harris lay in the morgue, his sons stood beside him, pausing for reflection. Thinking it too quiet and sombre, Jamie slipped outside to grab a pint of Guinness. Dipping his finger into the black nectar he moistened his father's lips with it. That's how the great man went to meet his maker, as he'd love to have gone, with the taste of a good pint on him.

Ten days later Harris was laid to rest. The mass held in London was beautiful, the coffin draped in an Irish flag, but Ann broke down at the crematorium. 'That was something else. To watch this vibrant, extraordinary man being on a conveyor belt . . . I just totally lost it and sobbed uncontrollably.'

Russell Crowe flew 5,000 miles from filming *Master and Commander* in Mexico to attend the service and was close to tears throughout. Afterwards he told journalists outside the church, 'I love him and I miss him. He was one of the greatest actors who ever walked this planet.' Crowe later joined Harris's family and friends in a London hotel and remembered his fallen pal by leaping on to the bar and raising a pint of Guinness after reciting the Irish ode 'Sanctity' by Patrick Kavanagh. Crowe had read the poem months earlier at the BAFTA film awards ceremony in tribute to Harris, who was then gravely ill, and was furious when the BBC cut it out of the broadcast. Hunting down the show's director Malcolm Gerrie, he pinned the man against a wall while unleashing a foul-mouthed tirade. Predictably the incident made headlines, cementing Crowe's bad boy persona.

This time Crowe's reading of 'Sanctity' was an emotional moment and he cheered on Harris's sons Damian, Jared and Jamie as they took it in turns to stand on the hotel bar and pay their respects. Mourners were determined to give Harris a huge send off and hotel staff had to call out for more Guinness as the revellers drank the place dry.

So deep ran Crowe's respect for Harris that he later fulfilled a promise he'd made to the dying actor to visit his home town of Limerick, drinking Guinness in some of Harris's old haunts, followed everywhere by a phalanx of journalists. Also there was Jared, who explained to reporters the close bond that existed between his father and Crowe. 'Dad saw himself in Russell – they were cut from the same cloth. And having met him I agree.'

Shortly after Harris's death a book of condolences was opened in Limerick that showed just how much he was loved by generations of people from all over the world. Alongside signatures of former colleagues and friends were childish scrawls from youngsters who knew him only from *Harry Potter*. One touching tribute read: 'From a nine-year-old girl who fell in love with Albus Dumbledore and her mother who fell in love with King Arthur. Thank you for that "One Brief Shining Moment."'

Others remembered the actor for his hellraising reputation, including more than a few landlords and barmaids. Colette Simms recalled how on her first week working behind the bar, she served Richard Harris her first pint of Guinness. 'He came into the bar for a quick drink because he was supposed to be leaving at three o'clock that day. But he didn't leave until three the following day.' It's a story that sums up Richard Harris perhaps better than most.

Curiously though for a man who loved his country with a passion, Harris's ashes were scattered in the Bahamas. A curious end to an extraordinary life.

When Peter O'Toole heard of Harris's passing he was deeply moved. 'A great spirit has gone, though I didn't expect him to die. I thought he was indestructible.' Even though sadly they never worked together, the two men had been friends and rugby game chums for 50 years, often cheering on Munster, Harris's favourite team. Harris didn't share O'Toole's love of cricket, however. 'Harris hated cricket. I mean he hated it. This tedious baffling English game. He found it insupportable.' In recent years, however, Harris had been barred from going to any of Munster's matches because he was considered a jinx. Local newspapers called it 'the Harris factor' because the team had lost every game in the last few years he'd attended. When Munster reached a cup semi final Harris again was barred, but he kept a keen watch on the result. 'I'll be hanging from every goalpost if they lose,' he said, which of course, they did.

'I went into his room afterwards,' O'Toole recalled. 'It was the last time we saw each other. The television was on and there was Harris watching cricket, after 50 years of cursing it. Then he turned off the television and put his head on the pillow, and I thought, "Well after the unnamable horror of a game of cricket, death must have been a walk in the park." And I'm now convinced that the long shadow on a cricket field is Harris.'

Last Man Standing

First Burton, then Reed and now Harris – all had gone; now only Peter O'Toole was left to fight the good fight. For a while it seemed O'Toole had checked out too when in 2001, mistakenly believing the great man had pegged it, confused fans bombarded websites dedicated to the Irish actor after he went on a TV show to talk about old age and plans for his send-off, including the fact he'd already chosen his own epitaph. Tributes poured in. One message read, 'I can't believe he's gone. What a man, what a talent.' The fan sites hurriedly issued a statement reassuring fans that O'Toole was still very much alive.

Perhaps sensing that O'Toole wasn't too far behind his comrades in retiring to the cricket pavilion of dead hellraisers, the Academy of Motion Picture Arts and Sciences decided in 2002 to bestow upon him their lifetime achievement Oscar. Chuffed? Not a bit of it. Over his whole career O'Toole had received seven nominations for best actor without a single win; it was a record he shared with Richard Burton. Back in the 70s the two men shared a plane flight. 'And we proceeded to get drunk,' Burton recalled. 'Peter asked me how many Oscar nominations I'd had. I said, truthfully, five. He said, holding up his fingers, that he'd had four. I know he's only had two. Does he think we're idiots?'

O'Toole stunned Hollywood by rejecting the honorary statuette, declaring in a note to the Academy that as he was 'still in the game and might win the lovely bugger outright, would the Academy please defer the honour until I am 80?' The board of directors sent a note back saying, 'We unanimously and enthusiastically voted you the honorary award because you've earned and deserved it.' The show's producer branded O'Toole 'silly' for not attending the ceremony; not half as silly as the Academy was for failing seven times to give the man a proper Oscar.

In the end O'Toole backtracked and decided to make a personal appearance after all, but almost missed out on picking up his Oscar after he threatened to leave the ceremony because of the show's strict no-alcohol rules. O'Toole had arrived in the green room and sauntered over to the bar to ask for a drink. 'We have lemon juice, apple juice, still or sparkling,' said the barman. O'Toole gazed at him with alarm. 'No, I want a drink.' The barman shook his head. 'No alcohol, sir.' O'Toole's face went ashen. 'All right, I'm fucking off.' One of the lackeys managed to stop him in time and eventually some vodka was smuggled in. 'I still like a little drink,' he told the press.

O'Toole was certainly still in the game and had seen something of a renaissance in his career. He sparkled as the elderly Casanova in a BBC drama series and was back making epic movies too, appearing as Augustus Caesar in a mammoth American TV production. Director Roger Young had only ever envisaged O'Toole for the role and was a huge fan. 'I flew to London to meet him, but I was so in awe of the man that I kind of drifted through the experience in a daze.' Arriving on location in Tunisia, O'Toole was given a large rented house by the ocean. Young paid him a visit the first day, just to hear his ideas about the script. 'I arrived at the appointed time and was escorted, by his assistant, through this large house out to the balcony where Peter waited. He sat in a chair at a table with the script laid out in front of him. I was terrified. I thought that Peter O'Toole could rip the director into little shreds of whimpering self-doubt if he wanted to, and I was afraid that he might want to, just to show who the boss was. He did nothing of the kind. He was charming, calm, soft spoken, and never arrogant. He never threw his weight around.'

Instead they just talked and when O'Toole finally showed signs of wanting to wrap up the meeting Young asked if he could be shown the way out, since he'd forgotten the path to the front door. 'I have no idea, darling,' said O'Toole. 'I don't go into the rest of the house. I stay in this room.' The room he was talking about was of tiny proportions with just a bed against one wall, a dresser, a closet and a bedside table. It was obviously meant for the maid. 'Mr O'Toole,' said Young (it took him a whole week to summon up the courage to call him Peter), 'I'm sure there is a master bedroom for you to sleep in.' O'Toole shook his head. 'No, no, I can't stand all that room. I'm fine here. I don't go into the rest of this house. Too large.'

When it came time to film O'Toole's scenes Young was so in awe that he couldn't find the guts within himself to give the star a note, a piece of direction, or even a suggestion for three full days of shooting. 'I could barely ask him to do a second take. Finally, on the fourth day, he said to me, rather loudly, so all could hear . . . "Darling, call me Peter. And tell me what you want." I'm not sure I can impart what a privilege that was. PETER O'TOOLE just said "Direct me." TO ME! So began one of the most enjoyable shoots I ever had.'

O'Toole also gained the respect of the entire cast and crew, largely because of who he was and the incredible reputation that he carried around with him, like a shadow, but also by his sheer professionalism. 'Peter often would take part in preparing the set,' recalls Young. 'If he wanted a prop, or a piece of furniture moved for the scene, he would just do it himself. There is a scene in which he gets into a bath. Peter helped fill the tub!'

It was a long tough shoot and about a quarter through it O'Toole got sick. 'We thought it was serious,' says Young. 'I visited Peter in hospital. He looked ill. I was afraid for him. The next day we started planning how to shoot around him. He was obviously going to be out for weeks. The day after that, he was back on the set! Ready to work. No little illness was going to stop him. He worked every day after that. If anyone showed concern for his health he simply waved them off. He's a strong man.'

Still, Young remained concerned about his star's fragile health, particularly as the role required dollops of stamina. In one scene Augustus Caesar faints on the hard cement floor of a temple. Young wanted O'Toole to begin his fall, and then he'd cut and let his double continue the stunt. O'Toole wanted to do it for real, knowing the shot would look better. 'I don't want you to take that fall, Peter,' said Young. 'Oh, darling, I'll be fine. Let's try it.' Young, cried 'Action' and O'Toole collapsed on the hard floor. After the shot the star said, 'Want to do it again?'

That dedication seemed to sum up O'Toole for Young. 'I've now worked with the best in the world. It doesn't get any better than that. He was professional, a gentleman, genius talent, and a great work ethic – a legend. It's an experience I'll never forget, sitting around talking about his films, David Lean, cricket, women, his children, various directors, Kate Hepburn, his books, and more cricket. I asked him to explain cricket to me one day and he said, "Oh dear boy, it would take months."'

Another epic followed, *Troy* (2004), where O'Toole played Priam, the father of Paris played by Orlando Bloom. It was a heavyweight film costing around the $175 million mark and also starred Brad Pitt and Sean Bean, another self-confessed O'Toole aficionado. 'First time I met him on the set,' recalled Bean, 'he was in a robe with a cigarette holder and he said, "Sean, how are you, dear boy?" He was just how I imagined him to be. It was a great moment.' From working class roots himself, Bean was a big fan of the old-school stars like Burton, O'Toole, Harris and Reed. 'They lived life on their terms, and why not? There are no rules saying you have to do this and you have to do that. They did it on their own terms and had a great time doing it.'

That was certainly still true of O'Toole, who, upon seeing the final result of *Troy,* labelled it, rather undiplomatically, 'a disaster', sending the PR brigade into a frenzy. Worse, he started to slag off the director, Wolfgang Petersen. 'That kraut, what a clown he was. When it was all over, I watched 15 minutes of the finished movie and then walked out. At least I had one good scene.'

O'Toole had never been the most subtle of people and old age hardly dented his un-PC ways. He had little time for the current crop of British stars like Hugh Grant. 'Ugh, that twitching idiot! Ooh, I mustn't say that, must I, but he's just a floppy young stammerer in all his films. How far is that line going to go? I watched that *Four Weddings and a Funeral* and thought, what the fuck is going on here?'

Amazingly, in 2007 O'Toole found himself in the running for a best actor Oscar yet again for his performance in *Venus* – his eighth nomination (you'd think they'd have finally caved in and given it to him – alas no). The film chronicled the curious, tender, almost wholly platonic romance between Maurice, an elderly thespian who has been reduced to playing corpses on TV (when O'Toole tells his ex-wife – played by Vanessa Redgrave – that he's been given a role as a corpse in a TV drama, she says, 'Typecast again?') and Jessie, a 21-year-old northern girl, sent to London to tend to her great uncle, Maurice's old acting mucker played by Leslie Phillips. O'Toole was delighted at the script and the idea of playing this odd romance: 'No one better for a dirty old man who falls for a sluttish young woman.'

Maurice's sexual interest hits the barrier of Jessie's revulsion, but slowly, as the characters reveal their vulnerability to each other, she starts to reward him with tiny tokens of favour. She bares her breasts for him when he's ill in bed and, in a daring scene, she slips a finger between her legs and allows him to smell, although naturally he wants to taste, too. 'Oh boy,' said O'Toole when reminded of it. It's a scene all our hellraisers would have been proud to play.

So O'Toole is the final one, the last surviving British reprobate. He has outlasted them all: an achievement the actor puts down to the O'Toole genes. 'My old man died when he was knocked down by a car. They took him to hospital and found he had nine mortal injuries. Nine! But he managed to die at home. When we went to the hospital we found a form which said, "The patient discharged himself." Discharged himself! Christ, he should have been dead nine times over.'

And so indeed should O'Toole; he knows he's been living on borrowed time for years, watching all his drinking pals from the 60s go under the turf one by one. 'The common denominator of all my friends is that they're dead,' he once said. 'I went to their funerals. There was a time when I felt like a perpendicular cuckoo clock, popping up and down in pulpits saying, "Fear no more the heat o' the sun." They were dying like flies.'

But like all our other hellraisers he has never once regretted the mistakes in life that he made, the boozing that almost killed him. 'I loved the drinking, and waking up in the morning to find I was in Mexico. It was part and parcel of being an idiot.' As with Burton, and to a lesser extent Harris and Reed, the accusation has been raised that O'Toole squandered his genius for fame, Hollywood and the bottle. When a reporter asked him to counter such claims he replied, 'Assholes!'

Our hellraisers never drank out of desperation or loneliness or some psychological problem. 'We weren't all brooding, introspective, addicted lunatics,' says O'Toole. 'And we weren't solitary, boring drinkers, sipping vodka alone in a room. No, no, no: we went out on the town, baby, and we did our drinking in public. We had fun!' Maybe it was even less complicated than that. 'O'Toole, Burton and I all drank to excess not because we had problems, but because we loved it,' said Harris. 'We liked to wonder what sort of trouble we could get into today. For us Alcoholics Anonymous was a joke. Can you imagine any of us at an AA meeting?'

Oliver Reed, too, never admitted he had a problem with booze. He drank. He fell over. No problem. If he wished he could stay on the wagon for months, but then go off on a marathon binge. Nor did he feel an ounce of guilt when inflicting his addiction upon others, even his own son, Mark, who he took along to a pub for the first time aged just 12. Mark downed seven pints and his father was immensely proud. Speaking years later Mark summed up Ollie Reed: 'My father never drank by himself. To him, beer was like a cup of tea. My father drank to have fun with people.'

And that's it, in a nutshell. OK, so in between the laughs, the falling down stairs and the pranks, marriage vows were trampled in the dirt, teeth were punched out of the faces of total strangers, and the odd police cell was occupied overnight, but at least it was done with style, a certain sense of panache, and nearly always for the sake of fun. I hope this collection of memories and anecdotes serves as a testament to four extraordinary lives lived extraordinarily.

Index

Also by Robert Sellers

Bad Boy Drive

The Wild Lives and Fast Times of Marlon Brando, Dennis Hopper, Warren Beatty and Jack Nicholson

They're the baddest bad asses Hollywood has ever seen: Marlon Brando, Dennis Hopper, Warren Beatty and Jack Nicholson. These are men for whom rules did not apply, men for whom normal standards of behaviour were simply too wearisome to worry about. These are men who brawled, boozed, snorted and shagged their way into legend-hood – but along the way they changed acting and the way movies were made forever.

Robert Sellers traces the intertwining lives and careers of movie mavericks Brando, Hopper, Beatty and Nicholson in this remarkable follow-up to the acclaimed *Hellraisers*. *Bad Boy Drive* is a whistle-stop tour of jaw-dropping sexual activity, misbehaviour of an Olympic standard, all-out excess and genuine madness. It's a wonder Hollywood survived.

'I don't know what people expect when they meet me. They seem to be afraid that I'm going to piss in the potted palm and slap them on the ass.'

Marlon Brando

'I should have been dead ten times over. I believe in miracles. It's an absolute miracle that I'm still around.' **Dennis Hopper**

'The best time to get married is noon. That way, if things don't work out, you haven't blown the whole day.' **Warren Beatty**

'You only lie to two people in your life: your girlfriend and the police.'

Jack Nicholson

Published by Preface

ISBN: 978 1 84809 122 1

£17.99